Identity Studies in the Social Sciences

Series Editors: **Margaret Wetherell**, Open University; **Valerie Hey**, Sussex University; **Stephen Reicher**, St Andrews University

Editorial Board: **Marta Augoustinos**, University of Adelaide, Australia; **Wendy Brown**, University of California, Berkeley, USA; **David McCrone**, University of Edinburgh, UK; **Angela McRobbie**, Goldsmiths College, University of London, UK; **Chandra Talpade Mohanty**, Syracuse University, USA; **Harriet B. Nielsen**, University of Oslo, Norway; **Ann Phoenix**, Institute of Education, University of London, UK; **Mike Savage**, University of Manchester, UK

Titles include:

Peter Aspinall and Miri Song
MIXED RACE IDENTITIES

Will Atkinson
CLASS, INDIVIDUALIZATION AND LATE MODERNITY
In Search of the Reflexive Worker

Mary J. Hickman, Nicola Mai and Helen Crowley (*editors*)
MIGRATION AND SOCIAL COHESION IN THE UK

John Kirk, Sylvie Contrepois and Steve Jefferys (*editors*)
CHANGING WORK AND COMMUNITY IDENTITIES IN EUROPEAN REGIONS
Perspectives on the Past and Present

John Kirk and Christine Wall
WORK AND IDENTITY
Historical and Cultural Contexts

Janice McLaughlin, Peter Phillimore and Diane Richardson (*editors*)
CONTESTING RECOGNITION
Culture, Identity and Citizenship

Ben Rogaly and Becky Taylor
MOVING HISTORIES OF CLASS AND COMMUNITY
Identity, Place and Belonging in Contemporary England

Susie Scott
TOTAL INSTITUTIONS AND REINVENTED IDENTITIES

Ruth Simpson, Natasha Slutskaya, Patricia Lewis and
Heather Höpfl (*editors*)
DIRTY WORK
Concepts and Identities

Margaret Wetherell (*editor*)
IDENTITY IN THE 21st CENTURY
New Trends in Changing Times

Margaret Wetherell (*editor*)
THEORIZING IDENTITIES AND SOCIAL ACTION

Valerie Walkerdine and Luis Jimenez (*editors*)
GENDER, WORK AND COMMUNITY AFTER DE-INDUSTRIALIZATION
A Psychosocial Approach to Affect

Identity Studies in the Social Sciences
Series Standing Order ISBN 978–0–230–20500–0 (Hardback)
978–0–230–20501–7 (Paperback)
(*outside North America only*)

You can receive future titles in this series as they are published by placing a standing order. Please contact your bookseller or, in case of difficulty, write to us at the address below with your name and address, the title of the series and the ISBN quoted above.

Customer Services Department, Macmillan Distribution Ltd, Houndmills, Basingstoke, Hampshire RG21 6XS, England

Mixed Race Identities

Peter Aspinall and Miri Song
University of Kent, UK

First published 2013 by
PALGRAVE MACMILLAN

Palgrave Macmillan in the UK is an imprint of Macmillan Publishers Limited, registered in England, company number 785998, of Houndmills, Basingstoke, Hampshire RG21 6XS.

Palgrave Macmillan in the US is a division of St Martin's Press LLC, 175 Fifth Avenue, New York, NY 10010.

Palgrave Macmillan is the global academic imprint of the above companies and has companies and representatives throughout the world.

Palgrave® and Macmillan® are registered trademarks in the United States, the United Kingdom, Europe and other countries.

ISBN 978–0–230–27504–1

This book is printed on paper suitable for recycling and made from fully managed and sustained forest sources. Logging, pulping and manufacturing processes are expected to conform to the environmental regulations of the country of origin.

A catalogue record for this book is available from the British Library.

A catalog record for this book is available from the Library of Congress.

To my mother, for her innumerable kindnesses

P. A.

To Charlie Song-Smith and Theo Song-Smith, who inspired this research

M. S.

Contents

Tables and Figures

Tables

Figures

Acknowledgements

Many people have made this research possible. We are especially grateful to all of the young people who participated in this project. Without their trust and interest in this project, this research would not have been possible. We would like to thank the Economic and Social Research Council (RES-000-23-1507, 'The Ethnic Options of "Mixed Race" People in Britain') for generously funding this research. We also thank the many colleges and universities in England which participated in this research by hosting the web link to the survey, and thus allowing us to advertise our research to their students. Dr Ferhana Hashem, who worked as a research assistant on this project, carried out a significant number of the interviews and kept the data on the project in good order.

Over the years, many people have offered helpful comments, support, and interest: Claire Alexander, Suki Ali, Michael Banton, Les Back, Ravinder Barn, Martin Bulmer, Chamion Caballero, Ros Edwards, Hamish MacPherson, Charlie Owen, and John Solomos. Scholars outside of the United Kingdom, including Maurice Crul, Becky King-O'Riain, Patrick Simon, and Linda Supik, also took an interest in the research and offered valuable encouragement.

In North America, we'd like to thank Melissa Herman, Minelle Mahtani, Ann Morning, Jennifer D. Parker, Nathaniel Schenker, Paul Spickard, Wendy Roth, and Debra Thompson – all of whom were encouraging, interested, or kindly supplied copies of relevant papers and reports. We also thank our colleagues at the University of Kent, for supporting this research.

Organizations such as People in Harmony, Intermix, Mix'd, and the BAAF also took an active interest in the research and helped spread the word about our research. Thanks to Val Hoskins in particular, who hosted the pilot study on People in Harmony's website.

At Palgrave Macmillan, we thank our editor Philippa Grand for guiding this project expertly, and the series editor, Professor Margie Wetherell, for taking an interest in the research and for her very informative comments on the manuscript.

Peter Aspinall would like to thank his mother, Kathleen Mary Aspinall, for her many kindnesses during the years over which this work was undertaken and his sister, Patricia Thompson, for her support. Thoughtful and stimulating conversations on the subject of race/ethnicity with George Ellison, Priya Davda, and associates at the Office for National Statistics helped maintain the momentum.

Miri Song would like to thank Murray Smith, and her children Charlie and Theo, for their belief in this project, and for their interest and patience over the years. Miri also thanks her parents, Moon-Won Song and Yung-Hee Park, for their love and support, as well as her siblings Vivian, Paul, and Joe. Miri's cousin, Paul Lee, also deserves thanks for his great sense of humour, good company, and invaluable poker tips. A number of friends also deserve a mention, for the numerous ways in which they helped Miri along this project: Miguel Alexiades, Abi Cooper, Cecily Fahey, David Herd, Pamela Kea, Daniela Peluso, Guy Roberts-Holmes, and Laurence Skillern.

1
Exploring 'Mixed Race' in Britain

Introduction

To what extent can we say that there is a 'mixed race' group in Britain today? What commonalities underlie the experience of being mixed, and in what ways does the growing population of mixed people comprise a group? This book explores the racial identifications and experiences of mixed race young adults in further and higher education in Britain. While studies of mixed people have grown in Britain in the last two decades, we still know remarkably little about this population. For instance, how do different types of mixed people identify themselves in ethnic and racial terms, and what sorts of identity options do they possess? Does the wider society validate mixed people's asserted identifications? Is being mixed race in Britain a racially disadvantaged status? To what extent is being mixed central to their sense of selves and their everyday lives?

Advocates of 'multiracial' people (the preferred term in the US), especially in the United States, have asserted that they have a right to be recognized as multiracial – as opposed to affiliated singularly with only one 'race' (see e.g. Root 1996). What is unknown, however, is whether the official recognition of 'mixed race' (the dominant term in Britain) or 'multiracial' people by the state actually heralds the emergence of a new racial identity (and/or group) which undercuts current racial classification schemes in which racial groups are still regarded as mutually exclusive entities (Bratter 2007).

By focusing upon Britain's mixed population, we are aware that this study of mixedness is situated in the context of specific social and migration histories. Clearly, the debates, policies, and discourses around mixed race people (and relationships) differ hugely across disparate societies. For instance, discussions of mixedness (or of ethnic and racial difference more generally) in Australia and New Zealand tend to centre on indigenous racialized populations, white settlers, and more recently arrived non-white migrants (such as migrants from East Asia), while 'New World' Caribbean societies' understandings of 'mixing' and mixed people are characterized by their own specific histories of colonization and racial categories and differences. Nevertheless, our study of young mixed people in Britain will contribute important empirical and theoretical findings to the existing body of research on multiracial people, which has thus far been dominated by studies of North America.

We use the terms 'mixed race', 'mixed', and 'multiracial' interchangeably throughout this book. There is no one terminology which is agreed upon among scholars (or among 'ordinary' people). What many scholars do agree upon is that these terms, like 'race', are all socially constructed, employed multifariously in a variety of discursive interactions (Harris & Rampton 2009) and subject to interpretation in particular ways and in particular societies. Who is considered to be mixed race or multiracial in the first place is by no means obvious and depends on the specific racial classification systems operating in a specific society (Aspinall 2009; Song 2009; Morning 2000). As DaCosta (2007) notes, the use of multiple terms also signals a heterogeneous group in the making, rather than a group in any fixed sense.

Furthermore, in our discussion and exploration of 'mixed race' people in this book, we refer to *both* race and ethnicity, and the often messy, and blurred boundaries between the two (Song 2003). Although some analysts have tended to differentiate clearly between these concepts, understandings and references to ethnicity and race can overlap with each other and are sometimes used interchangeably. While 'race' is now widely regarded as a socially constructed concept used to describe pan-ethnic population groups differentiated primarily by markers of visibility (in which Whiteness has traditionally constituted the norm), conceptualizations of race have typically referred to beliefs about biological differences among population groups. Recently, there have been attempts to reclaim the term 'race' to describe clusters representing important genetic differences between populations (Skinner 2007). 'Race' has been used historically to assign people into stigmatized categories, so that attributions of race are centrally about the exercising of power (see Omi & Winant 1994; Cornell & Hartmann 1998; Bashi & McDaniel 1996).

By comparison, analysts of 'ethnicity' have tended to emphasize collective assertions of shared culture, ancestry, and histories, whether imagined or real (see e.g. Bulmer 1986). Interestingly, unlike the United States, where the language and terminology of race is still largely uncontroversial (for example, the term continues to be used in the decennial US Census), many British analysts, and the Office for National Statistics (responsible for the census in the UK), pointedly refer to 'ethnicity' and manifest a clear discomfort with the language of 'race'. Indeed, the view that race should only be used in the contexts of racism and the history of race science is ascendant, rather than as a population category to describe differences based on visible markers like 'colour' or other racialized characteristics.

So while debates about the use of racial terminology continue in Britain (see Chapter 8), we would maintain that it is not always possible to differentiate neatly between 'race' and 'ethnicity' in our study of 'mixed race' young people, though these terms do carry disparate inflections and meanings in particular contexts and situations. Furthermore, the saliency in the use of 'mixed *race*' as a self-descriptor amongst our research subjects (rather than imposed terms like 'mixed heritage') gives the term legitimacy.

The growth of so-called mixed people and relationships today makes nonsense out of the idea that there exist discrete races that can be defined as mutually exclusive among people in multiethnic societies around the world (Parker & Song 2001) – though scientific debates continue concerning the legitimacy of population groups distinguishable as 'races' (see Kohn 1995; Herrnstein & Murray 1994; Gould 1996). And although we use the terms 'mixed race' and 'monoracial' to distinguish between those who are seen (or see themselves) as mixed from those who are (do) not, we recognize that population mixing has characterized the history of our species and is evident in our genetic make-up (Jones 1994; Spencer 2006).

Historically, mixed people have been pathologized as occupying a marginal location, in which they neither truly belong in one or another racial group (see Stonequist 1937; Furedi 2001). More recently, some analysts have argued that multiracial people's in-between status has resulted in their propensity to be especially racially conscious: 'The particular standpoint of multiracial persons, not being fully a part of a monoracial group, nor being completely recognized as a separate category, leads to an increased emphasis on racial issues for them' (Brackett et al. 2006:443).

Increasingly, research (especially in the US and Britain) has debunked depictions of mixed people as fragmented, marginal, and necessarily confused (see Phoenix & Owen 1996; Root 1992, 1996; Daniel 1996;

Spickard 1989; Olumide 2002; King & DaCosta 1996; Zack 1993). Nevertheless, much public policy in Britain has tended to see family breakdown or parental inadequacy as a direct result of racial mixing (Caballero et al. 2008). Arguing against what is perceived to be an essentialist, rigid, and now rather dated view of the dynamics surrounding racial identification, recent evidence concerning the racial identification of so-called mixed race people suggests growing latitude in how they may identify (or are identified by others), including a mixed or 'border' identification which refutes the primacy of one race over another (see Root 1996; Wilson 1987; Mahtani 2002; Herman 2004; Khanna 2010; Rockquemore & Brunsma 2002; Edwards & Caballero 2008; Ali 2003; Tizard & Phoenix 1993; Barn & Harman 2006; Okitikpi 2005; Barn 1999).

As found in many studies, having mixed ancestry does not necessarily mean that one identifies (or is identified) as a mixed or multiracial person. In fact, (arguably) the world's most famous mixed person, Barack Obama, apparently ticked 'Black' when he filled in his Census form – though the US Census now allows respondents to tick more than one category in its race question (Roberts & Baker 2010). Nevertheless, in the United States, where studies of the multiracial population are most numerous (at least in the Western world), a significant proportion of mixed people, including Black/White mixed people, are now asserting multiracial identities (see Root's 1992 and 1996 volumes; Brunsma 2006; Bratter 2007; Zack 1993; Harris & Sim 2002; Rockequemore & Brunsma 2002; Rockquemore & Laszloffy 2005; Roth 2005; DaCosta 2007; Khanna 2010; Dalmage 2000) – despite the historical legacy of the 'one drop rule', in which anyone with any known Black ancestry was labelled Black (Davis 1991). This growing latitude in identification is significant because it signals some degree of blurring and fluidity of racial boundaries (see Alba & Nee 2003).

A plethora of studies – both quantitative and qualitative – has identified a number of factors which influence the ways in which mixed people identify and understand themselves, including their socialization, ethnic composition of neighbourhood, socioeconomic status, physical appearance, and their locality and region, among others (see Rockquemore & Brunsma 2002; Harris & Sim 2002; Twine 2010; Tizard & Phoenix 1993). These many variables also intersect in both patterned and unpredictable ways.

Thus contemporary studies of race and ethnicity increasingly conceive of 'race' as a fluid concept which has been historically and socially constructed and maintained. Many analysts now recognize that racial statistics cannot always provide us with a picture of how race is actually experienced in 'real life' social interactions (Roth 2010; Troyer & Campbell 2007; Khanna 2004; Song & Hashem 2010; Harris & Rampton 2009; Earle & Phillips 2009). However, methodological innovations in how such data are collected and analysed are providing new insights. For example, post-census validation surveys and record linkage in census-based datasets (such as the Longitudinal Study) and other survey and administrative data are providing information on stability and change in self-assigned ethnicity over the short and long terms (Platt et al. 2005). Increasingly, data are collected in the census and surveys on multiple dimensions in the cultural question set, such as ethnic group, national identity, religion, and language (Burton et al. 2010), and the availability of census and survey microdata have facilitated exploration of how these variables and others of interest are related to each other at the person level (see Chapter 7). The UK Household Longitudinal Study, which is now a key vehicle for exploring the complexity of ethnic identity and other dimensions, is also undertaking new question development.

These datasets (and others in the US such as the National Longitudinal Study of Adolescent Health [Add Health], Current Population Survey, and Public Use Microdata Samples from the decennial census) have been exploited to show that people's sense or reporting of their racial/ethnic identities may be variable, and that there is a possibility that there is a mismatch between how individuals racially and ethnically see themselves, and how others see them, in a variety of settings (Khanna 2010; Roth 2010; Song & Aspinall 2012). Some British scholars, such as Ali (2003), Gilroy (2000), and Nayak (2008), have also emphasized the importance of adopting a post-racial perspective in the study of 'mixed' people and forms of interracial and interethnic co-mingling (and see Hylton et al. (2011) for a debate concerning critical race theory).

Yet in spite of the growing importance of mixed people and families in demographic terms and its entry into official data collection (see Aspinall 2003; Aspinall 2009; Panico & Nazroo 2011), relatively little is known about the life experiences of so-called mixed people in Britain, or how this diverse population identifies in ethnic and racial terms – information which is crucial for our understandings of cultural diversity and changing beliefs and practices concerning ethnic and racial difference. In the last two decades in particular, British studies of mixed people have grown significantly, focusing upon racial identification (Parker & Song 2001; Tizard & Phoenix 1993; Ali 2003; Katz 1996; Barn & Harman 2006; Ifekwunigwe 1999; Olumide 2002), family relationships (Song 2010; Caballero et al. 2008; Ali 2003; Twine 2010; Wilson 1987), and child welfare (Barn 1999; Okitikpi 2005). More recent analysis of the 2001 census and of ONS Longitudinal Study data has also resulted in studies of the residential geographies of 'mixed-ethnicity' families in Britain, showing variable concentrations of such families in distinct locations (Smith et al. 2011), and of neighbourhood ethnic mix and the formation of interethnic unions (Feng et al. 2010).

However, most studies of the mixed population in Britain have concerned (as in the US) Black/White 'mixture', and as discussed below, popular depictions of mixed relationships and people in Britain are likely to overlook the diverse experiences, identifications, and backgrounds of contemporary mixed people and their families.

Studying the mixed population in Britain today

A study of the mixed population in Britain is extremely timely for a number of reasons. *First,* there has been a marked growth in the number of mixed people and in the rates of interracial/ethnic partnering. In 2001, the England and Wales Census counted about 663,000 people (about 1.2% of the population) who identified themselves as 'mixed'. If mixedness is defined to encompass all those who are the offspring of parents in interracial/ethnic unions (as opposed to a measure of those who identified as being mixed), then the count is substantially larger: a recent analysis of the UK Household Longitudinal Study data (Wave 2, 2010) indicates that of those whose parents were of different ethnic groups, only 30% self-identified as 'mixed'. Thus, when based on parentage, the 'mixed' count is around three times larger than when captured in a self-identification question (Nandi & Platt 2012).

The recent release of the 2011 England and Wales Census data revealed that the 'mixed/multiple ethnic groups' grew from 1.2% in 2001 to 2.2% of the population in 2011 (ONS 2012). This growth has come about during a period of significant demographic change. For instance, those who chose 'White' as their ethnic group decreased from 94% in the 1991 England and Wales Census to 86% in the 2011 Census (ONS 2012). In absolute terms the White British population fell from 45.5 million to 45.1 million, while the White Other population increased from 1.3 million to 2.5 million. Furthermore, 12% of households with at least two people had partners or household members of different ethnic groups in 2011 (up 3% from 2001) (ibid.).

The mixed group is now one of the fastest growing sectors of the British population. The mid-2009 ONS experimental population estimates by ethnic group for England and Wales had indicated an increase in the size of the 'mixed' group of 46.8% between mid-2001 and mid-2009, with only the Chinese, Other, and Black African groups growing more quickly. However, the 2011 Census showed that in the inter-censal decade, the 'mixed' group had grown by 85%, varying from 80% for the White and Black Caribbean category to 110% in the case of the White and Black African category. This was a faster rate of growth than the Chinese group (73%) but not as high as the Black African increase (106%). Demographers have also identified that the mixed group will continue to grow at a high rate to 2020 and beyond. One set of projections indicate a 40% growth rate between 2001 and 2010, to reach almost 1 million, and 30% during 2010–2020 to achieve 1.2 million, although still smaller than the pan-ethnic Asian (3.5 million) and black (1.6 million) groups (Rees 2008). Another model predicts a 'mixed' population of 859,000 (2006), 2.23 million (2031), and 4.21 million (2056), representing *annual* growth rates of 3.82% (2006–2031) and 3.18% (2006–2056) (Coleman 2010), but exceeded by several other groups including Black African, Other Asian, and Other. Whatever the long-term increase, the inter-censal rise has been notable (Aspinall 2009). In the United States, the results of their 2010 census found a 32% rise since the 2000 census in the number of Americans who self-identified with two or more races, rising from 2.4% to 2.9% of the population (Humes et al. 2011): In the United Kingdom the inter-censal increase in 'mixed' numbers has been twice as high at 85%, with a commensurate increase in the contribution to the total population.

Britain manifests high rates of intermarriage among Western countries (Song 2009), and all second-generation ethnic minority groups exhibit a higher tendency to intermarry than the first generation, though individuals of Indian, Pakistani, and Bangladeshi backgrounds are less likely to do so than other groups (Muttarak & Heath 2010). In a recent analysis of the Labour Force Survey, nearly half of Black Caribbean men *in a partnership* were partnered (married or cohabiting) with someone of a different ethnic group (and about 1/3 of Black Caribbean women), while 39% of Chinese women in partnerships had a partner from a different ethnic group (Platt 2009).[1] There are now more children in Britain (under age 15) with one Black Caribbean and one White parent than children with two Black Caribbean parents (Owen 2007). A recent report by think tank British Future ('The Melting Pot Generation: How Britain Became more Relaxed About Race') found that the number of people concerned about mixed race relationships fell from 50% in the 1980s to 15% in 2012 (Ford et al. 2012).

In stark contrast with the United States, the relatively high rate of Black/White intermarriage in Britain accompanies various forms of Black/White 'conviviality' (Gilroy 2004) and social interactions (Back 1995; Hewitt 1986; Alexander 1996; Nayak 2003), especially in large, urban contexts. Recent research which maps more spontaneous forms of interaction, drawing on detailed linguistic ethnographies of young people in multiethnic settings demonstrate what 'conviviality' can mean, and how it takes multiple forms (see Alexander 2000; Nayak 2003; see chapters in Wetherell 2009). With growing cosmopolitan cultures in metropolitan areas, there is now more awareness of hybrid and multiple bases of identification, of which 'race' and ethnicity are a part, and more interest and scholarship in the intersection of various attributes such as gender, class, ethnicity, religion, and region. Furthermore, large metropolitan areas such as London (where a large proportion of mixed people and families live) are marked by 'superdiversity' (Vertovec 2007), so that the growth of mixed people and relationships can seem increasingly ordinary (Edwards & Caballero 2008; Caballero et al. 2007).

A heightened awareness and discourse around such conviviality and superdiversity has arisen at a time when British politicians (and British society more generally) have expressed concerns about the challenges to integration, the cohesiveness of neighbourhoods, Britain becoming a country of ghettos, and the idea that segregation may breed terrorism (the latter in relation to Britain's Asian Muslim population – which has been deemed problematic and a potential 'enemy within', especially since 9/11, but also since the London bombings of 2005). Such views have been robustly challenged, most notably by Finney and Simpson (2009). Against this backdrop, it may be tempting for some analysts to adopt an overly celebratory attitude towards 'mixing', as evidence of the diminishing significance of 'race' and racial boundaries (Parker & Song 2001; Song 2009).

Second, another reason why a study of the mixed population in Britain is timely is that the subject of 'mixing' continues to receive a lot of media and policy attention, suggesting rather ambivalent stances towards a more mixed society. On the one hand, 'mixing' in Britain is often depicted as evidence of its open and progressive social milieu. Indeed, the marketing of mixedness is not uncommon (DaCosta 2007; Cashmore 2008). On the British airwaves, we are increasingly aware of celebrities who are mixed, including the 2012 Olympics 'poster girl' Jessica Ennis, the fashion presenter Gok Wan, the Formula One driver Lewis Hamilton, and novelist Zadie Smith. A recent historical series by the BBC, 'Mixed Britannia', along with the popularity of programmes such as 'Who do you think you are?', signal a societal interest in ancestry and genealogy more generally.

Despite the fact that many (though not all) scientists refute the legitimacy of 'race' as a biological basis for differentiating among the human population, programmes and discussion about the scientific basis of racial differences persist. A 2009 Channel 4 documentary, 'Is it better to be mixed race?' explored whether there was a biological edge to having parents of different ethnic backgrounds – the idea of mixed people exhibiting 'hybrid-vigour' (Caballero 2005). So while it would appear that our growing awareness of mixed people and relationships renders them increasingly ordinary, we as a society continue to note the significance of a mixed background, marking such individuals as somehow novel and distinct from other people. There is still some residue of societal unease about the idea of mixing and racial transgressions.

For instance, in the 2006 film *Secrets and Lies* (directed by Mike Leigh), Hortense, a professional Black woman, whose adoptive parents have recently died, investigates the identity of her birth mother. What results is the shock Cynthia (the White birth mother) experiences when she meets Hortense for the first time. Although we, the audience, know what is coming (that they are of different 'races'), we are still primed to marvel at the fact that Cynthia could be Hortense's birth mother, especially when the two women are juxtaposed on screen together. Such films follow in the wake of decades of autobiographical writings (many of which concern the author's discovery of one's mixed ancestry) which have proliferated especially in the United States (see Spickard 2001 for an excellent review). Other media depictions of interracial couplings (especially concerning White working-class women and Black men), and their putatively hyper-sexualized nature, are still rife (Caballero et al. 2008).

There is no doubt that thinking about 'difference' and race 'mixture' is in flux in Britain today – but the evidence does not all point neatly in one direction, which suggests neither a glib image of 'happy families', nor a wholly negative picture of mixed people and families. There is debate, for example, about whether a Black and White child needs to identify as Black in order to develop a healthy sense of self, as has been argued by many social workers in the past (see Prevatt-Goldstein 1999). A related policy issue which is currently being debated in Britain concerns the long-standing prohibition of trans-racial adoption. David Cameron (the current PM of the UK) recently announced the government's 'adoption action plan', in which he vowed to dismantle the 'life-wrecking bureaucracy' that delayed efforts to place children in adoptive homes, referring to the current rules against the placement of children with parents considered to be of a different ethnic background (Morris 2012).

It is not uncommon to hear analysts and public figures articulating the view that mixed people are still somehow troubled about 'who they are'. In a speech from 2007, Trevor Phillips talked about mixed people being potentially disadvantaged and vulnerable to 'identity stripping', as a result of them growing up marooned between disparate communities – this sweeping generalization coming from the head of the new Equality & Human Rights Commission. On the other hand, the growth of mixed people and relationships has been seen by some to herald a more tolerant and open attitude towards 'difference' and multiculture, with an emphasis upon the transcending of racial boundaries and tensions (see Alibhai-Brown & Montagu 1992).

These examples reveal society's continuing fascination and preoccupation with the idea of a mixed race person and the alleged positives or negatives stemming from the transgression of racial boundaries, thus reinforcing the sense (however much it may be refuted in academic studies) that such people are somehow intrinsically different from everyone else who is presumed to be 'monoracial'. More than ever we need careful empirical studies of the mixed population to accompany more sensationalistic media and cultural interest in them and their experiences.

Third, a number of public figures and commentators have advocated the recognition of a mixed experience, as distinct from those of both White and monoracial minority people. As Yasmin Alibhai-Brown observes in her book, *Mixed Feelings*, '*It is foolish to generalise about mixed race families or to impose strong but false categories on them ... What is new however is that we now have a critical mass of young Britons who see themselves as mixed-race and who wish to challenge many of the assumptions that have been made about them for four centuries ....*' (p. 124). Nevertheless, the emergence of Internet websites and organizations in Britain (e.g. 'Intermix' and 'People in Harmony') reveals the relatively nascent awareness of and debates concerning the diversity among so-called mixed people.

Whether in relation to negative or rose-tinted depictions of them, the mixed population is all too often lumped together as one entity – regardless of specific ethnic and racial backgrounds, social class, region, gender, or family type. In the 2001 England and Wales Census's 'What is your ethnic group' question, individuals were able to choose from the following categories under the heading 'Mixed' (and the heading 'Mixed/multiple ethnic groups' in the 2011 census):

White and Black Caribbean
White and Black African
White and Asian
Any other Mixed background, please *write in*

The provision of the four categories explicitly acknowledges the diversity of the so-called mixed population (Aspinall 2003) and was a substantial advance over the free text provision in 1991 for capturing the increasing diversity of the population due to population mixing.[2] Yet it is in the nature of categorization that it always conceals some heterogeneity and evokes calls for yet ever finer granularity, against the constraints of topic coverage and consequent competition for space on the census form. As we will see in the chapters of this book, intra-group diversity in this segment of the population requires further research and regular monitoring as the group is growing at a fast rate and different patterns of in-migration since the early 1990s will result in new patterns of population mixing that may not fit neatly into the current Census mixed categories. To date, there has been no comparative study of disparate mixed people in Britain. In fact, comparative qualitative studies of multiracial people are still relatively rare, even in the United States. So our study is breaking new ground in identifying and investigating the different constituencies within this 'mixed' collectivity.

Furthermore, the official recognition and categorization of 'Mixed' people in the 2001 Census has significantly opened up this population segment for research as the census ethnic group categorization was adopted across government for use in surveys, data collection, and administrative reporting. See the work, for example, of Feng et al. (2012) on the tendencies of migration among mixed ethnic unions and Panico & Nazroo (2011) on the social and economic circumstances of mixed ethnicity children. Yet major areas remain to be explored. For instance, most studies of mixed people and families have not investigated the degree to which they encounter forms of racism. Furthermore, how meaningful or significant racial lines of difference are vis-à-vis other modes of belonging and identification, such as ethnic, religious, or regional forms of belonging (Song 2003; Caballero et al. 2008; Luke & Luke 1998), has been accorded little attention. We endeavour to provide new evidence on both these topics.

While practitioners and analysts acknowledge the growth of mixed people, there is no agreement about how they should be categorized in racial/ethnic terms, whether they should be differentiated from monoracial minority groups in terms of their needs and experiences (and thus require specific interventions), or whether different types of mixed people can be said to share a common status or set of experiences. This book aims to investigate the diversity of the mixed population in Britain by examining a youthful subset of educated individuals and to consider the social and political implications of this recognition.

Methods and data collection

The findings in this book are based upon an Economic and Social Research Council (ESRC) funded project, 'The ethnic options of "mixed race" people in Britain' (2006 to 2008).[3] This research examined the ways in which different types of mixed people, including Black/White, South Asian/White, East or SE Asian/White, Arab/White, and 'minority mixed' (those with no reported White forebears), chose to identify themselves in ethnic and racial terms. We employed an integrated mixed methods approach, in which we drew upon both survey and interview data and established the connections between the two approaches during the analysis and preparation of the results.[4]

While designing the research study we explored and evaluated a number of putative samples. A strategy of using 'focused enumeration' to derive a population-based sample was discounted as the mixed population is geographically dispersed. We also investigated the feasibility of a workforce sample (National Health Service employees), but encountered confidentiality issues in accessing the workforce annual census that records ethnic group. Once the study had started, we attempted to recruit a 'comparison group' of young people who were clients of a national social enterprise organization that catered for their employment and training needs: however, the slow rate of accrual resulted in an achieved sample that was too small for meaningful analysis.

We first adopted a cross-sectional study design, with the use of a semi-structured survey (largely administered online), followed by in-depth interviews with a sub-set of these survey respondents. Young adults were recruited from universities and colleges of further education across England (but the achieved responses were primarily from London). A stratified sample (based on location and size of the mixed race student population) was drawn from a sampling frame that integrated ethnically coded data for students in universities and colleges supplied by the Higher Education Statistics Agency and the Learning and Skills Council.

Ahead of the main survey, a pilot survey was undertaken in 2005–2006. A questionnaire was designed which encompassed question sets on the person's identity, terminology for the mixed group, how the mixed group is incorporated into ethnicity classifications, changes in racial/ethnic identity, and socio-demographic information. One of the main reasons for undertaking this pilot study was to provide information (primarily through an unprompted, free-text question on how the person identifies in ethnic/racial terms) on how to break down the census 'mixed' categories into a more finely granulated set for use in the main student study. The pilot questionnaire was hosted on a mixed race charity (People in Harmony) website and responses were also accrued through networking and snow-balling in the organization. A general population sample of 51 persons, unrestricted by age, was achieved, 47 of whom were in scope. The findings from this pilot were incorporated into the main study instrument.

This main student study is based upon 326 questionnaires returned to us from 36 higher education institutions, but mostly from those in London and the Southeast. While over 500 survey responses were received in total, many of these were out-of-scope, as the respondents did not match the sample criteria: the eligibility criteria included being a mix of two or more pan-ethnic (main) population groups (see below), aged 18 to 25 years of age and at least secondary school educated in Britain (i.e. from the age of 11). This minimum secondary school requirement was put into place because we wanted a sample of respondents who were socialized, and grew up, in Britain, as opposed to another society.

The aim of the research was to capture persons of 'mixed race' rather than of multiple ethnic backgrounds, such that respondents with, say, White European (English and French) parentage or Chinese and Filipina parentage were excluded from the sample. While such ethnic (and national) differences can be truly significant in family life, in terms of contrasting cultural beliefs and practices, our study's focus was on the study of people who were regarded as the offspring of two racially disparate parents, according to wider societal conventions – for instance, people who were Black/White or South Asian/White. Perceived racial transgression is what fuels the wider society's interest and fascination with 'mixed race' people – not individuals deemed to possess different but relatively uncontroversial parentage. While less common, our study also included individuals whose mixed ancestry was generationally removed, so that some respondents had a mixed race parent.

Participating institutions hosted a weblink to the online survey (that used the proprietary software of Bristol Online Surveys) and sent out an email advertising our research to its student body. Those who participated were a self-selecting group who self-identified as possessing a mixed heritage (though as we discuss, they did not necessarily describe themselves as 'mixed', or 'feel' that being 'mixed' was of particular importance) and/or had forebears of disparate 'races'. The respondents comprised 258 women and 68 men and encompassed the following mixes:

157   Black/White (e.g. Black African and Black Caribbean)
50   South Asian/White (e.g. Indian, Pakistani, Bangladeshi)
46   East or SE Asian/White (e.g. Chinese, Filipino/a, Japanese, Myanmarese)
40   'minority mixed' (no reported White forebears, e.g. Indian/ Chinese)
29   Arab/White (e.g. Egyptian, Iranian, Lebanese)
4   Other mixes not classifiable above
TOTAL = 326

Our survey data reflected the fact that that people with 'Mixed' ethnic identities in the 2001 Census were most likely to be living in the London region, but contained a higher relative concentration of students resident in London (around 60%). Their experience of being multiracial may have been different from that of students living in other regions, since London is particularly diverse and cosmopolitan. In such institutions, respondents (especially those who did not grow up in the area) may come into contact with other minority and multiracial individuals in large numbers, and thus, being mixed may be regarded as more ordinary than in other, less cosmopolitan parts of the country.

Furthermore, of these survey respondents, a sub-sample of 65 (27 men and 38 women) were then recruited for an in-depth interview.

Black/White	17
East or SE Asian/White	16
South Asian/White	10
Arab/White	15
minority mixed	7

Both our survey and interview samples were comprised primarily of female respondents, especially in the case of the survey. This gender imbalance in studies concerning ethnic and racial identification is not uncommon (see Lopez 2003; Portes & Macleod 1996). For instance,

Harris and Sim (2002) found that their female respondents were more likely than male respondents to self-identify with more than one race. Various analysts have suggested the possibility that women are more aware, and sensitive to, their racial status and their racialized interactions with others (Russell et al. 1992).

The in-depth interviews with the sub-sample of 65 respondents were crucial in illuminating not only how respondents thought about, but also experienced, their mixed status. Interview respondents were asked to describe their racial identifications and to discuss what role these identifications played in their day-to-day lives. The interviews allowed us to explore the ways in which respondents' understandings and experiences of being mixed could differ, both across and within the five mixed groups.

The in-depth interviews were conducted in a variety of settings, most commonly in public cafes/restaurants and university settings – depending upon the preferences of our participants. These interviews were recorded with a digital voice recorder, and most interviews lasted between 1.5 and 2.5 hours; each interview was subsequently transcribed. All of our respondents (including our larger survey sample) were given pseudonyms to protect their anonymity. An effort was made to assign similar ethnic or Anglo names to our respondents.

Aims of this book: Chapter outline

Chapter 2: Racial identification: multiplicity and fluidity

Given the prevalence of ethnic and racial categories on surveys, such as the Census, albeit now a mix of pre-designated and open-ended options, how confident are we that these modes of describing ourselves actually capture the ways in which mixed people see themselves? For many mixed individuals, there is no neat or easy answer to the question of how they identify themselves: a wide body of evidence indicates that people answer in a range of ways, from the use of terms like 'Asian' or 'mixed race' to detailed descriptions of their racial/ethnic origins, comprising two or more groups and frequently infused with terms that indicate national identity, colour, geographic origins, and faith. This chapter focuses upon the multiple and potentially complex ways in which multiracial respondents can identify themselves. In particular, we examine modes of identification which are unprompted – that is, when respondents are able to describe themselves in an open-ended fashion, in their own words. Furthermore, this chapter examines the potentially fluid and contextually specific nature of identification.

Chapter 3: Differential ethnic options?

In contrast with Chapter 2, in which we examine how respondents describe themselves in an open-ended fashion, we investigate whether mixed young people in Britain are willing to choose only *one* ethnic or racial group – the group they think best describes them. Such a 'forced choice' question has been used in the United States as an indicator of the identity options (and by extension, the sense of racial allegiance and membership) of disparate types of mixed people. Are there differences across specific types of 'mixes' in terms of whether they opt for their White or minority racial backgrounds (or a refusal to choose only one group), and if so, how can we explain such group differences? These questions enable us to explore how specific mixed people may perceive and experience their ethnic options in different ways. Furthermore, we also explore the difficulties involved in interpreting the choice of such 'forced choice' questions. The ethnic options of disparate mixed groups matter because they tend to reflect racial fault lines, the differential values and meanings associated with specific 'races', and society's continuing preoccupation with racial difference in everyday life.

Chapter 4: Does racial mismatch in identification matter?

How we see ourselves racially is not necessarily congruent with how other people see us, resulting in a form of racial mismatch. In this chapter, we first focus upon survey evidence of how respondents thought others saw them in racial terms. Not surprisingly, physical appearance (and how others see you in racial terms) was a central part of this dynamic. By drawing upon the interviews, we then examine how different groups of mixed respondents thought about and responded to how they were perceived by others. Were their racial identifications validated by others, and did it matter? The issue of validation is, for many, fundamental, because without validation of one's own racial identity by others, one cannot easily assert and 'own' that identity. Prior studies of mixed people in the United States have assumed that racial mismatch is almost always a negative and troubling experience – but was this the case in our own British study?

Chapter 5: Are mixed people racially disadvantaged?

Most existing studies of racism in Western multiethnic societies have conceived of racisms in relation to distinct, monoracial minority groups. As a result, very little is known about the forms of racial prejudice and discrimination experienced by mixed people. In this chapter, we draw on survey data to investigate the extent to which mixed people report experiences of racial prejudice and discrimination in the wider society. How may such experiences differ according to different types of mixed backgrounds? If these respondents feel racially stigmatized, *on what basis* do they feel they are marked? And in which specific contexts and situations do such encounters occur? By drawing on interviews, we then explore how mixed people make sense of, experience, and cope with forms of prejudice and discrimination. In doing so, we also explore the ways in which they may feel racially marginalized and/or excluded by co-ethnic monoracial minorities.

Chapter 6: How central is 'race' to mixed people?

For many decades, scholarship on race and ethnic minorities has assumed the centrality of 'race' and racial identifications – but is racial identity still a 'master identity' among our mixed race respondents? Not only may other attributes or dimensions of one's everyday life take precedence, but the blurring (and intersection) of racial, ethnic, national, and religious boundaries may challenge the primacy of racial identity, at least in some contexts. In this chapter we explore the relative importance of various identity dimensions for different ethnic and racial groups, first by reviewing existing surveys such as the British Citizenship survey. We then explore the importance of 'mixed' status for our respondents' sense of selves and their everyday lives. The meaning and significance of race and/or ethnicity may be shaped by many different factors, for example, through processes of disadvantage and discrimination, the specific locality within which someone is raised, or the nature and quality of one's relationships with relatives and/or co-ethnic social networks.

Chapter 7: Rethinking ethnic and racial classifications

One of the key research questions investigated in our study concerns the ability of official classifications to capture the ethnic and racial identifications of young 'mixed race' people, such as in the Census or other ethnic monitoring forms which are now rife in contemporary life. We argue that census ethnicity data are often reductionist, whereby respondents are asked to shoehorn their choices into the pre-designated categories on a 'best fit' basis. While many scholars of ethnicity have argued for its fluid, multi-dimensional, and socially constructed nature, ethnicity is captured in large-scale surveys typically at one point in time and through mutually exclusive categorization of ethnic group. This disjuncture between theories of ethnicity and measures of ethnicity used to map and document forms of demographic change in the wider society is perhaps not surprising, but it makes the study of a population (which is differentiated into ethnic and racial categories – such as 'mixed race') fraught with difficulties. Furthermore, given the official recognition of the category 'mixed' in Britain, can multiracial people be said to share particular concerns and experiences in common? Is their mixedness an important basis of collective identification? We draw on our in-depth interviews to explore this important question.

Chapter 8: Conclusion: what is the future of 'mixed race' Britain?

As demographic patterns shift, there is a pressing need to reflect upon the meanings and social significance of 'mixed race' identities and people. Mixed people in Britain have gained official recognition as a distinct sector of the population. Given this recognition, and the very fast growth in mixed people and relationships, multiracial people may increasingly become a group which makes specific political demands. What are the social and political implications of recognizing 'mixed' people as a separate category? Might it result in the creation of an intermediate racial category which reinforces a top-down racial hierarchy in which White privilege is retained, or does it signal a hopeful change towards the eventual dismantling of racial classification and the emergence of a post-racial society? How may the recognition of mixed people affect the ways in which we understand continuing forms of racial injustice? Furthermore, can we conceive of 'mixed race' without reifying 'race' and racial difference? We also consider what is yet unknown about so-called mixed people in Britain, pointing to the need for future research in this area.

2
Racial Identification: Multiplicity and Fluidity

Introduction

One of the most common questions that 'mixed race' people encounter from strangers is the 'what are you?' question, which is often prompted by attributions of a person's perceived racial/ethnic ambiguity. For many mixed individuals, there is no neat or easy answer to this question: a wide body of evidence indicates that people answer in a range of ways, from the use of single generic terms like 'mixed race' to detailed descriptions of their racial/ethnic origins, comprising two or more groups and frequently infused with terms that indicate national identity, colour, geographic origins, and faith.

This chapter focuses upon the multiple and potentially complex ways in which multiracial respondents can identify themselves. In particular, we focus upon modes of identification which are unprompted – that is, when respondents are able to describe themselves in an open-ended fashion, wholly in their own words. In the process of identifying themselves in a variety of ways, our mixed respondents are effectively joining in a national conversation about the nature of mixedness – in addition to engaging in self-identification. That is, even though these open identity descriptions are given in the context of a self-completion questionnaire, many are dialogically and relationally constructed and linked to wider public discourses. As we show below, our respondents could actively take issue with existing paradigms and discourses around ethnic and racial markers and systems of classification. Furthermore, this chapter examines the potentially fluid and contextually specific nature of identification. Depending upon the specific context, self-descriptions (and how respondents saw themselves) could vary, or several could be held simultaneously.

While there are now many conceptualizations of 'identity' which emphasize the socially constructed and dynamic nature of identities and identifications, by identity we mean '*the way we understand ourselves in relation to others and our social environment. Our identities are constructed through a reflexive process involving interaction between ourselves and others in our environment (e.g. families, schools, neighbourhoods, and houses of worship)*' (Rockquemore & Laszloffy 2005:4). In other words, identities are meanings that people acquire through social interaction with others (Song 2003; Stephan 1992), including our perception of in-groups and out-groups (Tajfel 1978). Identities are not static and are regularly negotiated and experienced vis-à-vis others in a multitude of settings. Although studies in the United States (see Brunsma 2005) increasingly distinguish between 'identity' (how people see themselves) and 'identification' (how people identify themselves in specific situations and surveys), we think there is evidence that even 'identity' (how people see themselves) can be fluid for some respondents (Doyle & Kao 2007).

The US literature from the late 1990s advanced new models concerning the identities of 'mixed race' individuals. Despite some variations, these models shared a number of aspects in common, namely that there is no one way for a multiracial person in the United States to racially identify, and that a hybrid border identity was possible – for example, see Root's (1996) 'border crossings' model and Renn's (2000) biracial/multiracial identity development model, to name only a few.

In recent years, Rockquemore and Brunsma's (2002) model, though based specifically upon 'biracial' Black/White university students in the United States, has been particularly influential. Their theoretical framework for the ways in which biracial individuals understand their identities delineates four possible identities: a *border identity*, located between predefined social categories (neither Black nor White, but a self-understanding that incorporates both into a hybrid category, and the most commonly found at 58% of the sample); a *singular* identity, in which an individual's racial identity is exclusively *either* Black (13%) or White (4%); a *protean identity*, where biracial individuals are able to cross boundaries between Black, White, and biracial (made possible by the fact that they actually possess each of these identities, and are not merely adjusting their behaviours) (the least common with only 4%); a *transcendent identity*, a self-understanding of being biracial that results in avoidance or rejection of any type of racial group categorization as the basis of personal identity (about 13% of sample).

The above models are all based upon the US population, and especially upon Black/White individuals, and while various aspects of these models are generally applicable to disparate types of mixed individuals in Britain, our own study sample comprises different types of mixed people (not only Black/White people). As we discuss below, given the considerable ancestral complexity of some of our respondents, we will consider how we may rethink such models in relation to the British context.

Another important theoretical strand concerning the identification of mixed individuals (again, based on US studies) focuses on the multidimensional aspect of identity, and whether mixed people's asserted identities are validated by others – the focus of discussion in Chapter 4. For instance, Harris and Sim (2002) have conceptualized the multiple nature of racial identities in terms of 'internal identities' (how we think of ourselves), 'expressed identities' (what we say we are), and 'observed identities' (what others think we are based on our appearance), as these are not necessarily the same (and see Roth 2010; Khanna 2010). The multidimensional aspect of racial identities becomes immediately apparent when we examine both the pilot and main surveys and interview data from our respondents.[1]

In this chapter, we focus primarily upon the ways in which our mixed race individuals *describe* their racial and ethnic identities to others – thus, a focus on what analysts (such as those above) would call expressed identities (or 'identifications'). But in doing so, we found that it is not always possible to differentiate as clearly, and neatly, between expressed (self-described) and internal (felt) identities as some models may suggest, as we discuss below.

Self-identification amidst growing diversity

A logical starting point in our study was a measure of how our mixed race young people described their racial/ethnic identities *in their own words*, unprompted by official classifications. Such open-ended questions solicit 'top of head' responses – what immediately comes to mind in the participant's response – and therein lies both their utility and validity when compared with other kinds of survey questions. They provide a subjective measure of identity relatively free of the biases of social categorization or the observer's view. This approach is somewhat novel in the United Kingdom – though the Northern Ireland and Scotland 2001 Censuses employed a free-text option to capture those identifying as 'mixed' (Aspinall 2009). There is a dearth of surveys that elicits a respondent's ethnic identity as an open response or free text. The only UK Government social survey to have used an open-response ethnicity question was the 2001 People, Families, and Communities Survey (Citizenship Survey). In Canada and the United States, by contrast, there is a greater plurality of methods.[2]

Asking about unprompted open response was judged to be important for a number of reasons. During a period of unprecedented ethnic monitoring and data collection in Britain, an almost universal characteristic of this practice has been the mandated use of the decennial census ethnicity classifications. As the ethnic diversity of Britain has increased, driven by immigration dynamics and population mixing leading to 'super-diversity', the census is no longer able to capture the new populations, not least because – unlike the United States and Canada – Britain has no tradition in its censuses of asking an additional ancestry or ethnic origin question.

Such diversity has increased dramatically over the last few decades through population mixing, the emergence of new mixed/multiple identities and affiliations, and migration from an ever-increasing range of countries. The census classifications (in 1991, 2001, and most recently, 2011) capture a number of broad groups that link to socially perceived ethnic differences in the wider society and longer-term processes of colonialism, discrimination, and disadvantage. What such classifications cannot capture is the sheer complexity of the ethnic composition of most of Britain's large cities and towns and, increasingly, settlements in rural areas (see Chapter 7). As Steven Vertovec (2007:7) has written: '*In Britain much public discourse and service provision is still based on a limited set of Census categories ... these categories do not begin to convey the extent and modes of diversity existing within the population today*'.

This increased diversity is due, importantly, to the growing rates of interethnic partnering and the growth of mixed people.[3] We considered that an entirely open-response question could be a modus operandi for large-scale ethnicity data collection and that the lack of consistency in recording of such responses need not necessarily be viewed as a drawback. Moreover, open response was likely to offer substantial insights into the country's super-diversity in a way that pre-given ethnicity categorization alone could not.

Capturing the 'mixed' group in open response: survey findings

Although open-response questions about ethnic and racial identities are important in capturing contemporary super-diversity, only a few surveys have used open-response formats in relation to the 'mixed' group in Britain. An analysis of Lincoln's 'Mix-d:uk' study (2008) – a library of photographs and self-descriptions used by 78 mainly young mixed race people opportunistically recruited from the general population in street settings – reveals that the majority (65.4%) used two terms (such as 'Caribbean/European', 'Welsh/Arabic', 'Irish/Zimbabwean'), but 16.7% used three or more terms (such as 'Afro-Celt/Jamaican', 'English/ Greek/Jamaican', and 'Jamaican/Irish/Italian'). The sheer complexity of terms, which could combine racial, ethnic, national, religious, and geographical identities, is illustrated by a handful of respondents: 'Black/White African/British', 'Egyptian plus Jewish/Salford plus Jewish', and 'Nigerian Spanish/Black Nigerian British'.

The *People, Families and Communities Survey 2001* (renamed the Citizenship Survey), which draws on open responses for 380 'mixed' persons, also illustrates the heterogeneity of unprompted 'mixed' open-response descriptions (see Table 2.1). Interesting differences emerge. While 20.0% of White and Asian respondents claimed a British or home country national identity, 11.9% of White and Black Caribbeans, 11.1% of Other Mixed, and just 6.5% of White and Black Africans did so. Religion did not comprise part of the identities of any of the mixed group – in contrast to Pakistanis, Bangladeshis, and Indians. Mention of the Caribbean, West Indies, or individual Caribbean countries featured in only 15.4% of the descriptions of the 'White and Black Caribbean' group.

By comparison, the Newham Young People's Survey, based on over 9,500 young people (mainly 11–16) in Newham (a London borough), listed all the descriptions given by those who eschewed the 2001 census pre-designated categories (and so comprised a residual group) (Jones 2006). A total of 6.4% (610) of the young people giving ethnicity descriptions ($n = 9,516$) chose one of the four census 'Mixed' categories. Of these 610, 160 (26.2%) selected the 'Any other Mixed background' option and 130 wrote in a description. This data, therefore, is not *entirely* open response but comprises free-text answers given within an ethnicity classification and is included here for the insights it offers.

One of the most important findings is the number of 'mixed' persons located in the 'other White', 'other Asian', 'other Black', and 'any other' open-response options, as well as in 'other Mixed', suggesting that ethnicity data collected using the census classification may significantly undercount how respondents define 'mixedness' and also the Census-defined mixed counts. Clearly, these young people more strongly reflect 'superdiversity' than would an older cohort, suggesting that mixes based on categories such as those in the census that have

Table 2.1 Responses to question on how you would describe your ethnic group and cultural background using 'your own words', *People, Families & Communities Survey, 2001*

Open-response answer	Answer for 2001 census 'Mixed' Category			
	White & Black Caribbean (*n* = 143)	White & Black African (*n* = 62)	White & Asian (*n* = 85)	Other Mixed background (*n* = 90)
Same as in ethnicity question	1	0	2	2
British	11	3	10	6
White British	0	0	0	0
English	3	1	4	2
White English	0	0	0	0
White	3	1	5	1
Welsh/British Welsh/ White Welsh	0	0	3	1
Scottish/White Scottish	1	0	0	0
Irish/White Irish	2	0	0	1
Caucasian/White Caucasian	0	0	0	0
Other mentions of UK regions, towns, etc.	2	0	1	1
Anglo-Saxon	0	0	0	0
French/Italian/Greek/ Swedish/Polish/other specific European	1	1	3	6
European/White European	0	0	1	4
British Asian (or Asian British)/British Indian, Br Pakistani…	0	0	11	4
British West Indian/British Caribbean, British Caribbean, British African, etc.	4	3	0	1
Asian/Indian, etc. (no mention of British/ English)	0	0	7	4
Caribbean/Jamaican, etc. (no mention of British/ English)	11	0	0	2
African/Nigerian/Zaire, etc. (no mention of British/ English)	0	13	0	8

Other non-European country (Chinese/Taiwanese/Vietnamese/ Sri Lankan/Philippine, etc.) (no mention of British/English)	1	2	15	18
Black	5	0	0	2
Black British/Black English	4	4	0	3
Black Caribbean/Black Jamaican, etc.	7	1	0	2
Black African/Black Nigerian, etc.	0	10	0	0
Mixed race/mixed culture/mixed origin, etc.	70	19	19	21
Mention of Muslim/Moslem/Islam/ Islamic	0	1	2	3
Mention of Hindu or Sikh	0	0	0	1
Mention of Christian/Protestant, etc.	0	1	1	2
Other mentions of religion	2	0	2	1
Reference to class (working-, middle-, etc.)	0	0	1	1
Reference to gender	0	1	0	1
Reference to other personal characteristics	5	8	6	10
Citizen of world/human being, etc.	7	1	5	0
Mention of parents' or grandparents' country of origin	5	3	4	2
Jewish	0	0	0	1
Other coding	3	1	2	6
Don't know	11	2	7	7
Refused	1	0	0	1
Not stated	6	3	1	0

Source: Home Office People, Families & Communities Survey (renamed Citizenship Survey), 2001. Dataset SN 4754, accessed via the Economic and Social Data Service (ESDS).

historical (including colonial) links with Britain may be of diminishing efficacy as self-descriptors.

Our main student survey

Given the well-documented 'order effects' in questionnaire data – the fact that a person's response will be influenced by the context of the questionnaire – an unprompted question about self-identification was the very first question posed on our main student survey. Respondents were asked: '*Please describe your racial/ethnic identity in your own words in the text box.*' By asking this question first, and providing ample space for a free-text response, we hoped to gain some measure of the respondent's spontaneous self-ascribed racial/ethnic identity (though, as we discuss below, such a self-ascribed identity could be subject to change).

Table 2.2   Characteristics of free text, unprompted descriptions of racial/ethnic identity

Characteristics	Count
'Mixed' only	5
'Mixed race' only	17
'Mixed race' and other description	69
'Mixed heritage' and other description	1
'Dual heritage' and other description	2
'Multiracial'	0
'Mixed parentage'	4
Mention of 'British'	67
Mention of 'English'	75
Mention of 'European'	8
One specific group mentioned	24
Two specific groups mentioned	197
Three or more specific groups mentioned	66
Use of 'half'[2]	78
Indication that respondent does not identify racially	3

Notes: Counts exceed total respondents as some responses encompassed more than one characteristic.
Source: Main student survey.

Our survey revealed similar findings to those reported in the surveys discussed above (see Table 2.2).

The substantial majority of our 326 survey respondents gave a specific description rather than a generic term only, like 'mixed race' or just 'mixed'. These descriptions varied substantially in length, with some fairly short, combining just a couple of terms (e.g. 'Asian White', 'Mixed White/Chinese') and others more extensive, involving multiple terms and identifications. Overall, 60% of respondents named two groups and 20% three or more groups. A quarter (24%) used the term 'half' (e.g. 'half Japanese half English', 'half White British, half Jamaican') and a small number fractionated their identities in more complex ways (e.g. 'three-quarters British, quarter Chinese', 'I am quarter English, quarter Irish, quarter Spanish, quarter Filipina'). Significant numbers – over a fifth in both cases – included the national identity terms 'English' and 'British' in their responses (and see Ifekwunigwe 2002).

What is distinctive about these unprompted open responses is their heterogeneity and frequent complexity, with some combining racial/pan-ethnic terms like 'black', 'white', and 'Asian' with ethnic/national origin terms such as 'English', 'Somali', 'Polish', and so on in the same description:

My mother is English (white) & my father is Sri Lankan (Asian). I was born & brought up in Wales, which is what I consider my nationality to be (Welsh).

I am mixed race – half Jamaican, quarter English, and quarter Portuguese.

My father is fully British while my mother is ethnic Chinese & comes from Hong Kong. I have fair hair and only slightly Chinese looks. I am always mistaken for full Caucasian. I only speak English but have been brought up in largely Asian influences.

English, Welsh, Swiss, Kiwi, Indian, Singaporean. I am of mixed parentage – this is a good thing.

I am mixed race, black & white, but only have black friends who all see me as black.

I am a white mixed race. Both parents are mixed race from a white and black mixture, & both are darker than me. I was born in Africa.

I am a Londoner, born & bred with an Arab (Egyptian) father & white European (French) mother.

Half British, three-eighths Vietnamese, one eighth French.

While some respondents used Census terms (e.g. 'White British') and other expressions that included racial terms like 'Black' and 'White', only 14 (of 326 survey respondents) explicitly referred to skin colour in their descriptions and are notable for their exceptionality (though references to physical appearance more generally were not uncommon). How one described oneself if one or both parents were themselves mixed, for example, could engender specific references to skin colour, especially in relation to concerns about whether or not they looked mixed or not:

My father is white Irish and my mother is mixed black Antiguan and white British. I call myself mixed race even though my skin is white.

My father is white and my mother is white/Asian therefore I would say that for the most part I am white yet my skin is not: it is a mixture therefore making it hard to place myself as white or Asian.

These findings show that nearly all respondents found a single generic label (like 'mixed') unsatisfactory and wished to describe their 'mixedness' more fully. While many respondents mentioned just two groups, a significant minority mentioned three or more. The descriptions sometimes combined 'mixed' terminology with national and/or ethnic identities or origins (as in *'I am mixed race – half Jamaican, quarter English and quarter Portuguese'*). Such evidence indicates that many mixed individuals are required to simplify their responses when using the Census 'mixed' categorization of dual groupings, such as 'White and Black Caribbean'.

Furthermore, the ways in which respondents described themselves in this open-response format shows that many respondents did not differentiate clearly between racial, ethnic, national, and regional modes of identification and belonging, suggesting layered and multiple modes of affiliation and belonging. These responses also show that when asked for unprompted self-descriptions, mixed individuals often comment upon their physical appearance and their awareness of the importance of their physical appearance to how they are seen by others (see Chapters 3 and 4).

The open-ended survey question in which they were invited to describe themselves wholly in their own words was also important because it provided some respondents with the opportunity to comment on the legitimacy of racial categorization per se, or the opportunity to contest the concept of 'race' and racial difference as a basis for differentiating among people. Brian, who had a South Asian and White background, wrote this:

> *Race seems to be a wholly artificial concept, historically used only for division. I do sometimes describe myself as English. I was born in that country and so were many of my mum's ancestors. I do sometimes describe myself as British. I have been known to describe myself as Sri Lankan, where my dad and many of his fathers ancestors were born. Often the best box to tick is British Asian. This is very vague, as I could just as well be Scottish-Malaysian than English-Sri-Lankan. I am always and definitely a member of the human RACE. One race.*

In this excerpt, Brian notes the variable and potentially multiple ways in which he can identify himself, drawing potentially on ethnic, racial, national, and even regional modes of belonging. Importantly, he implies that there is no obvious privileging of one status – racial, ethnic, national – over another. At the same time, he points to the arbitrary and socially constructed nature of 'race', suggesting that he does not accept the idea of racial difference: *'I am always and definitely a member of the human RACE. One race.'* Such a sentiment is similar to what

Rockquemore and Brunsma (2002) call a 'transcendent' identity in their biracial Black/White model – discussed more fully in Chapter 3. Brian also notes the potentially changeable ways in which he describes himself (his expressed identity) – though it is not entirely clear whether his internal identity (how he sees himself) is also subject to change in this excerpt.

Valerie, who was one of our 'minority mixed' respondents, also communicated what she thought about the idea of race and racial difference. In the first open-ended question, she described herself as 'Chinese (Shanghainese) and Indian (Gujarati) resident Londoner'. But in the interview, this respondent made it clear that, while she valued her wider family and her family ancestry, especially that of her Chinese mother, she did not see herself in terms of her parents' specific ancestries: *My mother told me that race doesn't matter. I am who I am, and as an artist I relate to all sorts of people with various backgrounds. I don't see those people in terms of their specific racial backgrounds, and they don't see me that way.* A number of different points appear to be made by Valerie, across the survey and the interview: In the survey, she suggests the importance of a highly specific description of herself, making reference to both her parents' ethnic and even regional backgrounds. Yet in the interview, she conveys the view that *'race doesn't matter'*, and that her racial identity is not particularly central to who she is. This example is illustrative of the complex, and not always congruent and neat, accounts given by respondents, especially when we looked at the range of responses offered by respondents who had participated in both the surveys and the interviews.

Why respondents identified themselves in specific ways

There is still relatively little research on why respondents write in the free-text answers in the ways they do, other than an understanding that such descriptions are likely to be spontaneous and to represent components of identification that are of particular importance to them. Thus, in our main survey, we specifically asked respondents why they identified in the ways they did in the free-text box, giving them the option to *multi-tick* across seven options (including a free-text field) (Table 2.3).

The response which attracted the most respondents (70%) was, *'my parents are from different racial/ethnic groups'* – though this could be combined with other responses, as we discuss below. Forty-three per cent of respondents chose, *'it is my own sense of personal identity'*. This distinction between the responses *'It is my own sense of personal identity'*

Table 2.3   Reasons respondents gave for identifying themselves in this way

Reason	Count
It is my own sense of personal identity	139
It is the way society sees me	53
It is the group I feel I belong to	53
My parents are from different racial/ethnic groups	228
My ancestors (forebears) before my parents were from different racial/ethnic groups	62
My friends/peers identify me in this way	50
Some other reason[1]	25

Note: [1]The following responses are a sample of those given: '*so that I can include all the countries which my parents come from in one phrase. I don't feel like pure English people so I don't want to be seen as one*'; '*a mixture of my perception of what I am and what others perceive me to be*'.
Source: Main student survey.

and '*My parents are from different racial/ethnic groups*' is important – and one which echoes Berthoud's (1998) distinction between *actual* parental ancestries and one's identity, as the two are not necessarily the same. Such a point was in fact made by various respondents, including a female respondent who ticked '*Some other reason*': '*It is my blood but not necessarily me, I consider myself British/Japanese because I grew up in the UK.*' More explicitly 'social' factors attracted substantially fewer responses. Around 16% of respondents chose: '*it is the way society sees me*' and a similar proportion chose '*my friends/peers identify me in this way*' and '*it is the group I feel I belong to*'.

The relative lack of importance accorded to a sense of group membership is noteworthy. In the United States respondents who selected 'multiracial' in the Current Population Survey supplement on race and ethnicity were asked the reason for choosing the multiracial category (Tucker et al. 1996). Across the panels 74–81% selected '*parents from different racial groups*', 70–78% '*ancestors from different racial groups*', and 52–57% '*specific group belong to is mixed*'. This probably reflects the fact that in the United States a strong multiracial movement coalesced around the issue of gaining representation in the 2000 US Census categorization. In Britain, by contrast, there was no organized mixed race movement in the years leading up to the 2001 Census and no sizeable lobbying by such organizations to obtain 'mixed' categorization, although a small number of local and national groups have emerged in the last decade.

Table 2.4 Identification with known ancestry

Racial/ethnic group(s) of:	Very important	Fairly important	Not important
My parents	209	94	23
My grandparents	126	138	58
More distant ancestors	55	127	140

Note: There were four cases of non-response on the '*my grandparents*' category and four on '*more distant ancestors*' category.
Source: Main student survey.

Interestingly, more distant ancestry was much less important than that of their parents in shaping their open-ended self-descriptions, with only 19% of respondents selecting '*my ancestors (forebears) before my parents were from different racial/ethnic groups*' (see Table 2.3). But since ancestry was revealed in pilot testing as an important factor in shaping respondents' racial/ethnic identity, the importance of this was further explored. Respondents were also asked about the importance of their ancestors' (forebears') race/ethnicity across three generations: their parents, their grandparents, and more distant ancestors (Table 2.4).

The importance of the race/ethnicity of one's ancestors as a factor shaping respondents' own racial/ethnic identity appears to diminish the further back one goes. This finding meshes with that of Morning (2000), who argues that multiracial ancestry further back in one's family tree (e.g. a multiracial grandparent) is likely to mean that someone with more distant multiracial ancestry is less likely to identify as multiracial than someone with parents who constitute an interracial couple.

While almost two-thirds (64%) of respondents thought the race/ethnicity of their parents was a very important influence (consistent with the 70% who chose the response '*my parents are from different racial/ethnic groups*' in the previous question), this fell to 39% in the case of grandparents, and just 17% in the case of more distant ancestors. Not all respondents necessarily knew the racial/ethnic group of some or all of their grandparents and more distant ancestors – a factor which, of itself, could diminish the importance of their racial/ethnic group(s).[4]

Nevertheless, 264 respondents reported that their grandparents' ancestry was either very or fairly important, and 182 respondents said that the ancestry of their more distant ancestors was either very or fairly important (Table 2.4). In fact, in the interview sub-sample, some respondents, such as Amelia, reported that their grandparents' ancestry was even more important than that of their parents:

Int: *You say you'd describe yourself as mixed race English and Burmese.*

Amelia: *And with a Maltese grandfather.*

Int: *Right. Can you say a bit more about which side of your family is Burmese and Maltese?*

Amelia: *My mother's mother is Burmese and my mother's father is Maltese. And my father is English. And I think my grandmother's mother was actually Indian, and her father Burmese.*

Int: *I was intrigued by the fact that, on this form [survey], you put your grandparents' racial backgrounds as more important than your parents'.*

Amelia: *[hesitates] Because my grandparents' race is so prominent to me, it's a much stronger influence than my parents'.*

Int: *Isn't your mother's race prominent too? She's Burmese/Maltese.*

Amelia: *Yeah. She's important, but I feel an even stronger connection to my grandparents.*

Int: *Is that because your grandparents talk to you about their heritage?*

Amelia: *Yeah, and it's the fact that my [maternal] extended family have a very strong connection to my grandparents (maternal grandparents). So the whole extended family is the Burmese. So the amount of contact I had with the Burmese was far greater than with my dad's [English] side. And her two sisters [grandmother's sisters] married Burmese men. And so all my cousins are Burmese, whereas.... [long pause], my grandmother didn't [marry a Burmese man], and so there's a dilution.*

As revealed in this excerpt, Amelia's own mother is 'mixed' (Burmese and Maltese), and Amelia hints at a concern about a gradual dilution of her Burmese 'bloodline'. Her maternal grandmother is the lynchpin in Amelia's sense of Burmese identity, because Amelia feels a strong attachment to not only her grandmother, but also her grandmothers' sisters, all of whom married Burmese men, and her 'fully' Burmese cousins. Thus, the symbolic and emotional importance that some respondents placed on their ancestors' ethnic and racial backgrounds could stem from an awareness and concern about ethnic and racial dilution – especially (though not exclusively) in the case of respondents who were the children of a mixed parent (and who appeared White to others, like Amelia).

Shifts in self-identification

The findings above have established that many mixed people choose to identify in non-standard and highly specific ways when the possibility of open-response self-description is offered. Furthermore, we can see that mixed individuals can also identify themselves in potentially multiple ways and may possess a variety of reasons for describing themselves in specific ways. An additional layer of complexity is added, moreover, when we consider how identification is subject to change over time and in different settings or situations (see Harris & Sim 2002; Doyle & Kao 2007). Herman (2004:743) notes that racial identification among multiracials is a 'moving target', as it changes over time and context – see also Kich (1992). As discussed earlier in the chapter, while ethnic identity more generally is conceptualized by many theorists as potentially fluid and subject to change, less is known about these processes in relation to disparate types of mixed people. We examine shifts in identification in relation to the following themes: change over time, situational/contextual changes, and the transition to higher education.

Change over time

In terms of how identification may vary over time on official forms, we found considerable fluidity when we examined longer-term change through transitions in the ONS Longitudinal Study: less than half of those identifying with one of the 2001 Census 'mixed' categories had used the free-text option to identify themselves as 'mixed' in the 1991 Census, which did not provide mixed categories (Platt et al. 2005). In the 1991 Census, people could identify as 'mixed' in either of the 'Black-Other' or 'Any other ethnic group' open-response options and around 230,000 did so. However, this number significantly under-counted the mixed population at that time, many of whom selected one of the pre-designated categories. We are also able to establish how those who chose a 'mixed' category in the 2001 Census identified in the 1991 Census as the ONS Longitudinal Study links individuals' census records. Analyses undertaken by Platt et al. (2005) and Simpson and Akinwale (2007) reveal the transitions between the two censuses (Table 2.5). Given that ten years separates the two censuses, it is possible that in 1991 ethnic group was assigned by the head of household for some household members (e.g. younger children) who (might have) later assigned their own ethnic group in 2001 (Fig. 2.1).

The transition matrices show that almost half (49%) of Longitudinal Study (LS) members identifying as 'White and Asian' in 2001 had identified as 'White' in 1991 (when 'White and Asian' was not available on

Table 2.5   Transition in ethnic group between 1991 and 2001

Ethnic group in 1991	Ethnic group in 2001			
	White & Black Caribbean	White & Black African	White & Asian	Other Mixed
Numbers				
White	367	98	487	325
Black Caribbean	194	7	–	26
Black African	9	41	–	13
Black Other	396	79	20	66
Indian	–	5	51	18
Pakistani	–	–	35	5
Bangladeshi	–	–	9	4
Other groups – Asian	3	–	31	58
Chinese	–	–	6	20
Other groups – Other	300	79	354	204
Per cent of 2001 group				
White	28.9	31.7	49.0	44.0
Black Caribbean	15.3	2.3	0.0	3.5
Black African	0.7	13.3	0.0	1.8
Black Other	31.2	25.6	2.0	8.9
Indian	0.0	1.6	5.1	2.4
Pakistani	0.0	0.0	3.5	0.7
Bangladeshi	0.0	0.0	0.9	0.5
Other groups – Asian	0.2	0.0	3.1	7.8
Chinese	0.0	0.0	0.6	2.7
Other groups – Other	23.6	25.6	35.7	27.6

Source: ONS Longitudinal Study; analysis by Platt et al. (2005).

that Census). Almost as many of the 'Other Mixed' group in 2001 (44%) also identified as White in 1991. However, around only 32% of 'White and Black African' (and 29% of the 'White and Black Caribbean' group) respondents chose 'White' in 1991. The odds ratio (OR) of the 'White and Black Caribbean' group identifying as 'White' compared with the 'White and Asian' group is 0.42 (95% CI, 0.36 to 0.50). When we compared the 'Black/White' group as a whole with the other mixes ('White and Asian' and 'Other Mixed'), the OR is 0.47 (95% CI, 0.41 to 0.55). That is, the Black/White mixes were less than half as likely to identify as 'White'.

There may be many reasons for the lack of stability of individuals' ethnic group affiliations in the Longitudinal Study Census data. Some change may be artefactual (question ambiguity and unreliability and changes in categories), while others may reflect real, conscious changes

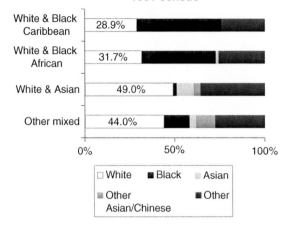

How LS 2001 Census 'Mixed' cohort members identified in 1991 census

Figure 2.1 Transition in ethnic group between 1991 and 2001

in affiliation. Simpson and Akinwale (2004) found that the latter (conscious change of affiliation) contributed little to the instability in the 1991–2001 Longitudinal Study data and that the limitations and ambiguity of the categories in 1991 (as opposed to 2001) was probably the main driver, concluding that '*mixed is one of the most ambiguous ethnic group labels*'.

With respect to changes over time, we asked our pilot sample if they had ever reported – or whether they could foresee a time when they might report – their racial/ethnic identities differently from the way they usually did now (and why). Of the 47 pilot responders, 45% said that they had reported their racial/ethnic identity differently than they had at some point in the past, and just over half (51%) had not. A number of respondents who were 'changers' mentioned that they had been constrained by the previous categorization that had been used on the Census and other forms:

> '*No set grouping to identify with in the 1980s & 1990s. I was "A.N.Other"*'; '*Original census (1991) and other forms may not allow mixed race – so tend to tick "other" or leave out*'; '*The categorisations were different in years gone by. I used to tick the box black other because that was the closest category*'; '*The questions have changed over the years. I used to refuse to reply to earlier questions because they were not inclusive of mixed race/heritage*'.

Others pilot respondents reporting changes in the ways in which they reported their racial/ethnic identities gave a variety of explanations, including the complexity and multifaceted nature of their identities, frustration with the unwieldy nature of official forms, as well as strategically motivated changes in expressed identities:

> *'Because I could not be bothered with the long winded process of explanation'; 'Because I'm lots of "things", British, Black Caribbean & mixed'; 'Better chance of acquiring a job at university union'; 'Didn't want to be pinned down on that particular form, so put "multiracial"'; 'I did not know my racial origins'; 'I used to say "mixed race", but now I always say English/Jamaican'.*

Fewer pilot respondents (26%) could foresee a *future* time when they might report their racial/ethnic identity differently: 40% could not and 28% did not know. Again the responses were heterogeneous, with references to the adequate provision of categories, assertions about the right to change ethnic/cultural allegiances, and being motivated by strategic considerations:

> *'I have the right to change my ethnic/cultural allegiances throughout the course of my life, and more than once'; 'If categorisation is changed to more accurately describe my ethnic origin then I would change, e.g. White British/English and Black African'; 'If for genetic screening or other reason, I would need to explore further my father's background'; 'Times change. Mixed race suits me now but other terms might be invented which are better'; and 'Well terms/trends are always changing. For my own identity, I will always say brown'.*

Situational/contextual change

Drawing on the models developed by US scholars discussed earlier, we were also very interested to see what would happen if we allowed our respondents to multi-tick across five categories concerning the relative stability or fluidity of racial identification (see Fig. 2.2). In our main survey, we asked our respondents: *Please look through the following statements. Which do you feel best describes you? [Please tick all boxes that apply].* A derivative classification was then used to report the choices of respondents in terms of the multiple positions they chose within the typology.

No simple picture emerges from our respondents' choices (Table 2.6). A considerable proportion of our respondents (a third) identified as

1. '*I identify with a single ethnic group at all times*' [*Single group*]
2. '*I identify with more than one single ethnic group, depending on the situation (e.g. sometimes as "Chinese" and sometimes as "White")*' [*Single groups situationally*]
3. '*I identify as "mixed race" (i.e. two or more groups in combination)*' [*Mixed race*]
4. '*I move between "mixed race" and the other options listed above, depending on the situation I'm in*' [*Mixed race & others situationally*]
5. '*I do not identify at all along race/ethnic group lines*' [*Transcends race*]

Figure 2.2   Statement which best describes you

Table 2.6   Choosing ethnic options with respect to dynamics and context

Statements respondent feels best describes them	Count
(1) Single group	30
(2) Single groups situationally	34
(3) Mixed race	106
(4) Mixed race and others situationally	48
(5) Non-racial/ethnic	43
(6) Multi-ticked responses:	
(1) & (2)	2
(1) & (3)	2
(1), (3), & (4)	3
(1), (2), (4), & (5)	1
(1), (3), (4), & (5)	1
(2) & (3) & (4)	12
(2) & (3)	15
(2) & (4)	8
(2), (4), & (5)	1
(3) & (4)	16
(3) & (5)	2
(4) & (5)	1
Non-response	2

Source: Main student survey.

'mixed race' (that is, *two or more groups in combination*). Around a tenth of respondents (a) indicated that they identified with a single group at all times (*single group*), or (b) that they identified with more than one single group, depending on situation (*single groups situationally*). However, almost 15% of respondents reported that they moved between 'mixed race' and the other listed options, depending on the situation they were in. Another 20% of respondents multi-ticked across the five options, indicating some degree of fluidity in the way they identified themselves. Thus, including those who identified with more than one single group (depending on the situation), almost half the sample (45%) utilized some kind of switching strategy or exercised more than one option. A small proportion indicated through their multi-ticking that they utilized three or more options.

Interestingly, 15 respondents ticked both '2' (single groups situationally) and '3' (mixed race), and 12 respondents ticked '2','3', and '4', suggesting that some individuals may identify both monoracially and/or as mixed race, depending upon the situation. This question also gave respondents the choice to indicate that they did not identify at all along racial/ethnic lines, and 43 respondents (13%) did so.[5]

With regard to situation and context, *both* the pilot and main surveys asked respondents if they described their racial/ethnic identities differently (and how) *in conversation with friends* to the way they reported it on *official forms*. In both surveys, around three in ten and four in ten respondents, respectively, indicated that they would describe their racial/ethnic identity differently *in conversation with friends* to the way in which they would identify themselves on *official forms*, suggesting, again, that 'Census ethnicity' is only one mode of racial/ethnic identification.

The responses highlight the potentially different meanings and motivations attached to identifications in what are, broadly speaking, 'private' and 'public' settings. In both the pilot and main surveys, more respondents claimed that they did *not* describe themselves differently in these two specific contexts than those who said they did. However, shifts in situational identification more generally is a much more salient phenomenon, as our sub-set of interviewees reported. Among the 65 interviewees, 39 reported that they often or sometimes identified themselves differently, depending on the specific situation. Typically, we are talking about subtle or small shifts in expressed identification or in internal identity, rather than cataclysmic shifts. It is important to remember, also, that those who reported no fluidity in identification included those who did not identify racially at all – that is, those who reportedly transcended race.

Of those (125 of 326 respondents) who claimed that they *did* describe themselves differently with friends (as opposed to on forms) in the main student survey, many indicated that they were inclined to provide more detail in describing their racial/ethnic identity in conversation with friends: *'When speaking to others I'll tell them that I'm also quarter Portuguese whereas in official forms I'm normally only able to tick white & Black Caribbean mix which tends to imply just White UK with black'; 'with friends I include my Italian roots but on official forms I just associate with "White" which I think could be taken as any nationality. I prefer to be able to include Italian in my "White" categorisation'; 'I prefer to say I am half Filipina than half Asian as a whole continent cannot locate accurately my heritage and my identity'.*

As one respondent, who had a Russian mother and a Ghanaian father, reported: *'On forms they only give the option White and Black African. With friends I would describe which [kind of] White'.* Perhaps not surprisingly, these respondents suggest that it is personally important to them that their friends know the specifics of their ancestry, rather than describe themselves in generic terms; this more personal information is not something one would share with just anyone or in every context, but rather, with one's intimates.

The responses above again indicate that the census 'Mixed' categories may be only partially or situationally meaningful to people thus labelled but are nonetheless employed by them in their dealings with officialdom – seemingly often as a shortcut. In contrast to the ways in which they may describe themselves to their friends, filling in an official form requires no personal interaction or validation.

Some respondents revealed that one reason why they described themselves differently on forms than they did with friends was that they simply could not be 'bothered' to go into exact detail about 'what they were', and therefore just ticked one of the boxes which were provided, if only because it was the easiest thing to do. In fact, many of the survey and interview respondents seemed rather cynical about form filling more generally, not only because of the perceived inadequacy of the offered categories, but because of the routinized nature of form filling in contemporary multiethnic Britain.

By comparison, a smaller number of the 125 respondents who reported a disparity in how they described themselves to friends (in comparison with how they did so on official forms) reportedly *simplified* their expressed identities in conversation with friends: *'To friends I identify as mixed race, but in official forms I am required to be more specific which I refer to as Black & Latin'; 'In forms I include that I am half white. Whereas with friends, they see me as black only and that's how I describe myself'; 'In more official forms I am more specific in my racial identity. With friends I am more general, as more or less know my background already'.*

Various processes appear to be at work in these accounts. It is clear that the majority of respondents who reported differences in their expressed identifications between the contexts of officialdom and friendships believed that the specifics of their actual ancestry was something to be shared with people they knew relatively well – it was not necessarily for public consumption. Yet for a small proportion of such respondents, we can conclude that amongst peers, knowledge about the specific ancestries of friends was not considered important or relevant in their friendship networks, especially in multiethnic settings, where being mixed may not be considered unusual or necessarily meaningful.

Clearly, differences in setting (between completing an official form and describing one's racial/ethnic identity to friends, or between being in a 'public' setting versus being with one's family) are likely to be one of many different and sometimes interacting situational and contextual influences on self-identification (see Lopez 2003; Harris & Sim 2002). And as shown above, the influence of changes in setting was not always predictable.

Reported fluidity of identifications was even more pronounced in the interviews[6]: some degree of fluidity in either or both their expressed identification or internal identity was reported by many of the 65 interviewees, with shifts typically (though not exclusively) occurring between 'public' and 'private' settings (e.g. school versus family home), between different groups of peers or relatives, or even in different countries.

The recognition and interpretation of changes in expressed identifications and/or internal identities was far from straightforward and could be ambiguous. In some cases, shifts in expressed identification could be largely automatic and strategic, and in many respects involved dynamics similar to those described in various forms of code-switching by ethnic minority groups more generally (see Ballard 1994; Song 2003), as illustrated below:

Int: *Do you ever change the way in which you describe your identity to others?*

Ahmed: *Let's say [to] the parents of a Caucasian Englishman, I may say that I'm a Londoner. Then to the parents of an Asian friend I may say that my family origins are from there......[being a Londoner] allows the other person to identify certain aspects of culture and society, so that means he's been schooled in the British education. He is familiar with British popular culture or British etiquette.....if employers were to ask me about my background, I would say British, but if I was probed about this, I would then go into more detail about my parents.*

In this case, Ahmed makes it fairly clear that he can present himself quite differently to disparate sets of people, depending upon the situation he was in; but there is no further suggestion that his internal identity actually changes in these varied interactions and settings. Shifts in how he described himself were motivated by a desire to enhance his social connectedness with disparate types of people (see Khanna 2011).

By comparison, Callum stressed no change in his expressed identity. He did describe a change in his internal identity, depending upon whether he was at home with his family, or whether he was in public settings. Callum was raised by his Filipino mother and Filipino stepfather (his English father left home when Callum was young, and Callum had had very little contact with him since). Callum reported that he felt (and thought of himself as) White British most of the time at university and with his friends, but when he was at home or with Filipino friends, Callum said that he could not help but feel more Filipino, with his mother and stepfather, and their Filipino food and customs. Clearly, there will be many cases in which such a neat distinction between a public and private identification will not hold, but such shifts in how one 'feels' goes beyond an instrumental shift in expressed identification.

Like Ahmed and Callum, it was not uncommon for respondents to emphasize the ethnic background that the respondent had in common with the person with whom they were interacting: Junko, who was Japanese and English, reported that when she is in Japan (interacting primarily with Japanese people), she emphasizes the fact that her mother is Japanese and that she speaks Japanese. But when she is in Britain, she emphasizes the fact that her father is British and that she has grown up here. When asked how she would describe herself, Junko responded: *I would say British and Japanese, but it depends, sometimes I have to say half Japanese . . . in Japan I would say Japanese and British.*

However, in Junko's case, it was not clear whether a shift in expressed identification also signalled a change in the way she thought of herself (and felt) in these two quite different settings. As her excerpt above implies, whether or not she also experienced a shift in internal identity may be largely shaped by how others react to her, and whether they accept her assertions of being either Japanese and British or British and Japanese. Reported shifts in identification could involve *either or both* expressed identification and/or internal identity for many respondents, and were likely to accompany the varied ways in which mixed individuals navigate issues of belonging in specific places. Thus, reported shifts in identification could be quite ambiguous – as it was not always clear whether certain shifts involved 'only' changes in expressed identification or whether they also involved shifts in internal identity. Indeed, individual respondents themselves did not always seem to know, or to have reflected upon, this distinction.

Transition to university/college

We know from a range of research findings that changes in personal circumstances may lead to a reconsideration of ethnic identity over time, including leaving home, partnering, changes in the ethnic composition of a person's household and the area in which they live, changes in exposure to racism, and shifts in social and political attitudes (Harris & Sim 2002; Root 1996; Rockquemore & Brunsma 2002). Thus both personal and wider societal triggers could be influential in engendering changes in identification at particular points in people's lives, such as in the transition to university/college. In our student survey, we asked our respondents: '*Since moving to college/university, have you changed how you identify in racial/ethnic terms in any way?*' Respondents were able to tick 'yes' or 'no', and those who ticked 'yes' were asked to write in what factors caused these changes.

In response to this question, 83 (of the 326) students (25%) indicated that they had changed the way they identified in racial/ethnic terms, since they had started higher education. For instance, one female respondent who chose 'yes' wrote in that '*Mixing with international students and people with different backgrounds*' had engendered a change in how she identified. Most responses to this question did not differentiate between changes in identification (expressed identities) and (internal) identity, so as discussed above, it was not always possible to discern the nature and extent of reported changes (equally, some who may have ticked 'no' to this question may have only based this response upon changes in (internal) identity, as opposed to changes in expressed identifications). For most respondents who ticked 'yes', the change had been a positive one, making respondents more able to identify with their various heritages and more comfortable in doing so:

> '*I am more open about my mixed race heritage, though still identify with a sense of "Britishness"*'; '*Realised you don't have to be one or the other.*

Being mixed is the best way'; 'Having met more mixed race Arabs, it has made me feel stronger about my Arab side because they've grown up also being made to feel included but at the same time "other". Also it's made me feel more comfortable in associating myself with my European ethnicity'; and 'More in touch with all of my backgrounds (not just two), more in touch with how that manifests not as two distinct identities I can move between (this is more for other non-mixed minorities) but the ways I can now recognise they manifest not as one part or two parts, but rather more like the dancer and the dance'.

By comparison, few survey respondents had changed their racial/ethnic identification for negative reasons and very few respondents had simplified their identity. Changes in identification were also explored in the sub-set of interviews with respondents who talked of the ways in which their move to higher education entailed new experiences, feelings, and modes of identification. For some respondents, especially those who had grown up in predominantly White neighbourhoods and attended primarily White schools, going to a more ethnically diverse university (such as most institutions in London) provided their first major immersion in a genuinely multiethnic and cosmopolitan environment. Such a transition resulted in some respondents' 'discovering' their non-White minority heritage, or a newly found appreciation of the idea of being 'mixed', when they encountered other mixed people. Such experiences could result in individuals rethinking their expressed and internal identities.

For instance, Patricia (Black Caribbean/White) had grown up in a mostly White town in the Southeast, and thought that she had 'fitted in' with her mostly White peers during her school years. But when she arrived at university, where there were many more Black and part-Black students, she gravitated towards this group, and realized that she felt much more at ease with these students than she had during secondary school:

Patricia: ... *like when I was in secondary school I sort of, I don't know the way to word this. Certain things you talk about, like . . . . I don't know. Certain things about your family and home, and like things to do about Jamaica and stuff I can talk about and joke about with my [university] friends because they sort of understand. But with my friends in secondary school they weren't really . . . there was no point in me saying things like that because they wouldn't even know what I was talking about.*

Int: *So they wouldn't understand.*
Patricia: *Yeah, they wouldn't really. So it's now I can sort of not hold [back]. I didn't think I was holding back before but it's like now I can fully sort of...*
Int: *Be yourself?*
Patricia: *Yeah. I...I don't know. It's strange because at the time at secondary school I did feel like I was being myself but now I'm looking back, I feel like, well, not really.*

Furthermore, in retrospect, Patricia realized that some of her White friends (in secondary school) had been racist towards her and that she had normalized such interactions and minimized their significance while she had lived in that milieu. While she had always acknowledged her racial ancestry in secondary school, she had effectively contained the meanings and significance of her Blackness in her predominantly White setting. But now that she had a lot of Black friends at university, she felt more able to embrace and assert her identification as 'mixed' *and* as Black.

Mike (Chinese/English) had also grown up in a predominantly White suburb in the Southeast and had had little exposure to other Chinese people; he explained that almost all of his cultural references were British when he was growing up. In the interview, Mike reported that he regarded himself as primarily 'British', but he also noted that '*the Chinese part of me has grown*'. Mike revealed that at university (in London), he was now feeling 'more Chinese', and that he had discovered his Chinese side, having made a number of Chinese friends for the first time. His sense of racial identity was clearly in process, at a key transitional moment in his life, pointing to the importance of contextual forces.

Like Mike, Leo's growing interest in his Iranian heritage coincided with exposure to co-ethnic students and cultural organizations at his university. Leo had grown up in a very White, semi-rural area and had had virtually no contact with other Iranians. But he was now at a university where he had become actively involved in the Persian society, dating a Persian woman, and learning to speak Farsi. He was now extremely proud and enthusiastic about his Iranian heritage and wished to highlight this part of his heritage. Yet when he went back home (where he'd grown up), he tended to revert to his 'former' English persona.

Well, when I'm at home in [x] and with my friends there, I'm very much like English. Like absolutely. No one even thinks different. Only my very close friends even know [that he's part Iranian]... A lot of them call me [a Persian name] for fun because they just think it's fun but they're... That's it. But I mean down here [at university] I'm a bit different.

Like Leo, Alan, who was Indian and English, also grew up in a very White setting, so that he felt (and identified) differently in his 'old' home setting and his current university setting:

For example I grew up in Essex, in [x]... they're all kind of White. And when I'm with them, like I identify as you know, supporting England, like watching football, taking an interest in... not English things but, you know, just generally I'd more identify with being British in my young life. And then coming to university and meeting lots of different people and then when I'm hanging with them, so I've got quite a few friends who are Sri Lankan and Indian and things like that...

But not all mixed young people found university to be a place where they could enjoy and discover a specific minority heritage or their mixedness. Natalie's sense of who she was (Black Caribbean and White English), especially her sense of being mixed, was destabilized by her arrival at a predominantly White university, in which being mixed or Black was anomalous.

Natalie: *It's as if I'm losing my sense of identity. When I came here, I was very... this is who I am, I'm mixed race... I'm white and I'm black and I've been influenced by both cultures. If I'd had gone to X University, I'd have felt more mixed, they could have related to me a bit more. But here I've come to a heavily populated white university. Some people have never had a mixed race friend or black friend and don't understand the culture at all. So they get a bit frightened by it. They associate... everyone seems to think I'm from the ghetto in [X] called [X]... Well no... and they all think I know every black person in the world... I've had to change the way I speak obviously, I feel I'm having a bit of a crisis of identity.*

Thus, while a mixed identity had been validated in her previous 'home' setting, a move to a mostly White university setting with a significantly different ethnic composition resulted in Natalie feeling racially objectified and unable to assert a mixed identity. By comparison, Anna, who considered herself to be 'mixed race' Black Antiguan and Irish (and whose mixed ancestry was acknowledged in her home town), reported

that since coming to university in London, she had stopped calling herself 'mixed race' to other people and had started saying she was Irish.
Because of her White appearance, Anna's claim to being 'mixed race'
was almost never validated by others (see Chapters 3 and 4): '*I got fed up
explaining my background so I started just saying I was Irish.*'

As in Natalie's and Anna's cases, changes in expressed identification
did not necessarily signal a change in internal identity, but could be
engendered by others' racial assignment of them. While Natalie's sense
of identity as a mixed person was destabilized by others' reactions to
her (in a mostly White university), Anna decided to describe herself in
a way which did not invite challenges or incredulity from others – even
though she stubbornly claimed that she was, and felt, mixed race.

Key themes in findings and conclusion

The diverse and often detailed ways in which our mixed race young
people described themselves can be seen as positioned acts of communication and argumentation, in which they commented upon and
contested existing, official categorizations and terms. In doing so, they
were effectively engaging in dialogue with discourses of ethnic and racial
difference, and many respondents were keen to convey the uniqueness
of their mixed ancestries and experiences.

Because of the frequently unique way in which respondents choose to
identify, unprompted free-text ethnicity data does not easily map on to
census categories. The findings of this chapter indicate that open-ended
(free-text) questions can yield important insights into super-diversity
in a way that fixed categorization cannot and should be employed
for research and policy purposes, if resources permit. However, such
data are not easily transferred into conventional categorization because
of inconsistencies in reporting free-text descriptions. This may not be
an impediment if one takes the view that the insights yielded by the
descriptions are what makes this kind of data useful, for example, the
revelation that multiple (three or more) identities are now an important
component of 'mixed' ethnicity, even though conceptualized by ONS in
the 2001 and 2011 censuses in terms of *dual* groups in the predesignated
options. While the politics of statistical proportionality require discrete
and stable categories, the shift to a focus on identity politics and diversity may propel ethnicity data collection in new and more democratic
directions (see Roth 2010). Increasingly, self-identification is inconsis-
tent with forcing people into prescribed categories (Prewitt 2005). Open
response offers a potential means of addressing the issue of essentialism

that category labelling in censuses may engender (Bonnett & Carrington 2000).

Several important themes emerge from the analysis of the survey and interview data. First, giving a *detailed description* of their 'mixedness' or multiplicity of heritages is important to respondents. For most respondents, saying that they are just 'mixed race' or mixed is not a self-description of choice. The majority gave detailed descriptions involving at least two groups. Many respondents chose to provide a description of themselves that was not constrained to Census pan-ethnic groupings (like 'White and Black Caribbean', 'White and Black African', or 'White and Asian'), although Census terminology was used by some. Terms reflecting national identity or national/country origins were also important. While some were content to use census terms like 'Black African', 'Black Caribbean', or 'Asian' in the description of their mixed heritages, many others chose to name national origins or national identities, such as 'Egyptian', 'Gabon', 'Guinea', 'Zimbabwean', 'Montserratian', 'Chinese', 'Pakistani', and 'Indian'.

The second theme is *multiplicity*. An assumption has been made in official data collection in England and Wales – that 'mixed race' or 'mixedness' in individuals is primarily a product of having parents belonging to different pan-ethnic groupings ('Caribbean', 'African', and 'Asian' in combination with 'White'). Three of the four (2001 and 2011) Census 'mixed' categories reference such pairings. Indeed, many local authorities and other statutory bodies have labelled these options 'dual heritage' on equal opportunities monitoring and other forms in recognition that they appear to be asking about parentage. Similarly, the terminology of the main government departments encompasses terms such as 'mixed parentage' and 'dual heritage', that is, involving two groups. 'Dual heritage', for example, is the second most frequently used term after 'mixed heritage' on the website of the Department for Children, Schools and Families (Aspinall 2009). However, the findings from our survey show that a significant proportion (20%) of respondents identify three groups in these unprompted, free-text descriptions. These findings indicate that the identifications and conceptualizations of mixed race among young people are more complex than current terminology acknowledges and that census terminology simplifies this complexity for many respondents.

The third theme in our findings is *fluidity* of identification – over time, and in disparate contexts and situations. Such fluidity in expressed identification and/or internal identity, which is situationally specific, should not be read as 'identity confusion' as such (though such a sense of uncertainty or instability about internal identity is of course possible). Rather, the changeable nature of identification at a key developmental and transitional period in these young peoples' lives is not surprising – at a time when they often encounter very different settings and people, than they have previously done. This was especially the case for young people who moved from primarily suburban or even semi-rural settings to universities in urban and metropolitan centres, such as London. Despite some exceptions, overall, moving to universities allowed a wider remit of identification than previously available for many types of mixed young people. However, our respondents were highly aware of how they were differently perceived in different contexts, by different sets of people.

In many of the responses to our survey questions (and in the subset of interviews), it was not always possible to distinguish clearly between changes in expressed identification and internal identity. It was clear that some respondents (in specific situations) could adapt their expressed identifications in strategic ways, so that there was no suggestion of a change in internal identity – for example Ahmed, who reported that he tended to emphasize different aspects of his ancestry or identity in different settings, such as in a job interview, or a respondent who claimed a mixed description for the purposes of some form of 'positive discrimination' on an official form. There was also evidence that some respondents could experience changes in internal identities, especially when they switched from one setting (and network) to another – such as Callum, who reported that he actually *felt* more Filipino at home, with his mother, sister, and step-father, than he did when he was at university – without necessarily changing the way in which they described themselves. However, there were also many excerpts with survey respondents (and in some interviews) in which it was not clear whether particular changes in expressed identifications were *also* accompanied by changes in internal identities; in fact, respondents themselves were not always clear about the depth or nature of reported shifts in identification.

It is important to differentiate between disparate triggers to shifts in identification – whether these be changing official categories and forms encountered at specific points in time, changes in one's setting or situations, or key transitional moments of their lives (like going to university), some of which are more likely to engender shifts in internal as well as expressed identities. So while Rockquemore and Brunsma (2002) refer to four types of identities in relation to their biracial (Black and White) respondents in the United States, in which a 'protean' identity is one, we found that the potential for shifts in expressed and/or internal identities was more widespread among our respondents. Thus, we conceive of both expressed and internal identities, more generally, as *potentially* changeable, and not a 'type' of identification as such.

While this chapter focused primarily upon the ways in which mixed individuals responded to open-ended questions about their expressed identities, in the next chapter, we turn to the question of how respondents make choices about their expressed identities, if they are able to choose *only one* racial or ethnic group to which they feel they belong – and how we should interpret such choices. Building on our findings about the varied, detailed, and often changeable ways in which our respondents can identify themselves when they are able to do so in an open-ended fashion, in the next chapter, we turn to an examination of how respondents identify themselves when they are asked to prioritize one 'best' race. We will also critically explore what such choices may mean in our respondents' everyday lives.

3
Differential Ethnic Options?

In the previous chapter, we found that there is often multiplicity, detailed specificity, and fluidity in the racial identifications of many mixed race young people in this study, especially if they are given the opportunity to respond in an open-ended fashion. But when asked to do so, are mixed young people in Britain willing to choose only one 'race' – the race they think best describes them? Such a 'forced choice' question has been used in the United States as an indicator of the identity options (and by extension, the sense of racial allegiance and membership) of disparate types of mixed people. Are there differences across specific types of 'mixes' in terms of whether they opt for their White or minority racial backgrounds or in their propensity to refuse to choose only one 'race'? And if so, how do we make sense of such group differences? These questions enable us to explore how different types of mixed people may perceive and experience their ethnic options in a variety of ways.

Various American scholars, and Mary Waters (1990) in particular, have argued that minority people who are not White possess fewer or no 'ethnic options' compared with White Americans, who can exercise choice about whether they are ethnic, or whether they are simply Americans (though see Song 2003). While White Americans can enjoy a symbolic ethnicity without being subject to racial assignment by others (Gans 1979), non-White individuals are said to be unable to assert ethnic identities of their choosing, in a positive, costless way. Can this thinking be extended to mixed race people, many of whom do not appear White (and who can be racially assigned in ways which are beyond their control)? Their very mixedness, and the identity options available to them, presents an interesting and yet under-explored area of study, especially in the British context (though see Khanna 2011 for a study of 'biracial' options in the US).

The theoretical literature on ethnic options frequently invokes the concept of 'agent autonomy' or 'agency', the possession of which enables the subject to conceive and pursue projects, plans, and values. To exercise 'options' requires an awareness of one's options and also that, in choosing, the knowledge that one is charting a course (Raz 1986). This core idea connects to debates about structure and agency: there has, in the first place, to be an availability of options and the possibility that such options can be validated by others (Nagel 1994; Song 2003).

Our choices are both constrained and constituted by social practices. As Charles Taylor puts it, a self only exists and an identity only emerges within 'webs of interlocution' (Taylor 1994:36, 39), that is, our actions belong to the practices that shape them and endow them with meaning. For example, individuals from disadvantaged social backgrounds may not perceive the same range of ethnic options to be available to them as someone with the privilege of material advantage (Fhagen-Smith 2010). Or a person living in an area with a high concentration of co-ethnics may be constrained in choosing an ethnic identity that diverges from the norm within that area (Holloway et al. 2012). In such ways the options that we are able to freely exercise are fundamentally shaped by the social matrix in which we live. If social practices give shape and meaning to talk about options, so too does the conceptual vocabulary of ethnicity.

Margaret Somers (1994) calls such practices 'public narratives'. Thus, the options available may, in themselves, be the product of institutions and practices external to the self. In recognition of these external forces, Elster (1993) refers to the process of choice-making as '*adaptive* preference formation'. It is usual, therefore, for sociologists to talk of the mutually constitutive character of agency and structure and the recursive nature of their interactions. Appiah (2005:107) frames the issue thus: ' ... *we make up selves from a toolkit of options made available by our culture and society*'. We do make choices, but we don't, individually, determine the options which we choose. What we endeavour to do in this chapter is to explore how this process of choice-making for mixed race individuals is constrained and enabled within these broader social practices, particularly when such individuals are asked to nominate only one race which best captures their sense of selves.

Standen (1996) termed this situation – the need to pick one identity or another – the *forced-choice dilemma* and it has been the subject of substantial empirical interest. How multiracial individuals respond when compelled to identify with only one component of their identity has been explored through a variety of methodological approaches. Several US investigators have analysed these options in large-scale surveys such as the Current Population Survey (CPS) Supplement and National Health Interview Survey (NHIS) which have allowed multiple-race responses and also asked respondents to specify one race as their primary race (Campbell 2003, 2007; Harris & Sim 2002; Herman 2004; Schenker and Parker 2003), the so-called *directly* forced-choice question. Typically, these studies use a range of socio-demographic and other covariates available in the datasets and contextual variables relating to the home context and area of residence in models to try to identify predictors of the primary race responses. Some of this work has been driven by the need to find better bridging methods between administrative data that reports multiple races and that using only single races.

There are other genres or approaches that provide evidence of how the exercise of ethnic options may be constrained. Longitudinal datasets that cover the transition period from the selection of only one racial/ethnic group to the use of 'mixed' categorization or multi-ticking can be exploited, so that the responses of individuals identifying as 'mixed' can be tracked back to a single racial/ethnic group assignment (Platt et al. 2005). We saw the utility of the ONS Longitudinal Study in revealing the transitions between the two types of question in Chapter 2. The longitudinal transitions and directly forced-choice questions are close relatives: the assumption is that the response to the forced choice question would be closely associated with the response that would have been given if only a single-race question had been asked. There are, too, those indirect measures of having to choose, notably those studies that look at how parents in inter-ethnic unions/marriages racially/ethnically assign their children (see Roth 2005 and below) (these studies assess to what extent such decisions have been forced upon them by historical 'rules of assignment' and prevalent social attitudes).

Although some common themes about attributions of marginality (and pressures to 'choose sides') can apply to all mixed people, various studies in the United States have emphasized different identity options of people with part-Black heritage, in comparison with those with other types of ethnic minority heritage. The main point of comparison which has emerged in the US literature concerns the ethnic options of Black/White versus Asian/White (or Black/White options versus those of Latino/White and Native American/White) people (see Harris & Sim 2002; Doyle & Kao 2007; Herman 2004; Tashiro 2002; Lopez 2003). In their analysis of a large dataset of adolescents in the United States, Harris and Sim (2002) ask respondents (who identify with more than one race) to choose a single racial category. The authors found that 86%

of White/American Indian adolescents selected 'White', while 75% of Black/White adolescents chose 'Black' as their best single race, again reflecting the enduring power of the 'one drop rule'. Nevertheless, it is noteworthy that 17.1% of Black/White adolescents selected 'White' as the race that best describes them. A further 8.5% of the Black/White respondents were not able (or refused) to choose one single race, and the authors interpret this as '*a commitment to being multiracial on the part of white/black youth that is not evident in the responses of white/American Indian youth*' (Harris & Sim 2002:622).

In Campbell's (2003) sample from the US Current Population Survey (CPS), 32% of Black/White respondents chose White (and 47% Black), compared with 27% of the Black/Hispanic respondents, and just 2–6% of multiracial respondents where Black was paired with American Indian or Asian or Other. Similar findings were reported by Parker et al. (2004): The proportions selecting 'White' varied from 74.0% in the American Indian or Alaska Native (AIAN)/White group, 41.2% in the Asian and Pacific Islander (API)/White group, and 26.9% in the Black/White group. Interestingly, while Black/White people are clearly less likely to choose 'White' than other mixed people, these studies suggest that those choosing 'White' are not insignificant – 32% in Campbell's (2003) study and almost 27% in Parker et al.'s (2004) study.

With respect to Asian/White mixes ('Asian' referring primarily to those of East Asian ancestry in the US), some analysts (Harris & Sim 2002; Tashiro 2002) suggest that Asian/White people in the United States may identify as *either* White or Asian, and that part Asian respondents possess more freedom and latitude in their identity options than do part-Black people. Herman (2004) found that more (43%) White-Asians chose Asian than they did White (33%) when asked to choose only one race, while Parker et al. (2004) showed that 39.6% of the API/White group selected 'API' and 41.2% 'White'. In addition, some US studies of how *parents* racially designate their mixed children suggest that children with one Asian and one White parent can be identified as *either* Asian or White (see Qian 2004; Brunsma 2005; Xie & Goyette 1997; Saenz et al. 1995).[1]

Clearly, such studies comparing the 'forced choice' questions of disparate mixed groups require more investigation, especially in settings outside of the United States. Given these stark and consistent findings that a higher proportion of Black/White mixed people in the United States choose 'Black' rather than 'White' in forced choice survey questions, we wondered: Is this also the case for part-Black mixed young people in Britain, and what are the perceived identity options of other types of mixed people, such as Chinese and White, or Arab and White?

And what about mixed people who have no White ancestry? We found no other studies that specifically addressed these questions in a British context. We also wanted to know why our respondents made the choices they did. The US models found that strong primary race predictors were age cohort and contextual variables relating to home context and area of residence. Importantly, they also showed that relationships between primary race and covariates to predict primary race might be changing over time (Schenker & Parker 2003).

While not officially codified, as in the United States, a less stringent 'one drop' rule seems to have operated, de facto, in Britain (Twine 2010; Ifekwunigwe 1999). However, as in the United States, some British studies show that Black/White people in Britain are increasingly able to exercise a range of identity options (see e.g. Caballero et al. 2008; Edwards & Caballero 2008). A prominent study of the identities of mixed (Black and White) adolescents by Tizard & Phoenix (1993:159) found that just under 50% of the 58 mixed race teenagers they interviewed thought of themselves as 'black'; the rest of these young people considered themselves to be 'brown', 'mixed', or 'coloured'. Some regarded themselves as *both* black and 'mixed race', or even 'half-caste' (also see Tikly et al. 2004).

While previous US surveys employing a forced choice question with mixed people have detailed modelled information about the associations between primary race and selected covariates and contextual variables, providing access to an understanding of *why* respondents chose one specific group or 'race', there is a lack of such evidence for the British context. This chapter explores the ways in which different types of mixed respondents choose (or don't choose) one group, and the reasons why they have done so, including the role of physical appearance, which is often not sufficiently addressed in studies which have employed a forced choice question. The chapter concludes by drawing upon in-depth interviews to explore what respondents mean when they choose specific groups. We argue that the interpretation of responses to a forced choice question is not necessarily straightforward and requires some probing, which reveals the sometimes complex and ambivalent views of our mixed respondents.

'Forced choice' questions

Various measures of ethnicity and race can be placed along a continuum of stability, with ethnic and racial self-identification using open response likely to be the least stable, and operational definitions of actual family origins the most stable (Aspinall 2001). From the perspective of self-identification, open response may be said to have high validity as it is unconstrained by categorization. However, given its instability and frequently high non-response rate, surveys usually rely on pre-determined classifications to capture self-assigned ethnicity. Any system of classification will impose limitations on how the respondent might wish to self-identify. The Office for National Statistics (2003:2) states: '*The ethnic group options presented to the respondent are not completely ones of self-identity, since the respondent is likely to have had no say in the names or the number of the different alternative ethnic groups in the "menu". Therefore, the freedom the respondent has to select their own group is constrained and influenced by the options on offer.*' Ethnicity classifications, therefore, present one form of 'forced choice' question, albeit indirectly forced. For example, the 1991 Census offered respondents only free-text options to declare their mixedness and the England and Wales 2001 and 2011 Censuses constrained respondents to a set of exact combinations or free text.

The genre of 'forced choice' question used in our survey is one that explicitly asks mixed race respondents to choose just *one* group, thereby trying to force the respondent to prioritize their affiliations by naming the group that contributes *most strongly* to their identity. We were interested to see if our respondents could and would name just one racial/ethnic group to describe themselves, and whether their choices varied across our different types of mixed groups. Responses to this question have been regarded as a telling indicator of the perceived ethnic options held by mixed individuals. We wondered whether the responses to this question would reveal a leaning towards one ancestry over another. Were our British part-Black respondents (as in the US) more likely to choose Black as their single group (thus suggesting a social convention that they identify as Black) and were the other mixed groups more likely to choose White? In addition to the 'forced choice' survey question, we analyse a supplementary survey question asking why the respondent identified with this group. We also examine the sub-set of in-depth interviews, which revealed a degree of complexity and tension in respondents' answers, which were not discernible in the survey responses on their own.

Directly 'forced choice' questions

Our survey respondents were asked: '*If you had to name just one racial/ethnic group – the one that contributes most strongly to your identity –*

which group would that be?' They were invited to write in the name of
the group or tick a 'can't say' box. Respondents were then asked to say
in free text why they identified with this group. Thus our questions
diverge from previous 'forced choice' questions in two important ways:
First, we asked respondents to nominate a group via an open response,
rather than a pre-given set of categories; second, we asked respondents
to explain why they chose (or did not choose) one specific group. Both
of these measures result in the 'forced choice' providing a much more
reliable and revealing question than if it is used in isolation (as in most
previous studies). In addition to the follow-up survey question, we also
probed our sub-set of interviewees about their responses to the forced
choice question – thus adding another layer of information and depth
to these responses.

For each of our main mixed categories (Black/White; East or SE
Asian/White; Arab/White; South Asian/White; minority mixed), we collapsed the responses into three main groupings (Table 3.1): (i) refusers,
comprising those who selected the 'can't say' option and those who
indicated that they saw themselves as mixed and therefore did not prioritize one group; (ii) those who chose 'White', including those who
wrote in a White description and those who gave a national identity
that *probably* implied a European nationality (such as 'English', 'British',
'Italian', and 'German'); and (iii) those who prioritized a minority ethnic
identity (Fig. 3.1).

Those who prioritized a minority group

Amongst the mixes containing White ancestry, Black/White respondents were more likely to prioritize their minority ethnic identity
(36.9%) than the others; for example, 27.6% of Arab/White, 22.0% of
South Asian/White, and 17.7% of East or SE Asian/White respondents
prioritized their minority backgrounds – though small numbers in some
of these sub-groups may affect the robustness of these findings. This
finding on the forced choice question appears to accord with most US
findings which contrast part-Black and non-Black mixed people. However, the basis for one's sense of a primary feeling of attachment or
belonging in a minority group could differ. For some respondents, a
strong attachment to a minority background or culture could be key,
while others who chose a minority group did so because of their experiences of being racially assigned to their minority 'race' and/or forms of
racism.

Not surprisingly, the influence of parents, especially that of the non-
White parent (if they had grown up with them), could be an important

Table 3.1 Responses to the forced choice question: numbers and row percentages

	Refusers		White prioritizers		Minority ethnic identity prioritizers	
	Cant' say	Mixed[1]	Prioritized White[2]	Prioritized English, British, Italian, etc.[3]	Prioritized minority ethnic identity	TOTAL
1. Black/White	42	18	27	12	58	157
	26.8%	11.5%	17.2%	7.6%	36.9%	100%
2. East or SE Asian/White[4]	9	1	18	9	8	45
	20.0%	2.2%	40.0%	20.0%	17.7%	100%
3. Arab/White	3	2	6	10	8	29
	10.3%	6.9%	20.7%	34.5%	27.6%	100%
4. S Asian/White	9	3	19	8	11	50
	18.0%	6.0%	38.0%	16.0%	22.0%	100%
5. minority mixed	7	2	0	3	28	40
	17.5%	5.0%		7.5%	70.0%	100%
TOTAL[5]	70	26	70	42	113	321
	21.8%	8.1%	21.8%	13.1%	35.2%	100%

Notes: 1. Those who wrote in 'mixed race', 'mixed', or gave a mixed description are included as refusers as they chose to prioritize both groups and not one as asked. 2. 'White' and descriptions including White, such as 'White British' and 'White English'. 3. These are European national identities, including 'British', 'English', 'Welsh', 'Irish', 'Italian', and so on, but without the descriptor 'White'; clearly, some of the terms, like 'British', may have been used to imply 'Black British' in the case of group one. 4. One respondent in the East/SE Asian category left the question blank – thus, the row totalling to 45. 5. Four cases that could not be allocated to the five-category system are excluded from the analysis.
Source: Main student survey.

factor in moulding the identity of many respondents. For instance, Leo, who had an Iranian mother and English father, chose 'Iranian' in the forced choice question. When probed about his response to this question, Leo reported that: '*Mum was very proud of being Persian, whereas Dad didn't really care about being English.*' In Leo's case, his father's English background was simply regarded as a bland default mode – whereas his mother's Iranian background was notably distinctive against the mainstream culture. Thus respondents who grew up in households where their minority parent's culture was central to home life, as in customs and food, could be especially influenced by that parent – though in many cases, as we'll see below, the minority parent's culture was largely symbolic or eclipsed by the wider force of mainstream British settings and practices. Furthermore, as these young people got older, and spent more time with their peer group, the influence of parents could wane.

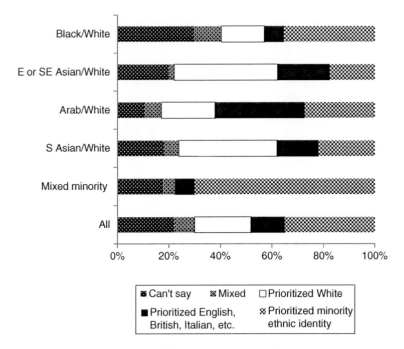

Figure 3.1   Forced choice racial/ethnic group
Source: Main student survey.

Many of the reasons offered by those who chose a minority 'race' (especially part-Black respondents who did so) focused on the importance of societal perceptions of them – particularly the ways in which they were racially assigned by others:

> *'Viewed in that way by society'; 'My features. I do not look mixed race. Have been taught about heritage'; 'My colour & looks are more obvious than the white side of my identity'; 'because of my skin colour I'm seen as black to everyone else'; 'Because that's the way society sees me, they don't see or want to recognise "another part of you" '; 'The way society views me comes into play here; race is something I deal with on a daily basis even if I know that genetically/biologically I am just as much White as I am Black.'*

Those who chose a single minority race reported that they tended to be seen, racially, as non-White, and/or sometimes referred to experiences of racial prejudice and a sense of being a racialized minority. Some of the part-Black respondents who chose Black or some variant, such as Jamaican, referred to the predominantly Black social networks and milieus in which they participated and inhabited. Danny, who had a Black mother and White father, said that he was usually seen as Black by other people. Furthermore, in the interview, when asked why he chose Black in the forced choice question, he revealed that his social world was primarily Black:

> *I don't know, everything in my household...Music, friends, I don't know.... Yeah, the only White person I know is my dad, really, so that everybody else is Black. At family parties you get a load of Black people and only a couple of White people.*

Keith, who had a White English mother and a Black Jamaican father, chose 'minority (Black)'. He revealed that, especially in public settings, he had experienced forms of racial prejudice as a Black man. In addition to being consistently pigeon-holed as Black, he had to contend with the negative social value attached to being Black and male. Keith knew he was 'mixed race', but he clearly experienced the world as a Black person (Waters 1999; Rockquemore & Brunsma 2002). As Keith put it:

> *1) When White people give you funny looks when you walk past them as if you're about [sic] rob them; 2) taxi drivers always ask you for the money upfront because they think you're going to run off without paying; 3) security follow you around the shop as soon as you walk through the door, stand right behind you and pretend they're tidying up, etc.... If you are treated like this [as a Black man] all your life it will affect the way you see yourself, how you see and feel about the people that see you in that way, and for me, who you choose to identify with.*

In the interview, Keith also stressed that he felt much more accepted by other Black people, than White people. The cumulative nature of these experiences with the White world (Feagin 1991), in which he was always seen as Black, reinforced his sense of being Black, even though he acknowledged his mixed heritage. Keith came from a working-class background, and his sense of occupying a disadvantaged minority position was also shaped by his class, culture and economic circumstances. Even in cases where Black/White respondents were from middle-class backgrounds, or had not suffered blatant forms of racism, such respondents were often racially assigned as Black by the wider society (see Chapter 4), and this could shape or reinforce their racial identities.

Nevertheless, coming from a more privileged background could matter in the case of some of our Black/White respondents, who reported a greater sense of autonomy about how they were seen by others, and who felt more insulated from forms of racial prejudice (see Chapter 5). Such respondents could embrace their Black ancestry in a more wholly positive way, without being (as) subject to the negative meanings and values associated with some Black people, especially disadvantaged and uneducated Black men. For instance, Sandy came from a middle-class background in which both her Barbadian father and White English mother were educated professionals. In response to the forced choice question, she wrote: *'The black Caribbean (Barbadian) side of my family'*. In her interview, she revealed that she felt very positive about her Barbadian ancestry (which she thought was 'cool'), and indicated that she had never experienced any negative interactions due to her Barbadian background. In this respect, Sandy's attachment to her Barbadian side was similar to that of Leo, above.

By comparison, many of the *non*-Black respondents who chose their minority background explained their choices rather differently from some of the part-Black respondents discussed above (such as Keith and Danny). As in the case of Leo (who celebrated his Iranian heritage), and Sandy, above, discussed earlier, most of the non-Black respondents who prioritized a minority group identity did so as a means of highlighting a valued minority culture and heritage, rather than because it had been socially imposed upon them by others. For instance, Mia, who had an Indian mother and English father, chose 'Indian/Malaysian' in the forced choice question. Mia reported that people did not know how to place her, based upon her physical appearance, and that she did not get racially assigned in any consistent fashion (see discussion in Chapter 4).

In her interview, she explained that: *Mainly at home I was brought up with White emphasis, like basically brought up White, even though my mum is Indian.* But in secondary school, and especially at university, where most of her friends were Asian and Arab, she primarily identified as a mixed person with Indian heritage. One key motivation for this was that she thought that English culture was completely 'bland': *It's sort of like when people say, what's the English culture like you can say…Say, like, India you have Indian dance, like in England you have Morris dancers. Do you know what I mean?…Like there isn't culture…. There's nothing particular to England. There's nothing to really identify with.*

For Mia, her Indian ancestry made her feel special – this is resonant with Mary Waters' discussion of White Americans' ethnic options, invoked in a wholly positive way. And unlike the Black/White respondents discussed above, Mia *chose* to emphasize her Indianness – it was not imposed upon her.

In some cases, respondents chose their non-White backgrounds to signal their sense of attachment and affiliation with their minority heritages, despite (or because of) the fact that the wider public tended to see them as solely White (these cases are discussed in more detail in Chapter 4). So in addition to their familial upbringing and their class backgrounds, the contexts and motivations for choosing a minority race in the forced choice question tended to differ for those who were seen, and thus racially assigned, as non-White versus those who were seen as White by the wider public. And as discussed in the previous chapter, given the potential fluidity of expressed and internal identities, especially at key transitions in their lives, it is important to remember that some of the respondents who chose a specific minority race (or 'White', as discussed below) could, in theory, make a different choice at another point in their life course.

Interestingly, 28 of the 40 'minority mixed' survey respondents prioritized one 'race' over another (as opposed to refusing to choose, e.g., by asserting a mixed identity). Of the minority mixed respondents who were part-Black and prioritized one group (18 of 40), 13 prioritized 'black' and 5 some other minority ethnic group, mirroring findings in the United States. For instance, Herman (2004:737) found her 'double minority' respondents who were Black/Asian and Black/Hispanic tended to choose Black over Asian and Hispanic; thus, a racial trumping of one race (Black) over another was in operation.

Nevertheless, as illustrated below, minority mixed respondents who chose one group reported a range of reasons for their choices, with many of them pointing to parental upbringing, cultural exposure of specific backgrounds, and physical appearance. The following are a selection of answers given to the question '*Why do you identify with this group*' by those minority mixed survey respondents who wrote in a prioritized group (in parentheses):

'Father's ethnic origin tended to have more dominant and significant impact on my upbringing & cultural values' [Asian Indian]; 'It's [Jamaican] the most dominate of the three races I'm mixed with'; 'have been brought up by Bengalis and with them' [Bengali]; 'the appearance' [Asian]; 'I can speak Urdu and feel that I'm more Pakistani in some ways' [Pakistani]; 'Because I am closer to my mums family because my dad and his family ain't been around much' [Asian]; 'I was brought up by my mother' [Filipino]; 'father's culture is more predominant in family household, and

> *I can speak Farsi (father's mother tongue) but not Cantonese (mother's mother tongue)' [Iranian].*

In fact, the experiences and perspectives of our seven minority mixed *interviewees* were quite varied: three of the seven minority mixed interviewees would not choose a single group, indicating that they were equally attached to both ancestries (or transcended racial identification). The other four minority mixed respondents chose one minority heritage over the other (one as Black, two as South Asian, and one as East Asian). Of these seven minority mixed respondents, four had part-Black heritage – but of these, only one chose Black. For example, Salma had a Pakistani mother and a Black Sudanese father. When posed with the forced choice survey question, she had chosen 'Asian'. When asked about this choice in the subsequent interview, Salma explained why she had chosen this, despite her reluctance to choose only one group:...*when I said Asian, I mean in my cultural upbringing. I speak Urdu at home and our family and friends are mostly from the Asian subcontinent such as India, Pakistan...We have no links with family in Sudan at the moment or our family in Afghanistan.* For the minority mixed respondents with part-Black ancestry, it is likely that they were racially assigned as Black in the wider society. However, as in Salma's case, such respondents did not necessarily choose 'Black' in the forced choice question.

Those who chose 'White' or a variant of 'White'

For those that were willing and/or able to identify a single group, the cases of individuals who chose 'White' or a European nationality are interesting, because they provide some measure of the extent to which such respondents felt able to claim a White identity – one which is historically and traditionally seen as off-bounds for most mixed people.

Black/White individuals were least likely to prioritize White in the forced choice question: just 17.2% chose White (including 'White English', 'White British', etc.) and an additional 7.6% wrote in British, English, or European national identities (together, almost 25%). In contrast, 40.0% of the East or SE Asian and White group prioritized 'White' and a further 20.0% British, English, et al. national identities (together, 60%). Similarly, 38.0% of the South Asian/White group named 'White' and an additional 16% commensurate national identities (together, 54%). The Odds Ratio (OR) of Black/White respondents naming 'White', compared with the East or SE Asian/White responders, was

0.32 (95% CI, 0.15 to 0.71). These diminished somewhat when White and commensurate national identity responses were combined: OR 0.23 (95% CI, 0.11 to 0.49). By comparison, the Arab/White group was some-what different, with those who prioritized a British, English, and so on national identity (34.5%) outnumbering those who prioritized 'White' (20.7%) – though as discussed below, there was much overlap in what respondents meant when they chose 'White' and European national terms. Only 3 of 40 minority mixed respondents chose a British or European nationality (and none chose 'White', which did not comprise part of their mix), with most (28 of 40) choosing one of their minority backgrounds, as discussed above. The three minority mixed respon-dents' choice of a European national identity is likely to signal their primary sense of identification and belonging in Britain, as opposed to a specific claim to Whiteness as such.

While relatively uncommon, almost 25% of our Black/White respon-dents chose either 'White' or a European nationality, such as 'British' or 'Irish'. A number of such respondents tended to explain their choices in similar terms. One female respondent, who had a Jamaican mother and English father, chose 'English/British' in the forced choice question. As an explanation, she wrote: '*both my parents were born in England and I have lived here all my life*'. Her choice of 'English/British' clearly refers to her sense of cultural belonging in Britain, but does not simplistically suggest that she is unattached to her Black Jamaican heritage. Another female respondent, who described herself as '*mixed Irish, Italian, and black African*', chose 'Italian' in the forced choice ques-tion. By way of explanation, she wrote: '*My first name is Italian, I speak Italian, my mother was born in Italy, out of all my relations, I see my Italian ones the most.*' In this latter case, her strong attachment to her mother's Italian family and culture trumps her identification with a Black group.

It is important to note that her choice of 'Italian' primarily signals a strong cultural attachment to her mother's side and should not be understood as a straightforward proxy for 'White'. Nevertheless, respon-dents who chose 'White' (or a variant) or a European national identity in the forced choice question share, as we discuss below, an assertion of cultural and national belonging in the wider society, and such a choice signals the primacy of such an affiliation over a minority racial attachment as such.

Interestingly, neither of these Black/White respondents said that they felt they were members of a group which was racially discriminated against, and when queried about whether they identified with a national group, they both reported: 'English' (they had the option to say that they did not identify along national lines at all, among other choices). While we are clearly looking at a handful of examples here, these cases suggest that it is not incidental that these Black/White respondents who chose a European national group in the forced choice question did not feel subject to forms of racial prejudice or discrimination – unlike the case of Keith, above. Thus even among Black/White respondents, there could be real variation in how respondents understood and experienced their identities and senses of belonging.

This finding is striking in itself, though in the United States, as noted, varying proportions of Black/White people are reported to identify as 'White'. US surveys tend to offer only racial and ethnic classifications, not open-ended responses which may allow for national terms of belonging, such as 'American' (Song & Hashem 2010). As with those who chose a minority race, like Danny, parental influence and upbringing (such as the case of the respondent who especially related to her mother's Italian background), the ethnic composition of one's neighbourhood, and social networks were also fundamental in shaping the choice of 'White' or a term implying a European nationality. A predominantly White setting, and in some cases, an upbringing by a White mother, could strongly shape respondents who chose 'White' or a variant. Lara, who had a Black African father and White English mother, and who grew up in a predominantly White town in the North, explained in her interview:

> *I would say predominantly White background. Yeah, cos we've always had people from different backgrounds around all me life, but it's been predominantly a White upbringing, White city culture, the way I dress, the people I hang around with, things I eat, the places I go to, predominantly White I suppose.*

So, unlike Danny, discussed above (who had chosen 'Black', and was primarily surrounded by Black people), Lara's Black father had left when she had been a young child, and thus Lara had primarily been surrounded by White people and family, in a primarily White town. While she knew that she had a Black African father, and that she did not *look* White, she recognized that her everyday life and surroundings were mostly White – in terms of both people and what she considered to be White cultural practices. Lara's choice of White is rather exceptional, since, as discussed below, there are strong societal norms which tend to prohibit Black/White people from claiming a White identification or allegiance.

Nevertheless, being raised by a White mother (without much contact with a Black father) did not necessarily result in identifying primarily as White. For instance, Clara was raised primarily by her White Russian mother and had had limited contact with her Black African father. She grew up speaking Russian, and she reported that her upbringing by her mother was wholly European. However, as she grew older, in secondary school and now at university, Clara described herself as 'Black African' in the forced choice question, explaining that she felt more accepted by Black, than White, people and relatives. She also reported that most people saw her as a Black person. In comparison with Lara, who lived in a very White setting, Clara's social network in London became increasingly Black, as she grew older, and had more contact with her Black peers.

Why do a substantial proportion of non-Black mixed respondents choose 'White' or a European national identity? On the basis of these responses to the forced choice question, it would appear that these non-Black mixed respondents see themselves as White or European – but was this in fact the case? Insights into how respondents answered the forced choice question were gained from the follow-up question which asked: '*Why do you identify with this group?*'. These answers reveal very strongly that the context of a person's upbringing was very important to those selecting White or a commensurate national identity (and in this respect are very similar to the explanations given by the Black/White respondents who chose 'English/British' and 'White' discussed above):

> '*Grown up in England, English schooling. Although father is Arab, he is very Anglicised*'; '*I'm more English than Indonesian because I've lived here all my life*'; '*Have been born & brought up in Wales & with quite "White" values, etc. Do not know any different, never lived an extended time in Sri Lanka*'; '*I was born & brought up in white middle class England. My family that I know is white (my mother's family I have never met)*'.

As shown in these responses, those choosing White emphasized that, if forced to choose only one group, 'White' (referring primarily to a sense of national and cultural belonging in Britain) made much more sense than did a minority background, especially if the minority heritage was associated with a distant overseas society with which they had had little contact or knowledge. Many of these respondents were aware of the fact that their ties with an overseas heritage were often tenuous, however symbolically important they may have been, and they noted their unfamiliarity with both the language and customs of their minority parent (especially in the case of those with a White parent).

Although it was relatively uncommon in this study, a few respondents who chose 'White' reported (sometimes sheepishly) that they lived their lives as White people and that most people assumed they were White. For instance, Callum reported that he chose White because he believed that he looked White and that most people did not discern his Filipino ancestry. For these individuals, their physical appearance as White was fundamental to their choice of 'White', in addition to the fact that these individuals were also wholly immersed in British culture and networks, often with predominantly White social networks.

However, unlike Callum, we found that most of the non-Black respondents who chose White distanced themselves from the idea of being *racially* White. In fact, as we'll see in Chapter 4, only a minority of these respondents reported that others actually saw them as unambiguously White; the majority of non-Black respondents reported that they were seen as physically indeterminate, somehow 'different', or foreign. For most of these respondents, identifying White or White British as the group that contributes most strongly to their identity meant that they were first and foremost British in *cultural terms*.

For instance, Nazy, of Iranian and English parentage, chose 'White', and her explanation for this choice was typical of respondents in this group. In response to the follow-up survey question which asked why she chose this group, she wrote: '*I have an olive complexion and so rarely class myself as White; however, I was born and raised in Britain and so identify with that culture*'. While it may appear that she is contradicting herself (in the forced choice question she nominates 'White', but then in response to the follow-up question she says she does not look White), it is clear that Nazy uses the term 'White' to refer to her sense of Britishness, as opposed to being White, racially, and phenotypically. But without our knowledge of how she responds in the follow-up question, we would not have known what she meant when she nominated the term White.

Given that these young people typically had limited exposure to their minority backgrounds, and had grown up in Britain, their primary sense of belonging in Britain was over-determined. This understanding of 'White' differs from the more delimited understanding of White (as a racial identity) in most US studies (Song & Hashem 2010). In another case, Mai (who was Chinese Malaysian/English), chose 'White' in the survey and responded to the follow-up question about why she chose this group: '*Brought up in a mostly white school, and first university. Most*

of my friends are therefore White. I look more White British than Malaysian.'
When probed in the interview about her choice of 'White', Mai said this:

> *I was thinking about it . . . . I wouldn't put it into . . . what colour you are, in a categorising system. I put it more into your culture. My friends who are of Chinese origin, now at X's [medical school] are from the same background as me, so they view themselves, not as being White but as British. We've all had the same upbringing, we've all done the same things, they've grown up here, they don't have a Chinese upbringing.*

Although Mai indicated (in the survey) that she looked more White British than Malaysian, she reported in the interview that most people saw her not as White (or as Chinese), but as physically indeterminate. Like Nazy, Mai understood the term 'British' in a race-neutral way – being British was not about being any one 'color', as she pointed to the very diverse student body milling about us. Yet, when asked why she chose the term 'White' as the group which contributed most strongly to her sense of identity, it is telling that the term 'White' is still the dominant image and meaning associated with being British. Mai had grown up in a small and very White village, in which she and her family had stood out. As she pointed out, she did not look White; yet she felt she belonged in mainstream White Britain.

By comparison, Mohammed, who had an Egyptian father and Irish mother, grew up in a very multiethnic part of London. In choosing 'British', he stressed an inclusive and non-racial understanding of what it meant to be British:

> Int: *You put down that the one single identity most central to you is British.*
> Mohammed: *It's wherever you're born. It's home for me.*
> Int: *And being British doesn't mean you're of any particular color or background?*
> Mohammed: *Um, I don't think color is . . . . It's if you speak the language, you're part of the culture . . . there's a new culture emerging in London, Britain, just the youth culture, urban . . . . Before, it was seen as Black or African. Now I just see people just take it as their own [in fact, his speech is heavily inflected with 'Black' modes of speech]. Before, when I was growing up, it was like, 'Why are you trying to be Black?' And now, everyone is using it.*

Mohammed explained that choosing the term 'British' transcended any narrow notion of race, and that this term incorporated everyone who had grown up in the cultural melange he experienced in London. For him, taking a strong interest in his Muslim faith melded unproblem- atically with his interest in hip hop and his multiethnic friendship network.

Thus, in isolation, the forced choice question can obscure impor- tant information about why someone chooses a particular group or category, or what such a choice means in practice. Without further infor- mation, especially via an interview, the responses to such a question could be misleading. For instance, Paul (East or SE Asian/White) chose 'Irish (or European)' in the forced choice question and wrote this in response to the follow-up question: '*My English is better than my Chinese, I look more Western than Asian, I was educated in the West.*' But in the subsequent interview, he revealed a very strong attachment to being a mixed person, who was invested in *both* his Chinese background and his mixedness (and less so his Irish heritage). This example illustrates the importance of the interview and the triangulation of different forms of data. Although the follow-up survey response explained his choice of 'Irish (or European)', it did not provide a complete picture of what Paul was like, or how he saw himself as a person.

Although Paul had grown up immersed in European cultures and set- tings, what came across in the interview was a very strong sense of being 'Eurasian', and mixed race: '*Eurasiannation [a website] saved my life! For the first time I felt like I connected with a lot of other people like me – that there was actually a Eurasian identity.*' He was also very invested in his Chinese roots – he had lived in China, learned Mandarin, and was now studying Chinese at the MA level. His closest friend was also a Eurasian man with whom he regularly discussed their Eurasian experiences. Paul explained that he did not feel able to call himself Chinese because he did not feel sufficiently ethnically authentic in claiming that he was 'Chinese', given his upbringing in European settings. This case exempli- fies the multilayered forms of belonging and identification experienced by some of these respondents – forms of belonging which cannot easily be captured in survey questionnaires on their own. And as illustrated in Mai's case, above, respondents could be very reflexive about the mean- ings of the ethnic and racial terms they employed (and which could be attributed to them).

Furthermore, the choice of 'White' (or of a minority background) did not necessarily mean that others necessarily validated people's sense of themselves (discussed more fully in Chapter 4). Some non- Black respondents, like George, who chose 'White British', reported that their sense of their White backgrounds as most central to themselves was not validated by others, often due to their indeterminate physical appearance and attributions of foreignness. For example, George, who was Chinese and White English, complained of being seen 'only' as a Chinese or a foreign person, because he saw himself as very British. He'd had very little exposure to Chinese culture and people, and had grown up in a mostly White northern city, where he had *'stuck out like a sore thumb'*. Based upon his appearance (though his name was wholly Anglo), he had encountered a lot of racial taunting at school, and was highly aware of the fact that the 'public' saw him as a non-White foreigner. This treatment of him angered and depressed him. His experiences of racism had made him all the more determined to assert his White British side:

> *You will probably not find anyone more patriotic than me or my brother.... We're super patriotic.... It's a repeated bitterness, actually, to be honest, because it's that thing of trying as hard as you can to be British and never having done anything else, and then realising that that life is always going to be beyond your control.*

In fact, some respondents who chose White or a European nationality term could do so in order to distance themselves from what they perceived as a stigmatized status in Britain. For instance, Nira chose 'British' in the forced choice question, explaining that she felt first and foremost British. Nira's English mother and Egyptian father divorced when she was young, and she had since cut ties with her father, whom she said had not been a good father or husband. In addition to the fact that she was estranged from her father, Nira reported in her interview that she wished to distance herself from her father's Arab culture and the negative symbolism associated with being Muslim and Arab:

> *With Islam, my dad, it's very male dominated. And I just feel that it's not right. And inequalities. That sort of area, where I think I'm very Westernized. I mean, you have inequalities in the workplace [in the UK], and stuff like that. But women have more chances. And obviously, I don't believe in terrorism [laughs ruefully].*

Thus survey findings which report that mixed individuals choose 'White', and then straightforwardly interpret this choice as signalling individuals' identification as a White person, run the risk of obscuring what such choices mean in the everyday lives of such respondents. Without further probing of such choices, and what they may mean, such forced choice formats can provide a misleading and overly simplistic picture.

Those who refused to choose

Significantly, almost a third of respondents ($n = 96$) indicated that they could (or would) not prioritize just *one* racial/ethnic group that contributed most strongly to their identity: while some respondents insisted that they were mixed (26) and refused to prioritize one group over another, more (70) simply ticked the 'can't say' option. The reasons for choosing 'can't say' were not investigated in the survey but may have included those who were unable to name a single group and those that transcended racial categorization and thinking. Interestingly, *Black/White* (38%) respondents comprised the group with the largest proportion of respondents who refused to choose, followed by 24% South Asian/White, 22% East or SE Asian/White, while around 17% of Arab/White respondents did so (though again, there were relatively few Arab/White respondents).

As discussed above, only 9 of 40 minority mixed survey respondents refused to choose. And even though four of the seven minority mixed interviewees chose one group (in the survey), six of these seven interview respondents reported a strong mixed identity in their *interviews*, which suggests that neither non-White 'race' necessarily took precedence over the other. For example, Tara, who had an East or SE Asian mother and an African father, insisted that she could not prioritize one race over the other: '*My parents have made it quite clear that they won't impose their own individual beliefs on me or my brother. So I do feel half African and half Asian.*' In Tara's case, there was no automatic privileging of her Black side over her Asian side. Nor did she feel that she should have to make such a choice.

As for other types of mixed respondents, Richard (South Asian/White) refused to choose one 'race' because he did not identify along racial lines: '*I'm just me...I mean, no ones cares*'. When asked about his cultural upbringing in London, it became evident that Richard's parents had de-emphasized the idea of ethnic or racial difference in their family:

So they just raised me as neutral, which is British really...I just don't think they were that bothered about it. I think my parents have the attitude that your nationality doesn't really define you as a person, which is the way I see it really.

Not identifying along racial lines was, by definition, a derogation of the importance of race or ethnic difference for these individuals. This did not mean, though, that their ethnic or cultural attachment to one or both ancestries was unimportant, but that racial and ethnic signifiers of difference, per se, did not mean very much to these respondents.

Like Richard, some of the Black/White respondents refused to choose because they explicitly disavowed the concept of race or racial difference. Many of the 17 Black/White interview respondents who refused to choose also insisted that they were 'mixed', and neither Black nor White. They understood their mixedness as a refusal to recognize the legitimacy of racial categories and boundaries. When asked why she had ticked 'can't say' to the forced choice question, Keisha, who had a White English mother and Black Ugandan father, said this in her interview:

> *I think it's a question as a mixed race person I wouldn't answer. Because the fact is that I'm half White and half Black, and that puts me in a very specific ethnic box . . . . so to choose one to me would be denying one of my parents . . . . Cos my mum and dad have split up and there's a very dodgy relationship with my dad, because my mum has been so influential, to say choose Black and to deny her, would be denying the parent who really has brought me up.*

Because she was especially close to her White mother – the parent who raised her, and to whom she felt real loyalty – the social expectation that she identify monoracially (as Black) was even more problematic and offensive to Keisha. Interestingly, most of the Black/White interview respondents claiming a multiracial identity were women. While we cannot explore this finding more fully in this book, it may be that part-Black men are even more normatively constrained from claiming a mixed heritage than are women (cf. Lopez 2003; Harris & Sim 2002). Like Keisha, Natalie found it impossible to just choose one 'race':

> *I feel I'm not one or the other, but I know I'm both. For example, my older sister X, who's fully Black, she said to me, 'say if White and Black people were at war, and there was a group of White people who were on one side of the street and a group of Black people who were on the other side of the street, which one would you go ter [sic]?' I said I couldn't go to either, because I don't feel fully part of one defined group.*

These interview excerpts from Keisha and Natalie evoke philosopher Naomi Zack's refusal to choose between her Jewish and African American ancestries:

> ...given a choice, it is ethically better to not-be both black and Jewish. In that sense, not-being both identities presupposes that one cannot be either one alone. The resulting distance from one's own racial and ethnic identity opens a space to question the ethical assumptions and implications – which is to say the good faith – of any racial or ethnic identity.
>
> (Zack 1996:141)

Other types of mixed respondents also expressed a strong sense of being 'mixed' and of an inability and principled refusal to have to nominate only one side over another. Of Iranian and Irish background, Sara observed,

> *Because I feel so attached to both sides, I can't detach myself from one completely. Yeah I just feel very, very, half. Yeah. I remember two summers ago we went to Slovenia .... And there was this man by the lake painting .... He was a lovely man. And my parents were saying where they were from and then he said to me, 'Oh you should, if someone asks you where you're from you should say you're 100% Irish and 100% Iranian', and that stays with me because I really, I really do feel that in a way.*

Thus, those who refused to choose one race either identified as 'mixed' and refused to prioritize one part of their heritage over another and/or claimed to refute racial thinking and categories more generally. Interestingly, while part-Black respondents were most likely to choose their minority race, they were *also* most likely to refuse to choose and to embrace a mixed identity or to transcend racial identification. It is possible that recent media attention to the numbers of Black/White entertainers and sports stars has put Black/White mixedness 'on the map' and enhanced their sense of belonging to an emergent group in Britain. For example, Carrie (who had a White father and Black mother) refused to choose only one 'race' and insisted that she was 'mixed race'. She reported that she had been influenced by the Spice Girls singer 'mel b': *Well this is cheesy but mel b from the Spice Girls, who is a mixed race person, wrote an article when I was 13, which basically supported the idea of mixed race being A RACE, and not feeling u[sic] had to conform to any other race; from that I built my views with additional reading.*

Clearly, Carrie's sense of being mixed race was encouraged and legit-imated by the existence of a Black/White mixed pop star. Furthermore, for many Black/White young people growing up in urban settings the sheer numbers of other mixed people like themselves has contributed to a collective sense of being 'mixed race'.

Discussion

Of the five types of mixed race groups in our study, some differences in how these groups responded to the 'forced choice' survey ques-tion were observed. The majority of East or SE Asian/White, South Asian/White, and Arab/White respondents chose White, or a European national term, followed by about half that proportion who said they couldn't choose one group; of these groups, relatively few chose their non-White heritage (about 22% East or SE Asian/White and 24% of South Asian/White).

By comparison, our Black/White respondents were most likely to choose their minority (Black) identity (37%). However, there was also a great deal of variation among the Black/White sub-group: this group also evidenced the highest *refusal to choose only one group, either by refusing to choose or saying that they were mixed race* (38%). Furthermore, almost 25% of our Black/White respondents chose either *White or a European national term.* Many Black/White respondents who chose White or a European national term articulated similar reasons for choosing such terms to those expressed by part East or SE Asian (and South Asian) respon-dents. This finding points to the greater sense of ethnic options that part-Black individuals appear to possess in Britain than in the United States. Black/White Britons may feel more able to sideline or navigate around 'race' (e.g. by refusing to identify racially or transcending racial thinking) and/or to claim a national affiliation and sense of belonging – especially in multiethnic, metropolitan settings where being 'mixed' is not at all unusual (see Back 1996; Gilroy 2004).

Thus, in addition to the typology of racial identification found by Rockquemore and Brunsma (2002), which were based upon Black/White 'biracial' individuals in the United States, in the British context, we would add a national mode of identification (e.g. British, English), in which one's sense of national belonging (or even attachment to another European heritage) can take precedence over racial and ethnic identifica-tions in certain social situations – though the meanings associated with national and racial (and ethnic) identifications are not mutually exclu-sive and can shade into each other. By choosing 'White' or a European nationality, many of our respondents described themselves in terms of nationality and cultural belonging in Britain and saw their nationality as being more salient than their racial or ethnic identities. Furthermore, a British (or White British) identity could take precedence, since they grew up in Britain, surrounded by British norms and cultural practices. Most of these young people did not feel that they could claim an ethnically authentic affiliation with some distant ancestral culture, for instance, in Hong Kong or Pakistan. This discourse of national belonging may also be gaining currency at a time when numbers of young people may question the legitimacy of racial ideologies and categories in their everyday lives.

This finding chimes with broader patterns of national identification found by the Office for National Statistics: in 2004, the majority of ethnic groups in Britain who were not White described their national identity as British, English, Scottish, or Welsh. This included almost nine of ten (88%) mixed people, 86% of the Black Caribbean group, 83% of the Pakistani group, and 75% of the Indian group (ONS 2011). While people from the White British group were more likely to describe their national identity as English (58%) rather than British (36%), the opposite was true of the non-White groups, who were more likely to identify themselves as British, as opposed to English. Of the mixed group, 37% identified as English and 52% identified as British (ibid.). While these figures suggest that 'British' is regarded as a more race-neutral term by non-White Britons than 'English', given how widely adopted it was, it is perhaps significant that our young, well-educated sample mentioned 'English' slightly more frequently than 'British' in their *unprompted open response descriptions* of their ethnic/racial identity – though one explanation for this is that our respondents were indeed from England (see Chapter 2).

Additional light can be cast on the issue of national identity – as a *separate* strand – as we asked our survey respondents in a final subset on personal details if they self-identified with '*a particular national identity/group*', inviting them to multi-tick across the options of 'British', 'English', 'Scottish', 'Welsh', 'Irish', and a free-text 'Some other (such as 'Indian', 'Nigerian', 'Chinese', etc., for example)'.[2] Of our respondents 304 (93%) ticked one or more options (see Table 3.2).

These data show that 66.8% of our student sample chose 'British' (singly or in combination) and 34.5% 'English' (singly or in combination), similar to the ONS figures but with a higher incidence of 'British'. Of those selecting these terms singly or in combination, 'British' was selected more often as a stand-alone national identity (that is, *singly* rather than *in combination*) (66.5%) than English (46.6%). Overall, those

Table 3.2 Respondents self-identifying with a particular
national identity/group via multi-ticking

National identities	No. (%)
'British' (singly or in combination)	203 (66.8)
'English' (singly or in combination)	105 (34.5)
'British' (singly)	135 (44.4)
'English' (singly)	49 (16.1)
'British and English' (in exclusive combination)	45 (14.8)
'British', 'English', 'Scottish', 'Welsh' (singly or in a combination with any others)	259 (85.2)
'Irish' (singly or in combination)	8 (2.6)
Some other (singly or in combination)	63 (20.7)
Some other (singly)	42 (13.8)

Note: The categories in the above typology of national identities are not
mutually exclusive.
Source: Main student survey.

ticking any of the terms 'British', 'English', 'Scottish', or 'Welsh' (singly
or in a combination with others) amounted to 85.2%, similar to the ONS
figure of 88%. Just 13.8% of our respondents chose some other stand-
alone identity (without reference to 'British', home country national
identities, or 'Irish').

Furthermore, the meanings of the racial and national categories chosen by respondents appear to be very much in flux, with some overlap
and inter-changeability evidenced in the use of various terms. The interview excerpts also revealed that there is slippage and blurring between
the use of racial, ethnic, and national terms. In comparison with the
United States, different understandings of the term 'White' emerged
in our study, to connote a sense of belonging in mainstream Britain
(and a distancing from their minority background, especially if it was
associated with a distant ancestral homeland) – though, of course, the
very fact that 'White' was associated with Britishness for many of our
respondents is not incidental. Nevertheless, based on the interview and
free-text survey data very few respondents appear to have used the
term 'White' to refer to White *racial* membership, even though many
respondents understood the privileged status of Whiteness.

While their sense of belonging in Britain seemed no less strong
for many part-Black respondents, their consistent and persistent racial
assignment as Black by the wider public meant that they were regularly reminded of their 'race' (though some Black/White respondents

managed to deflect or disregard this). Black/White respondents tended to *differentiate* their racial and national identifications more clearly than the other groups. For most part-Black respondents, being British sat alongside their racial identifications as mixed or Black, with no necessary tension between the two (though in a few cases, experiences of racism had attenuated feelings of Britishness). Therefore, it is important not to overstate group differences between part-Black people who may have chosen 'Black' or who refused to choose, from other non-Black mixed respondents who chose 'British' or 'White British' – because despite disparate responses to the forced choice question, a shared sense of being British was a strong undercurrent across all the mixed groups, and served to moderate the force of differently expressed racial identifications.

We also need to rethink the differential ethnic options said to be held by part-Black versus part-Asian people, as found in previous studies. In their studies of how various multiracial adolescents in the United States racially identify, various analysts concluded that, in comparison with Black/White young people, East Asian/White respondents possessed a wider range of identity options. Based on our findings on the forced choice question (and the interview sub-set), the identity options of Black/White respondents in Britain also appear to be more constrained than those for other mixed groups. However, we need to qualify a stark contrast in the purported ethnic options of part-Black versus non-Black mixed people – at least in the British context.

The fact that one was *not* consistently pigeon-holed into a category (as in the case of many part-Black individuals) did not automatically translate into an ability to assert a racial, ethnic, or national identification which was *validated* by others (see Chapter 4). So while non-Black mixed individuals in our sample generally possessed more latitude in how they identified themselves, their asserted identifications were not necessarily validated by others.

In this chapter, we examined the complexity involved in interpreting the racial identifications of mixed young people, when they have been asked to choose one group or race which they feel most strongly contributes to their identities. As shown in the examples throughout this chapter, the broader social setting in which respondents grew up, parents and the home lives of our respondents, as well as peer networks, could be fundamental in shaping the identities and experiences of respondents.

We found that the responses to the 'forced choice' question, in combination with the follow-up question asking them to explain their choices, were revealing and provided a fuller understanding of these choices (especially in comparison with US surveys which did not employ such a follow-up question). However, the choice of specific racial terms, such as White, Black, or British, could obscure the nuances and variations in the meanings and usage of these terms, not to mention the diversity of experiences as multiracial individuals. Such question formats do not necessarily reveal the strength of such identifications, or the potentially multifaceted layers of belonging (national, regional, faith communities) which can accompany a racial sense of self (see Chapter 6). Thus, special care is needed in the *interpretation* of chosen racial terms, as they are used by a variety of mixed respondents; in this respect, the in-depth interviews were important in this process, as our respondents were often reflexive about their understandings and experiences of ethnic and racial terms and identifications.

While the variable responses to this survey question were revealing, especially in terms of differences in the responses between part-Black and other non-Black mixed respondents, the interviews illustrated that there is no automatic correspondence between the choice of specific groups or terms with particular modes of behaviour, thinking, or overall social experiences. The chosen terms do not speak for themselves, as they require careful unpacking and interpretation. By using a mixed methods approach, we were able to draw upon both survey findings and a sub-set of interviews, providing a more complete and nuanced understanding of the ways in which (and reasons for why) mixed individuals identify themselves. As we will see in the next chapter, even when mixed individuals perceive a variety of ethnic options and choose to describe themselves in particular ways (such as mixed, British, or Chinese), other people do not always validate the ways in which they identified themselves.

4
Does Racial Mismatch in Identification Matter?

In the previous chapter, we found that different types of mixed groups tend to perceive (and claim) a disparate range of ethnic options, but that people's responses to the forced choice question require careful interpretation. In this chapter, we first focus upon survey evidence of how respondents thought others saw them in racial terms. Then we draw upon the interviews to examine how different types of mixed respondents thought about and responded to how they were perceived by others. Were their racial identifications validated by others, and did it matter? Addressing these questions allows us to discern the extent to which different types of mixed people are able to assert their chosen ethnic and racial identities and to understand the degree to which others' validation is or is not important to them.

Studies of expressed and observed racial identifications

As first discussed in Chapter 2, some recent scholarship has substantially advanced our understanding of expressed versus observed (or internal–external) dialectic of identification, extending exploration of the ground where 'self-image' meets 'public image' (how others see you) in relation to the mixed race population. Analysts such as Harris and Sim (2002) have conceptualized the multiple nature of racial identities in terms of 'internal identities' (how we think of ourselves), 'expressed identities' (what we say we are), and 'observed identities' (what others think we are based on our appearance). Similarly, Jenkins' (1996) internal–external dialectic of collective identification describes the interaction between (internal) self-definition and definition by others (external) (see also Nagel 1994).

The ways in which others identify us in the context of everyday life may be determined to a large degree by our physical appearance, which is the identity attribute most readily accessible to others. As discussed in a growing number of studies (see Rondilla & Spickard 2007; Doyle & Kao 2007; Song 2010; Roth 2010; Brunsma & Rockquemore 2001; Khanna 2004; Khanna 2010; Herring et al. 2004; Herman 2004; Hunter 2007), one's physical appearance is central to how one is perceived in ethnic and racial terms.[1] Debates about whether or not humans are predisposed to make sharp distinctions between in-group and out-group members (see Dawkins 2004), and whether such a predisposition accounts for the recognition and continuing preoccupation with 'race' and racial differences, are still ongoing.

Most importantly, this process of category identification happens without the consent of the observed. The extent to which the identities held by individuals are validated by others has been comprehensively investigated in the work of Brunsma and Rockquemore (2001), which reveals a strong association between socially mediated appearance and how Black/White Americans construct their identity. Khanna (2004) also found that 'reflected appraisals' – individuals' perceptions of how others see them – were very influential in shaping the racial identifications of Asian/White adults in the United States ('Asian' in the US primarily meaning a person having origins in any of the 'original' peoples of the Far East, Southeast Asia, or the Indian subcontinent).

In fact, there is growing evidence of disjuncture between expressed (and/or internal) and observed identifications among mixed race individuals (see Campbell & Troyer 2007; Shih & Sanchez 2005; Rockquemore & Laszloffy 2005). This disjuncture between how one sees oneself, in racial terms, and how others perceive that person can become problematic, because how one sees oneself may not be validated by others (Campbell & Troyer 2007; Appiah 2005). The issue of validation is, for many, fundamental, because without validation of one's own racial identity by others, one cannot easily assert and 'own' that identity (Rockquemore & Brunsma 2002).

Identity denial by others can be not only distressing, but can involve persistent efforts to assert a desired (and validated) identity in the wider society (Cheryan & Monin 2005). A lack of validation of one's asserted identity also matters because the negative consequences for some can be significant. In their study of Black/White biracial children in the United States, Rockquemore and Laszloffy (2005) argue that what is important is not the specific racial identification per se – for example as Black, or multiracial, or White – but the *pathway* to an identity: '... *individuals can develop a racial identity in both healthy and unhealthy ways. In other*

words, there are many possible pathways leading to the same racial iden-
tification . . . . It is our contention that health is not defined by the racial
label a person adopts, but rather it is a matter of the pathway one travels
to arrive at that label. More specifically, health is determined by the degree
of acceptance associated with the pathway one travels to a particular racial
self-understanding' (p.19). While the authors are primarily referring to
a multiracial person's acceptance of her ancestry, this pathway to a
healthy identity could also be importantly shaped by others' acceptance
and validation of that person.

However, in addition to the possibility that misrecognition or identity
denial by others can be a negative experience, another possibility which
has received little attention thus far is that observed identification by
others may not always figure that prominently (or may be of variable
importance) in how individuals come to see themselves. In fact, there
may be no uniform desire or expectation among mixed young people for
identity validation. A further possibility is that some mixed people may
even enjoy others' inability to 'place' them. In this chapter, we argue
that *misrecognition occurs in a meaningful way if something of value (such*
as racial identity) in an agent's sense of self is not recognized or validated by
others.

Survey results

In the main survey, respondents were asked: *'How do you think others*
(the general public) see you in racial/ethnic terms?' and they were invited
to *'tick one box only'* from four response options (Table 4.1). They were
then asked questions about the intersection between these perceptions
and the way they, personally, identified in racial/ethnic terms.

Across the different mixes the Black/White group had the highest proportion (37.6%) who chose 'mixed race', compared with around 17.5%
in the East or SE Asian/White and minority mixed groups. One reason
why a significant proportion of Black/White young people may have
reported that others saw them as mixed race is that the 'public' is more
aware of the existence of Black/White mixed people than that of other
types of mixed people; furthermore, as will be discussed below, the term
'mixed race' may invoke a dominant image of a Black/White person,
as opposed to, say, an East or SE Asian/White person. Some non-Black
mixed respondents may believe that the term does not apply to them
and so discount the possibility of the general public seeing them as
'mixed race'.

Table 4.1 How do you think others (the general public) see you in racial/ethnic terms?

	Black/ White ($n = 157$)	E/SE Asian/ White ($n = 46$)	Arab/ White ($n = 29$)	S Asian/ White ($n = 50$)	minority mixed ($n = 40$)
As mixed race	59 (37.6%)	8 (17.4%)	3 (10.3%)	14 (28.0%)	7 (17.5%)
As belonging to a single group[1]	61 (38.9%)	13 (28.3)	9 (31.0%)	18 (36.0%)	16 (40.0%)
As having an ambiguous racial/ethnic identity	28 (17.8%)	19 (41.3%)	14 (48.3%)	17 (34.0%)	11 (27.5%)
Don't know	9 (5.7%)	6 (13.0%)	3 (10.3%)	1 (2.0%)	6 (15.0%)

Note: [1] This option was accompanied by the instruction: *'Please write-in which group'*. This sub-group analysis is based on 322 respondents as four subjects could not satisfactorily be assigned to one of the five main groups.
Source: Main student survey.

Interestingly, while Black/White respondents were most likely to report that they were seen as 'mixed race' by other people, a significant proportion of these respondents thought the general public saw them as belonging to a single group (38.9%), as did 40% of minority mixed – many of whom were part-Black. Almost half (48.3%) of those in the Arab/White group and 41.3% of the East or SE Asian/White group thought others would see them as having an ambiguous racial/ethnic identity; however, the proportion who reported that others saw them as racially ambiguous was notably low (17.8%) in the Black/White group. This finding accords, as we'll see below, with interview data in which *non-Black* respondents often reported that others saw them as racially indeterminate.

Respondents who selected *'as belonging to a single group'* were asked to write in the group to which they thought others assigned them. Of the 58 Black/White respondents who wrote in a group (three who selected this option did not), the overwhelming majority – two-thirds – indicated 'black' in their write-in descriptions (such as 'Black', 'Black people', and 'Black Caribbean'), while very few wrote in 'White'. A minority of respondents reported that they were seen as something *other than* Black. For instance, five Black/White respondents indicated that they were seen as 'White', two as 'Asian', and one as 'Middle Eastern'. A further dozen Black/White respondents gave conditional responses, such as: *'some don't know until they ask me'*; *'black people see me as white and vice versa'*; *'generally as a mixed race person that acts white'.* Several responses reveal the situational complexity of the gaze of others:

> *It depends who they are, e.g. with a southern African husband and light skin some people assume that I'm from South Africa/Zimbabwe or Botswana = coloured/black. Some West Indians think I'm a light West Indian (if I'm nowhere near my husband at the time). Most white patients (especially elderly ones) just see me as black. Other people see me as mixed.*

> *I am usually judged by my features and hair, which tend to lead people to conceive of me as black; however, things such as my accent, dress and choice of study have led others seeing me as white.*

Amongst the 13 East or SE Asian and White respondents who selected *'a single group'*, 8 (62%) specified a 'White' identity (including variants, such as 'White British' and 'English') and 5 a minority identity (four 'Chinese', one 'Oriental'). Of the nine Arab/White respondents who selected a single group, 1/3 indicated 'White' or 'White British', the other answers being heterogeneous ('Asian or Arab'; 'Arabic', 'as half Arab but they forget I'm half English'). Amongst the 16 South Asian/White respondents who chose a single group and gave a description, 7 (44%) specified 'White' (or variants, such as 'White British'), 5 indicated 'Indian', followed by a variety of responses such as *'sometimes Greek, sometimes from an Arab nation'*. Finally, as one might expect, none of the minority mixed group who responded to the 'which group' question thought the general public saw them as 'White'; instead, a range of minority identities were mentioned, including 'Black', 'Asian', 'Pakistani', 'Chinese', and 'Far Eastern'. These findings suggest a significant degree of variation in how the respondents (especially the non-Black mixed) thought the general public saw them.

Respondents were then asked: *'Has the way others (the general public) see you had an effect on the way you, personally, identify in racial/ethnic terms?'*. Those who replied 'yes' were then prompted to write in the ways in which they were affected. For each of the mixed groups, a higher proportion of respondents reported that their identifications were *not* affected by how others saw them. This finding is interesting in light of what the sub-set of interviewees reveal in Table 4.3.

In Table 4.2, around 36% of Black/White and 37% of the East or SE Asian/White mixes indicated that the way the general public saw them did have an effect on the way they identified in racial/ethnic terms; the

Table 4.2 Has the way others (the general public) see you had an effect on the way you, personally, identify in racial/ethnic terms?

	Black/ White ($n = 157$)	E/SE Asian/ White ($n = 46$)	Arab/ White ($n = 29$)	S Asian/ White ($n = 50$)	minority mixed ($n = 40$)
Yes	57 (36.3%)	17 (37.0%)	12 (41.4%)	13 (26.0%)	9 (22.5%)
No	73 (46.5%)	21 (45.7%)	16 (55.2%)	28 (56.0%)	23 (57.5%)
Don't know	27 (17.2%)	8 (17.4%)	1 (3.4%)	9 (18.0%)	8 (22.0%)

Note: This sub-group analysis is based on 322 respondents as four subjects could not satisfactorily be assigned to one of the five main groups.
Source: Main student survey.

Table 4.3 How mixed race groups respond to others' perceptions of them

	Misrecognized	Positive	Indifferent
Black/White	8	2	7
East or SE Asian/White	4	7	5
Arab/White	3	1	11
South Asian/White	1	3	6
minority mixed	1	2	4
Total = 65	17	15	33

Note: Interview sub-set of 65.

proportion was somewhat higher in the Arab/White category (41%) but lower in the minority mixed (almost 23%) and 'Asian/White' (26%) categories. When asked in what ways the perceptions of the general public had affected their personal identities, 107 respondents gave an answer. While difficult to classify in some cases, 61% of respondents indicated that these effects had been negative (stereotyping, racist interactions, etc.), 21% neutral (neither positive nor negative in their effect), and 18% positive, though the question may have selected for the sub-group with negative experiences or most consequential effects. The comments of respondents reveal that even negative effects could sometimes have positive consequences in evoking resistance and strengthening their resolve to identify in the way they wished, as discussed in the interview data below.

Amongst Black/White respondents, some saw congruence between their self-image and public image as positive, while others contested others' categorization of them as solely Black: one respondent wrote in,

'*I enjoy socialising with the group I most look like*'. However, some felt the need to assert their 'mixedness' when their public image did not confer that recognition: '*I look very white which makes asserting my mixed race heritage very important*'; '*It makes me even more aware of my mixed identity in those situations... I give them another perspective & how to think and not simply to judge an individual by their physical appearance*'. Some East or SE Asian/White individuals reported themes of racial ambiguity and a sense of confusion about how they should see or categorize themselves: '*Yes in terms of labels I don't look mixed race, I look white, people say/assume I'm white or British so for a while I was a bit confused, especially when ticking the ethnic origin boxes on questionnaires (when younger)*'. One respondent's public image had '*created a sense of isolation and confusion, and a desire to fit into one ethnic group, especially when I was a child*'. The assertion of one's desired identification was also important for some in the minority mixed group: '*I felt like I had to define myself when I got to university as people would assume automatically that I was of Asian origin.*'

As we will see in the interview data below, how respondents were seen by others could jar with how they saw themselves, and this could engender a desire to 'correct' people and assert their preferred identification. Arguably, everyone is somehow affected by how other people see them in ethnic/racial terms, whether one acknowledges this or not. However, not only were respondents differently racially assigned by others; it also became evident that they were not all equally influenced (whether positively or negatively) by others' perceptions of them.

Interview findings

Following the survey questions, we were able to probe further in the interviews about how different types of mixed respondents felt about how they were perceived by others. Were their racial identifications validated by others, and did it matter? Addressing these questions allowed us to discern the extent to which different types of mixed people are able to assert their chosen identities and to understand the degree to which others' validation is or is not important to them. While the small number of respondents in each of the five groups does not allow for a systematic analysis of group differences, the in-depth interviews provide important insights into how different types of multiracial people perceive and experience their identity options.

As was illustrated in the survey findings above, the ways in which our mixed respondents were seen by others could vary considerably: while some were consistently pigeon-holed into a single racial category (such as 'White', 'Asian', or 'Black'), others were seen in a multitude of ways, as *physically ambiguous* individuals who were not readily assigned to existing racial categories. For this latter group, a common theme reported in studies of mixed people is that many people do not know how to 'place' them in the existing taxonomy of racial categories.

Many of the interview respondents reported that there was frequently, or sometimes, a disjuncture between their expressed and their observed identifications. That is, there was a mismatch between how they saw themselves and how others saw them in racial terms, and respondents' phenotype (and how this was perceived by others) was central to this process. How respondents saw themselves was not necessarily based upon a respondent's *actual* parentage or phenotype; reported mismatch or disjuncture was quite widespread and could occur whenever others' perceptions clashed with how respondents *wished to be seen*. Nevertheless, this mismatch did not always result in a sense of misrecognition. We relied upon respondents' own reports of how others saw them. We did so by asking them (a) how others saw them in racial terms; (b) how they felt about how others perceived them. In the interviews, we asked respondents for specific examples of how they were seen by others and how this made them feel.

While a mismatch between expressed and observed identifications was widely reported across all the mixed groups, their responses to this mismatch tended to vary according to three possible responses: (a) for 17 respondents, the disparity between how others saw them and how they saw themselves posed a regular source of irritation or stress in their day-to-day lives, resulting in a negative sense of misrecognition; (b) for 15 respondents, this mismatch, based upon others' inability to 'place' them, was actually experienced positively, not negatively; (c) yet 33 interviewees were reportedly indifferent to how others saw them, and did not pay much attention to, or take seriously, others' perceptions of them.

Of these three possible responses, only the first type of response actually constituted a sense of misrecognition. This is because individuals who felt primarily positive or indifferent did not expect others to be able to 'place' them or validate their desired identifications, and they were more able to deflect or disregard other people's perceptions of them. By comparison, those who felt misrecognized reported that a lack of validation of their asserted identity (which was of importance to them) was difficult and distressing. Rather than attempt to discern whether our respondents were actually accurate about how other people racially assigned them or not (which would not be possible, retrospectively), we wanted to see *how our interviewees responded to others' perceptions of them and how this made them feel.*

Negative experiences of misrecognition

For 17 respondents (eight Black/White, three Arab/White, four East or SE Asian/White, one South Asian/White, and one minority mixed), others' racial perceptions of them were experienced as misrecognition. How others racially assigned them jarred with how they saw themselves and this was a recurring concern in their day–to-day lives. The nature and basis of such misrecognition, however, was variable.

Racially assigned into a minority 'race'

Significantly, eight Black/White respondents (of 17 Black/White respondents) and one minority mixed (Black/East or SE Asian) respondent objected to the fact that they were usually seen as (monoracially) Black, as opposed to mixed. One of these respondents, Carrie, who had a Black African mother and White English father, saw herself as being mixed race. Yet she felt that her mixed identity was rarely validated, by either Black or White people: '*It annoys me, because I can't control it. Black people want me to say I'm black and if I don't, I'm supposedly ashamed to be Black. Some White people will just say I'm Black, without thinking also. I hate being generalized, and it gets harder I think as you get older.*'

In another excerpt, Carrie was asked how she would describe herself:

Carrie: *I think it's easier to say Black than it is to say White. I couldn't say I am White, but it's perfectly ok to say that I'm Black, which is a bit strange. I'm not so comfortable with that.*

Int: *Why is it ok to say that you're Black but not White?*

Carrie: *White is seen as you have to be completely White to be White, but Black, it's as if, if you're anything in particular, you're Black. That's the way I see it. I don't like it, but that's my experience of it anyway.*

Without being aware of the historical legacy of the 'one drop rule' in the United States, Carrie reported that a de facto rule was in operation in Britain for Black/White people such as her. Few people validated her mixed identity, and Carrie felt highly annoyed and constrained by other people's insistence that she was Black. And although she did not wish to be seen as White, she was bothered by the fact that being White was clearly off limits to her. The reported inaccessibility of either a White or a 'mixed' identity for some Black/White individuals like Carrie was pronounced (cf. Khanna 2011).

Another Black/White respondent, Tina, saw herself as 'mixed race':

> *For instance one of my friend's friends that I met, he was like, 'oh where do you come from?' I was like, 'Oh, I'm mixed race.' He was like, 'Oh, so you're Black?' I was like, 'No, I'm mixed race.' And it was like you're kind of just telling me what race I am . . . . . Yeah, and I've found a lot of people have done that but it doesn't, it doesn't define for me who I am . . .*

While Tina did not find the idea of being Black inherently objectionable, she resented other people's refusal to acknowledge the fact that she was mixed race, not only Black. Tina's reported upset about how others racially assigned her clearly stemmed from the fact that she wanted recognition of her mixed status. Because her mixed identity was rarely validated, and was of personal importance to her, she experienced this mismatch as misrecognition.

In another case, Keith (discussed in Chapter 3), who was Black Caribbean and White English (and who grew up in a primarily White town in the Midlands), reported that while he acknowledged his mixed background, he did not feel able to claim a mixed identification, because in many contexts he was solely seen as Black. In addition to being pigeon-holed in this way, he had to contend with the negative social value attached to being Black and male. Like Tina, Keith's sense of misrecognition stemmed from others' placement of him as Black (as opposed to mixed race), but over time, he had come to terms with the idea of being *both* mixed and Black. Furthermore, his sense of misrecognition was based upon the fact that while the wider public attributed negative imagery and meanings to him, on the basis of his perceived Blackness, he saw himself as an ordinary mixed (and Black) young man in higher education.

Unlike Keith, Tara, one of our 'minority mixed' respondents, objected to others' perception of her as Black, and the expected script of behaviour this racial assignment entailed. Tara had a Sierra Leonian father and a Malaysian mother, and she considered herself to be 'mixed race' *and* 'Afro-Asian' – a hybrid identification recognizing both sides of her heritage. Because she grew up in a middle class, predominantly White suburb of London, she reported that she was very comfortable around White people, and that she did not think about being 'different' in most contexts. Yet Tara was aware that most White people saw her as Black, and she felt constrained by other peoples' expectations that she behave in a particular way: '*My [White] friends say I'm the Whitest Black person they know*'. Although she was simply being herself, her White friends at university perceived her as acting against type – since she was seen primarily as a Black person. Tara was also upset by some Black peoples' expectations that she act more 'Black'. All of these respondents objected to what they perceived as a negation of their individuality – they were simply perceived as racial types.

Misrecognized as white

Problematic experiences of misrecognition also arose for a minority of respondents who were seen as White. In comparison to those who were only seen in relation to their non-White ancestries, 4 of the 17 respondents who reported that they were consistently misrecognized complained of being seen as *White*, though they did not identify in this way. For instance, two Black/White women said that they were almost always seen as White, though they identified as mixed race. Anna, who considered herself to be 'mixed race', was resigned but frustrated by the fact that other people did not see her in this way:

> *If I say I'm mixed race everyone, black and white, wants an explanation which I do not want to give. Black people sometimes think I am 'trying to be black' and white people find it 'exotic'. I think of myself as a mixed race person with white skin but usually, in order to not have to explain myself, I will just be whatever anyone wants to see me as.*

Because of the disjuncture between her White physical appearance and her identification as mixed race, Anna expressed her concerns about the gradual Whitening of her family and the dilution of her Black ancestry: '*I hope some of my mum's side of the family, it's been more mixed with white . . . . so it's got whiter and whiter as we've got younger . . . . . I did used to think, you know I hope someone brings some black back in so we don't lose that heritage.*' In fact, at the time of interview, Anna had recently married a Black African man; her choice of partner appeared to be indicative of her attachment to her Black heritage.

An Arab/White woman and an East or SE Asian/White woman identified as Palestinian and 'Burmese' (she did not use the term 'Myanmarese'), respectively, but were usually seen as White. For instance, Miriam, who had a Palestinian mother and White Belgian father, was blonde and blue-eyed, and this made her assertion of Arab identity very difficult, not only in relation to the public but also with her Arab relatives: ' . . . *It's also very difficult in a family to not look the same [as others], to not be seen as an Arab fully...it does play a big role in how I identify myself and why I choose to call myself an Arab. It's more to say, well, I am here too, you know, I do count.'*

As in the case of Miriam, all four of these respondents reported that such misrecognition was especially difficult because their ties to their non-White side of the family were stronger than those with their White family members. These respondents encountered outright incredulity (and sometimes hostility) when they claimed their minority ancestries (see Mengel 2001). Because they felt a very strong attachment to their minority backgrounds, scepticism about their minority ancestry was often painful. Thus although they were not insensitive to the privileges they enjoyed as a result of a White appearance, others' placement of them as White was distressing to these respondents.

Attributions of foreignness and indeterminate physical appearance

While part-Black respondents were most likely to report that they were pigeon-holed into their minority race (racialized as Black), other types of mixed respondents tended to emphasize misrecognition stemming from attributions of foreignness, often due to their indeterminate physical appearance. Some of our East or SE Asian/White respondents reported this to be the case. As discussed in Chapter 3, George, who was Chinese and White English, complained of being seen 'only' as a Chinese or a foreign person, because he saw himself as very British. Similarly, when Lori (Filipino/English) was asked how other people saw her, she responded:

Well I would hope most people wouldn't really notice my race. I don't really notice it in people. Some people are sort of dubious of my background or they don't really know where I'm from so them [sic] people will ask because they're curious and I suppose other people will just...well some people have been a bit ignorant and they will just say Asian and they don't know whereabouts or whatever.

Later in the interview, Lori reported that she disliked the fact that other people saw her as somehow foreign, and 'different', especially because, like George, she had grown up wholly in Britain and considered herself to be both British and 'mixed race'.

Thus, while many East or SE Asian/White respondents like George and Lori saw themselves as British (though not 'White' in racial terms), this was not always validated by others, given his 'Chinese' and her 'foreign' physical appearance. As another Chinese and White English respondent, Alison, noted, '*I'm often asked where I'm from – this implicitly denies me the right to be British because of the way I look*'. Many of the respondents who described themselves as being British associated membership in the British mainstream with being primarily 'White' in *cultural* terms – though for most respondents, this did not mean they regarded themselves as White in *racial* terms. In these cases, identification as British eschewed a racial emphasis and was based upon a sense of *national and cultural belonging* (see Chapter 3).

Therefore, the *basis* of misrecognition for East or SE Asian/White respondents who reported this was that they were denied membership in the nation, as British people – rather than a desire to disassociate themselves with their minority heritage per se (though, as we'll see below, a minority of our respondents did wish to do this). In other words, misrecognition occurred in these cases because they were seen by others as somehow 'different' (as somehow not really British), when they did not feel, or wish to be seen, as different – the opposite basis of misrecognition from that experienced by those respondents who were seen as White (when they wished to be seen as something more, or other, than simply White and/or British). In the latter case, these respondents wanted recognition of their membership in their non-White minority group.

A minority of respondents wanted to distance themselves from what they seemed to regard as a stigmatized minority background. For example, Chris (Arab/White) was often assumed to be 'different', based upon his reportedly ambiguous appearance. Others' curiosity about his background tended to bother Chris, who identified, simply, as 'British':

> Int: *How do others respond to the knowledge that you're part-Arab?*
> Chris: *I think in this day and age it's not really an issue. I do wish sometimes that I could erase it and be British, British, British.*
> Int: *Why's that?*
> Chris: *I just think it's typecasting me. It's labelling me as something that I feel sometimes I'm not. . . . I don't think my race really makes too much difference.*

These individuals strongly objected to the ways in which they were misrecognized and the lack of validation of their desired identities. As illustrated above, the basis for a sense of misrecognition could vary: some (especially Black/White respondents) felt consistently pigeonholed into one race (usually Black, but in some cases, White), while others (such as some East or SE Asian/White or Arab/White respondents) were seen as physically indeterminate and 'different', and thus regarded as foreign and not British. Furthermore, while some respondents felt forcibly *assigned* into racial categories, others (such as the respondents who were only seen as White) felt *denied* membership in minority communities. Despite these disparate dynamics, all of these respondents could be upset or irritated by the fact that they were objectified and reduced to a racial type.

Positive about how they were seen by others

In comparison with the 17 respondents who found other peoples' perceptions of them to be very problematic, 15 of the 65 interviewees articulated primarily positive experiences about how they were seen by others. Seven of these 15 were East or SE Asian/White, 3 South Asian/White, 2 'minority mixed', 2 Black/White, and 1 Arab/White. These respondents, most of whom were seen as physically indeterminate, reported that they enjoyed instances of mismatch and the fact that people were unable to discern their ethnic and racial heritage.

Selina, who had a Black African father and White English mother, found other people's curiosity about '*what she was*' rather enjoyable at times:

> *No, it doesn't bother me at all. I'm the same with other people. I find it interesting....As long as it's not for any horrible reasons, and most of the time people are just interested....A couple of times, I was in Topshop in London and two of the shop assistants were watching me. I was like I've not stolen anything, and eventually they came up to me and said.... 'where are you from?'....basically they thought I was Cantonese and White because they said I looked Asian, and I've had that before.*

Many of these respondents, and in particular female respondents, said that they enjoyed the attention they received from others *because* of their physical ambiguity; for instance, they were considered 'exotic'. The guessing game involved in people's reactions to them was often a good 'conversation starter'. As one male respondent put it, '*The girls love it!*'. Hari (Indian and White English) said that his physical appearance aroused curiosity: '*I quite like it because...it's like it makes me a bit more, I suppose, mysterious. It's sort of quite glamorous...Yeah, from my point of view it's quite nice, that sort of uniqueness...*' Although some male respondents, such as Hari, reported that they liked being seen as exotic, the awareness that being mixed, and thus physically alluring, appeared to be gendered.

Duke, who had a Black mother and White father, reported that he liked the fact that many people were unable to place him ethnically and racially:

> *Well it's confusing but I kind of like it because it means that if I meet somebody before I've talked to them, the first thing when somebody looks at you...exactly they start thinking things straight away...I don't think people know what to think when they see me, but I like it...it keeps it open for me.*

Like Hari and Duke, Ellie, who had a Burmese mother and English father, spoke of how other people were unable to categorize her:

> Int: *And how would you say that the public see you based on your appearance? What do you think people assume that you are?*
>
> Ellie: *Well I kind of...It varies because they either see me as possibly South East Asian/English. They're not sure. I mean in England I just assume that people assume that I'm from India or somewhere like that.*
>
> Int: *Oh do people usually think that you're from the Indian subcontinent?*
>
> Ellie: *Yeah. Places like that. I mean most people just aren't sure. I mean I've been...Even when I've been to other countries people have thought that I come from all over the place. I went to China and people tried speaking Chinese to me. Yeah.*

When asked how she felt about others' reactions to her, Ellie reported that she liked the fact that she was not easily racially assigned; this made her feel distinctive and interesting to others. Crucially, the curiosity these respondents encountered was experienced positively, in contrast to the respondents (who were seen as physically indeterminate) who reported negative attributions of being foreign or odd looking. Some of the respondents who felt positive about how they were seen by others articulated thoughts which were reminiscent of those expressed in Waters' (1990) study of White Americans, in which many White Americans tried to highlight an ethnic ancestry (e.g. Irish, Italian, Polish) in order to feel more distinctive, and not 'just' American. While our respondents were mixed, and not White, as in Waters' study, their perceived status as 'exotic' – different, but not *too* different – effectively afforded them privileges ordinarily associated with Whiteness (Frankenberg 2003; Twine & Gallagher 2008). In other words, there was no liability or 'down side' to being mixed for these individuals.

Although most of these respondents were unable to control how others saw them, and could not effectively invoke specific identifications at will, they enjoyed the fact that they were not easily categorized – in contrast with some of the Black/White respondents who identified as mixed, but felt pigeon-holed into the Black category. For these 'positive' respondents, others' curiosity and/or inability to place them could be a source of fun or amusement because (a) their sense of belonging in Britain was primary and secure, and not challenged by others; (b) how others racially assigned them was not considered to be stigmatizing – rather, the fact that others found it difficult to 'place them' made them feel special and distinctive.

In comparison with some of the respondents who objected to the often denigrating meanings and imagery associated with, for example, Blackness, or with being somehow foreign and racially indeterminate, these mixed individuals highlighted the positive aspects of their racial and ethnic ambiguity. Nevertheless, it seems that part East or SE Asian/White respondents (7 of 15) were especially prominent among those reporting positive experiences resulting from instances of mismatched identifications. While not within the scope of this chapter, a variety of positive and negative meanings (albeit potentially double-edged) could apply in relation to different types of 'mixture' (Song 2001).

Indifferent to how they were seen by others

In comparison with respondents who reported either negative or positive experiences in terms of how others perceived them, 33 of the 65 interview respondents (7 of 17 Black/White, 11 of 15 Arab/White, 6 of 10 South Asian/White, 5 of 16 East or SE Asian/White, and 4 of 7 'minority mixed') claimed to be indifferent to how they were seen by other people. For example, Beth refused to identify racially, claiming that she transcended racial categorization. She also reported that she was not particularly concerned with how others saw her; she was seen in many different ways, ranging from 'mixed race' to Mediterranean and Middle Eastern: '*I personally forget most of the time that I have an ethnicity, but I am lucky to have been successful academically and study in a world where I don't feel that such things are important....as I say, it's not an issue that even occurs to me unless someone raises it*'. As a child, she had grown up in a Northern town, and had lived in a predominantly White neighbour-hood, in which she had felt consciously different, being part-Black. But in London, where she has lived the last ten years, she reported that she felt very ordinary.

This lack of concern could also derive from the fact that 'race' was not particularly central to their sense of selves and/or the fact that their race was less salient than their overriding sense of Britishness, or their religion, studies, or regional identification (e.g. as a Londoner) (see Chapter 6). This derogation of racial difference was typically mentioned in terms of everyday life in large urban centres like London. As one South Asian/White respondent, Brian, put it, '*You don't really expect peo-ple to be White in London!*'. Or as Kareem (Pakistani and Arab) observed, '*I am what I am ... I'm just technically another person just walking*'. Nor did they think that their peers necessarily paid much attention to their exact parental heritage, given their common upbringing as British.

Peter (Vietnamese and White English) identified as a 'mixed' person, but had grown accustomed to the varied ways in which he was seen by others. He said that he was usually seen as ambiguous – sometimes South American, 'Oriental', or Mexican, but how others saw him did not matter very much to him: '*When I think of me, I don't think .... The first thing is not race. It's not an issue.*' While he would readily note his parental heritage on official forms, his racial and ethnic heritage did not figure centrally to how he saw himself.

Of course, claimed indifference to how they were seen in racial terms should not necessarily be taken at face value. In comparison to those Black/White respondents who were consistently seen as 'Black' (and who experienced this racial assignment as misrecognition), it is rela-tively easy for respondents who are not consistently pigeon-holed (or who may 'pass') to claim that race is not an issue (Waters 1990; Song 2003). Nevertheless, there were a significant number of respondents across all the mixed groups (most of whom did not appear White), including some who were consistently seen as Black (but who saw them-selves as being 'mixed'), who reported that they were indifferent to how they were seen by others.

Such a claimed indifference to how others racially assigned them did not necessarily mean that these respondents had not experienced forms of racism, especially in school, during their childhoods and adolescence (see the next chapter), but they were able to contain and minimize the significance of such negative experiences. Those who grew up in primarily White, non-urban locations (like George) were less likely to report indifference to mismatch than those who had grown up in more cosmopolitan settings. Yet the move to a more ethnically diverse university setting afforded such individuals an opportunity to re-evaluate their 'mixedness', and the relative importance (or not) of others' perceptions. Some respondents who reported indifference, like Beth, articulated the view that they had transcended race and racial thinking and identification, but only after a childhood and adolescence in which she had felt negatively racially marked in a mostly White town. So for some respondents reporting indifference, this could entail a process of change, in which they gradually became indifferent towards the varied and sometimes unpredictable ways in which people would see them. Even so, most of these 'indifferent' respondents recognized the contextually specific ways in which being 'different' could still matter, especially in settings outside of multiethnic London, where one could, as one respondent put it, be vulnerable and outside of one's 'comfort zone'.

Discussion

In this chapter we have focused on the interaction between expressed (and internal) identities and observed (assigned) identities based primarily on phenotype. How respondents felt about others' perceptions of them tended to vary according to group membership, and was not just due to differences in individual predisposition (though of course, this, along with other factors, clearly influenced how these young people reacted to others' perceptions of them).

This chapter extends existing studies by examining not only the potential disjuncture between expressed and observed identities for mixed individuals, but also *the variable ways in which mixed people may feel about how they are seen by the wider public*. Previous literature on this topic has tended to assume that the mismatch between expressed and observed identification is usually problematic, but our study of mixed race people in metropolitan Britain suggests that such mismatch was not problematic for all our respondents. While some people experienced this mismatch very negatively, as a form of misrecognition, others experienced this mismatch mostly positively, and yet others, with indifference. Crucially, such variation in responses was found *both* across and within all the mixed groups.

Although such a disjuncture between expressed and observed identifications was commonly reported by the 65 interview respondents, not all of them particularly cared about their racial assignment by others (especially if these were in superficial social encounters). More than half the Arab/White, South Asian/White, and 'minority mixed' respondents claimed to be indifferent to how others saw them and played down the importance of race for their sense of selves and their everyday lives, while 40% of Black/White and 30% of East or SE Asian/White respondents claimed indifference.

How should we interpret this reported indifference to misrecognition? In addition to the fact that they did not *expect* the wider public to validate their expressed identifications, these respondents tended to note (a) the fact that they were British, regardless of 'colour', thus emphasizing the growing importance of national belonging over membership in a 'race'; and (b) the relative unimportance of race in cosmopolitan, metropolitan settings such as London, where degrees of conviviality and mixing were high, and where being of any hue or mixture was regarded as unremarkable – at least in many situations.

Importantly, claims to indifference were not devoid of a recognition of continuing forms of racial prejudice and disadvantage, especially in certain institutional contexts; so these claims should not be interpreted as naïve denials of the existence of 'color-blind' racism (see Bonilla-Silva 2003). Rather, these respondents tended to articulate the view that they refused to take racial thinking and ideologies seriously and/or that they were able to deflect such thinking and prejudice in their everyday lives.

Despite the fact that a significant proportion of respondents (higher when explored in the interviewed subset) across all the groups reported indifference to how others saw them, we found some differences between groups in terms of how they responded to other peoples' perceptions of them. In comparison with the other mixed groups, a higher proportion of part-Black respondents (47%) felt misrecognized than any other group (the second highest was 25% of East or SE Asian/White respondents). As discussed in the previous chapter, while a substantial proportion of Black/White respondents saw themselves as 'mixed race', many of them were pigeon-holed as Black (as found in the US). Their feelings of misrecognition were based upon a lack of validation of their mixed heritage and upon the perceived negative social values attributed to their Blackness. So while Black/White respondents do possess a range of ethnic options (as evidenced in the variable responses of our Black/White respondents to instances of racial mismatch), Khanna's (2011) argument – that (Black/White) individuals' assertions of biracial status (in the US) are recognized by both Whites and Blacks when they strategically employ racial symbols – may be a bit too optimistic.

Clearly, the British 'public' recognizes someone with some Afro-Caribbean heritage as a 'Black' person, even if they note variations in skin tone and other physical features – though there were of course exceptions, as in Duke's case, discussed earlier. Certainly no such rule applied to the other types of mixes in our study, so that they were less likely to be consistently pigeon-holed into a single category, such as 'Black'. Variability in individuals' phenotype, while noted as being of importance, for example in relation to skin colour (and other facial and hair) variations among Black people, has not been emphasized enough in studies of other types of multiracial people (though see Rondilla & Spickard 2007; Roth 2010; Khanna 2004; Doyle & Kao 2007; Hunter 2007).

As discussed in the previous chapter, non-Black mixed respondents were often seen to be physically indeterminate and racially assigned in a wide variety of ways. This was experienced negatively by some as misrecognition, by some with indifference, and for others with positive social values and encounters. What some Black/White respondents found to be problematic (pigeon-holed into Black category, attribution of negative values associated with Blackness) differed from what non-Black mixed respondents found to be problematic about their misrecognition by others (being seen as 'foreign' and thus not really British, being seen as physically odd). Thus a key distinction between respondents who experienced instances of mismatch positively, as opposed to negatively, is that the former (a) did not expect others to validate their expressed identifications; (b) did not perceive their racial assignment by others to entail racial prejudice or negative social value. This latter point is important, because those emphasizing the positive aspects of mismatch between expressed and observed identification are likely to be people who effectively enjoyed the privileges of Whiteness, but with an additional 'exotic' twist. Respondents who were reportedly indifferent did not expect others to validate their expressed identities; furthermore, they may have been less invested in their ethnic and racial ancestries than those who felt misrecognized, or positive (though clearly, more research is needed on the dynamics differentiating these different kinds of responses).

As discussed in the previous chapter on ethnic options, the fact that one was *not* consistently pigeon-holed into a category (as in the case of East or SE Asian/White individuals) did not automatically translate into an ability to assert a racial, ethnic, or national identification which was *validated* by others. Misrecognition could therefore entail not only a negative experience of mismatch but also an *unwanted* ethnic or racial attribution in the case of respondents who identified primarily as British, in cultural and national terms.

Theorizing on the dynamics of racial mismatch also needs to consider the experiences of mixed race people who are consistently misrecognized as White, as opposed to a monoracial minority or multiracial identity. Although they benefited from their White skin privilege more generally, such misrecognition could be upsetting if their minority heritage was meaningful to them (and especially if they had been raised primarily by their minority parent and extended family). Thus, one's ethnic options can be constrained in a variety of ways, and can involve a lack of acceptance and validation in relation to minority group membership (Campbell & Troyer 2007; Song 2003; Mengel 2001). So while we must continue to be alert to the continuing privileges of Whiteness, the emergence of new nationalisms which exclude people on the basis of cultural and phenotypical 'foreignness' must not be overlooked.

Even if growing numbers of mixed people report that they are indifferent to others' racial perceptions of them, it is clear that assertions of belonging within a society (and validation of belonging) remains very important – whether that be recognition of belonging within the nation or membership within a minority group. Those who are 'indifferent' are, for whatever reasons, already secure in their sense of belonging in Britain (or at least in their day to day locality) and it is clear that such a secure sense of belonging, especially on their own terms, is far from widespread (or is contextually variable). Because this study focused upon the experiences of young adults, it is of course possible that their attitudes towards instances of mismatch (or their own racial identities) may also change in their life course.

5
Are Mixed Race People Racially Disadvantaged?

Introduction

Having explored how our sample of mixed race respondents identified in ethnic and racial terms using a variety of question/answer formats, and how they responded to experiences of racial mismatch, this chapter looks at how our mixed young people perceive and experience forms of racial prejudice and discrimination, both inside and outside of university settings. As recently documented in the BBC documentary series 'Mixed Britannia', and in studies of particular mixed communities (such as by Benson 1981 and by Lewis 2009), mixed race people and relationships were historically subject to both institutionalized and 'everyday' forms of racial discrimination and vilification, causing moral panics, when such mixing was seen to threaten the fabric of respectable society. While such attitudes and practices have changed greatly in Britain, in the 21st century, it would be naïve to assume that mixed people and unions no longer engender societal concern or objectification.

As discussed in the previous chapter, processes of group identification and social categorization (by others) are mutually implicated in, and feed upon, each other. Racial assignment by others may appear to be limited to the naming or labelling of these individuals but such interactions may have far greater ramifications and can be much more intrusive. They may encompass what Appiah (2005) calls 'treatment as', that is, treatment 'as Black', 'as Asian', and so on, which may be experienced negatively in a variety of ways. When negative, 'treatment as' may involve adverse behaviour in everyday social interactions (discourteousness, offensiveness, labelling, etc.), stigmatization, and social exclusion. When such treatment is, indeed, race-based, it tends to be systematic and patterned and constitutes a form of racism, so that some races are seen to be inferior or superior in relation to others. Though there are now plural forms and definitions of racism, our understanding of the term refers to the belief that people who are seen to be members of disparate 'races' possess inherent differences in their characteristics and capacities; racism also entails practices and behaviours which stem from beliefs about such putative inherent racial differences.

Particular forms of phenotypical variation have become selected for attention, especially those arising from the historical legacies of colonialism and slavery (Young 1994; Jenkins 1997; Cornell & Hartmann 1998). That is, certain physical differences are arbitrarily constructed as socially meaningful and are used as markers of racial differences which are believed to reveal evidence of relative inferiority and superiority, whether in relation to intelligence, beauty, and the capacity to be hard working, among many other characteristics (Spickard 1992).

In this chapter, we draw on survey data to investigate the extent to which mixed race people report experiences of racial prejudice and discrimination (and racisms more generally) in the wider society. How may such experiences differ according to different types of mixed people? If these respondents feel racially stigmatized, *on what basis* do they feel they are marked? And in which specific contexts and situations do such encounters occur? By drawing on interviews, we then explore how mixed race people make sense of, experience, and cope with forms of prejudice and discrimination. In doing so, we explore the ways in which they may feel racially marginalized and/or excluded by monoracial minorities, in addition to White people.

Existing studies of mixed race people and racism

While there is now a significant body of literature concerning the racialized experiences of minority ethnic people in Britain (see Anthias & Yuval-Davis 1992; Miles 1984; Song 2003; Solomos 1993; Back 1995; Solomos & Back 1996; Gilroy 1987; Alexander 2000; Pilkington 2003; Modood 1996, Troyna & Hatcher 1992 – to name only a few), very little is still known about forms of racial prejudice and discrimination experienced specifically by mixed race people in Britain.

In Britain, it is known that White working-class mothers of mixed race children (usually Black/White) experience social disapproval and are concerned about the racism their children will encounter (see Barn 1999; Twine 2010). We also know that Black/White mixed children of White mothers and Black Caribbean fathers are disproportionately vulnerable to entering into the social care system (Barn 1999; Okitikpi

2005; Owen & Statham 2009). There is also evidence that Black/White pupils in schools encounter low teacher expectations and racist stereo-typing from teachers and monoracial peers (see Tikly et al. 2004). By comparison, much less is known about other types of mixed race children in Britain, so the discourse of disadvantage is thus far quite specific to that of Black/White children. And while we have some survey information (e.g. based on the British Social Attitudes survey) about the wider public's attitudes towards immigrants and ethnic minority people (see Heath et al. 2010), very little is known about how mixed race people are regarded in this country.

Across the Atlantic, in the United States, there is a large litera-ture concerning attitudes towards monoracial minority groups, but not multiracial people (see Campbell & Herman 2010; Krysan 2000; Schuman et al. 1997). Anti-discrimination policies are framed in relation to specific monoracial groups, and there are no laws which specifi-cally protect multiracial groups (Campbell & Herman 2010). In fact, the head of the leading civil rights organization in the United States, the NAACP, recently argued that there '... *has not been a history of dis-crimination [specifically] against "mixed race" people*' – that is, because Black/White people in the United States have historically been seen as Black, there is no history of mixed people experiencing discrimina-tion specifically on the basis of being mixed (or 'multiracial') (quoted in Younge 2010:77). In their survey of attitudes towards multiracial people in the United States, Campbell and Herman (2010) found that about half of the monoracial minorities and most of the White respondents they surveyed opposed including multiracial people in anti-discrimination policies in the United States. Though this survey did not differentiate between disparate types of multiracial people, this finding suggests that most Americans do not believe that multiracial people actually expe-rience racisms or forms of racial disadvantage – despite the fact that the authors found that the multiracial people in their survey reported similar levels of discrimination to other monoracial minorities.

On the one hand, some scholars in the United States have argued that most multiracial people suffer less racial discrimination than monoracial minorities, because they may appear more White, or may have material privileges associated with having a White parent and wider White family network (see Yancey 2006; Gallagher 2006; Bonilla-Silva 2004; Keith & Herring 2004). There is evidence of 'colorism' and its role in racial discrimination by the wider (predominantly, though not exclusively, White) society (Rondilla & Spickard 2007; Hunter 2007). Some studies have shown that those multiracial people with darker skin perceive more racial discrimination and are more likely to identify with their minority race (Brunsma & Rockquemore 2001; Espino & Franz 2002; Phinney et al. 1990; Tizard & Phoenix 1993; Tashiro 2002). Lighter skinned people have been found to suffer less discrimination and are in higher level jobs (see Herring et al. 2004). In fact, even among mixed race siblings, differences in physical appearance, with some siblings looking more White than others, can result in entirely different ways in which they are racially assigned by others (see Song 2010).

Diana Sanchez and colleagues (2011) also found that those with knowledge of proportionally greater black ancestry (for instance, having a Black father and a mixed biracial mother, versus two parents who are both biracial) in a multiracial person increased the likelihood that they would categorize such multiracial individuals as Black and regard such individuals as experiencing racial discrimination and possessing stereotypically 'Black' traits. So in addition to someone's physical appearance, knowledge of a person's specific ancestry and 'blood quantum' can influence how they are seen, racially, by others.

On the other hand, some emerging studies suggest that it would be overly simplistic to assume that multiracial people are straightforwardly less subject to racial prejudice and discrimination (see e.g. the psychological studies by Cheng & Lee 2009). Herman (2004) found that part-Black biracial adolescents in the United States *perceived* just as much discrimination as their monoracial (Black) counterparts; she suggests that they may experience as much discrimination without benefiting from the acceptance and membership in a monoracial minority group (see also Bracket et al. 2006). Herman concludes: '*Thus, it seems that biracials, particularly those with some Black heritage, experienced the disadvantages but not the protective benefits of minority group membership*' (738).

In fact, some recent research suggests that we need to broaden the ways in which we assess the racialized experiences of mixed race people. What is not known is whether the racial discrimination reported by mixed race individuals is qualitatively similar, or somehow distinctive, to that reported by their monoracial counterparts, and such information is not easily discerned in large-scale surveys. Moreover, the ways in which multiracial individuals cope with negative racial interactions is bound to vary by the specific type of multiracial background, region, gender, and age (as discussed throughout this book).

The specific standpoint of multiracial persons may be potentially revealing, since such individuals are not fully a member of any one monoracial group (Rockquemore & Laszloffy 2005); nor are they completely recognized as a separate category, and this can lead to a heightened awareness and emphasis on racial identification and belonging (Brackett et al. 2006). And unlike monoracial minorities, such as African Americans (with no *known* recent non-Black ancestors), multiracial individuals may encounter prejudice and forms of racisms from 'both sides' – from both the wider, usually White society, and from monoracial minority communities (see Mengel 2001; Root 1996; Herman 2004). Their 'in-between' status, in relation to monoracial groups, may mean that their sense of social distance, both vis-à-vis White people and monoracial minority groups, is variable and subject to many factors, such as physical appearance, their exposure to minority and White people growing up, and class background (see Smith & Moore 2000).

The potential perception of racial prejudice or discrimination matters on several counts: Not only is it distressing to be on the receiving end of discriminatory attitudes and behaviours, and the sense of marginalization and exclusion which can accompany such encounters, but the perception of prejudice shapes one's own sense of self, and one's sense of belonging (or marginalization) within the wider society. Melissa Herman (2004) suggests that the more discrimination one experiences, the more one internalizes the racial categorization of others (744). Perhaps not surprisingly, for such individuals, their 'race' is likely to be more salient than for mixed individuals who are not negatively racialized on the basis of their appearance. And as discussed in the previous chapter, those who were not subject to negative racial experiences were more likely to be indifferent to instances of racial mismatch and to how others saw them. Tashiro's (2002) study of older, mixed race African American/White American and Asian American/White American individuals also found that respondents who had experienced the most racism tended to identify most with their non-White heritage.

One major limitation of existing studies about the racial discrimination or disadvantage experienced by mixed people is that most of it concerns only one type of mixture: Black/White mixed people, or it does not differentiate between disparate types of mixed people (e.g. Campbell & Herman 2010). Survey studies concerning the racial discrimination experienced by mixed race people cannot probe the racial diversity and complexity *within* disparate groups. For instance, two people with the same racial 'mix' may have a very different physical appearance, whether they are Black/White or East or SE Asian/White – not to mention how their appearance and habitus is mediated by social class, gender, and locality. Furthermore, much more information is needed about the specific contexts in which mixed race individuals perceive and experience prejudice or discrimination. In this chapter, we draw upon both survey data and in-depth interviews to illustrate some of the diverse ways in which different types of mixed race young people perceive, make sense of, and cope with, a variety of racialized encounters.

Findings

In the United States, one would expect there to be less recognition of racism directed against non-Black mixed people, such as towards East or SE Asian/White individuals, since theorists in the United States argue that there is less social distance between Asians and Whites, and less virulent racism directed against Asian Americans than at African Americans; as such, multiracial Asians (most of whom are part-White) would be less likely to experience or perceive racial injustice (see Yancey 2006). However, in the British context, there has been growing awareness of the diverse ways in which specific minority groups can be racialized – racisms can be varied and multifaceted in their manifestations and effects (see Modood 1994; Song 2004). This is all the more pressing an issue in the post-9/11 and 7/7 world, in which forms of Islamophobia are now more prominent than before – as evident in the results of the Citizenship Survey below.

In the 2007–2008 Citizenship Survey, respondents were asked: '*Which groups do you think there is more racial prejudice against, compared with 5 years ago? (Code all that apply)*'. Notably, both Muslims and [South] Asians were frequently chosen in this question, and interestingly, more Eastern Europeans (29%) than Black people (17%). Compared with 2005, in 2007–2008 Muslims and Eastern Europeans were mentioned by a greater proportion of people as experiencing more racial prejudice today than five years ago (Table 5.1).

In our own survey, three questions were asked about racial prejudice and experiences of discrimination, followed by in-depth interview questions with a sub-set of the sample. Firstly, respondents were asked: '*Do you think there is a lot/some racial prejudice against any of the following groups?*' (multi-ticking of 14 categories was allowed).[1] Secondly, respondents were asked: '*Would you describe yourself as being a member of a group that is discriminated against in this country*' (answered 'yes', 'no', or 'don't know'). Those who responded 'yes' to this second question were then asked: '*Which group is that?*' (an open response – '*please write in*').[2] Thirdly, respondents were asked: '*How often are the following*

Table 5.1 Groups experiencing more racial prejudice today compared with five years ago, 2005 and 2007–2008

	Mentioned (%), 2007–2008	Mentioned (%), 2005
Asian people	39	41
Black people	17	16
Chinese people	1	
White people	9	7
Mixed race people	2	
Hindus	1	
Jews	1	
Muslims	44	37
Sikhs	2	
Asylum seekers/refugees	13	29
New immigrants	17	14
Eastern Europeans	29	12

Notes: Base: Core sample, England and Wales, People who say there is more racial prejudice (2005:4,733; 2007–2008: 5,233).
Source: Ferguson et al. (2007–2008).

people unfair or negative to you because of your race/ethnicity' on a five-point scale ranging from 1 = 'almost never' to 5 = 'almost always'. The groups were 'Your peers/fellow students', 'University/college lecturers', and 'Other adults'.[3] This last question provides the most direct measure of discrimination experienced by respondents, tapping into their own perceptions of racial/ethnic discrimination.

The groups that respondents most frequently chose as being the targets of racial prejudice were Muslims, Asian people, Black people, and asylum seekers/refugees (Table 5.2) – thus findings which broadly accord with those in the Citizenship Survey above. At least three-quarters of respondents in the five mixed groups chose 'Muslims' and at least three-quarters chose 'Asian people'. Interestingly, Barbara Tizard and Ann Phoenix's (1993) study of Black and White mixed young people in London found that they regarded Asian (as opposed to Black) people in Britain as the primary targets of racial hostility. Asylum seekers/refugees and new immigrants were also selected by at least seven-tenths and one-half of our respondents, respectively, across the five groups. Lower proportions selected 'Chinese' (around 38–59%), while between 25% and 45% across the mixed groups selected 'White people' – perhaps a surprisingly high figure. Amongst religious groups other than 'Muslim', more selected 'Jews' than 'Sikhs', 'Hindus', and 'Buddhists'.

Table 5.2   Do you think there is a lot/some racial prejudice against any of the following groups? (Please tick all boxes that apply)

	Black/ White (*n* = 157)	E/SE Asian/ White (*n* = 46)	Arab/ White (*n* = 29)	S Asian/ White (*n* = 50)	minority mixed (*n* = 40)
Asian people	129 (82.2%)	35 (76.1%)	22 (75.9%)	38 (76.0%)	33 (82.5%)
Black people	123 (78.3%)	34 (73.9%)	18 (62.1%)	34 (68.0%)	34 (85.0%)
Chinese people	60 (38.2%)	27 (58.7%)	13 (44.8%)	27 (54.0%)	16 (40.0%)
White people	48 (30.6%)	21 (45.7%)	9 (31.0%)	13 (26.0%)	10 (25.0%)
Mixed race people	82 (52.2%)	17 (37.0%)	9 (31.0%)	14 (28.0%)	21 (52.5%)
Buddhists	37 (23.6%)	8 (17.4%)	6 (20.7%)	8 (16.0%)	7 (17.5%)
Hindus	48 (30.6%)	14 (30.4%)	9 (31.0%)	12 (24.0%)	8 (20.0%)
Jews	74 (47.1%)	29 (63.0%)	16 (55.2%)	26 (52.0%)	19 (47.5%)
Muslims	120 (76.4%)	35 (76.1%)	25 (86.2%)	41 (82.0%)	33 (82.5%)
Sikhs	59 (37.6%)	18 (39.1%)	10 (34.5%)	19 (38.0%)	15 (37.5%)
Asylum seekers/ refugees	130 (82.8%)	38 (82.6%)	21 (72.4%)	46 (92.0%)	33 (82.5%)
New immigrants	113 (72.0%)	32 (69.6%)	17 (58.6%)	38 (76.0%)	29 (72.5%)
Other	14 (8.9%)	3 (6.5%)	3 (10.3%)	5 (10.0%)	5 (12.5%)
Don't know	9 (5.7%)	4 (8.7%)	0	1 (2.0%)	0

Note: Percentages are column percentages; this sub-group analysis is based on 322 respondents as four subjects could not satisfactorily be assigned to one of the five main groups.
Source: Main student survey.

Those whose mix included 'South Asian' selected 'Asian people' less frequently (76%) than part-Black people (82%), although part-Asian people selected 'Muslims' more frequently (82%) than did part-Black (76%). Black/White mixes chose 'Black people' more frequently than the other mixes with the exception of 'minority mixed'. The East or SE Asian/White mixes chose 'Chinese people' more frequently than did the other mixes. So with some exceptions, each type of mixed group demonstrated a heightened awareness of racial prejudice against their own group. For example, while almost 59% of East or SE Asian/White people believed that Chinese people (the proxy for 'their group' in this case) were racially targeted, 54% of South Asian/White, 45% of Arab/White, and 38% of Black/White people believed this to be the case. It is noteworthy that the highest percentages who thought there was a lot/some prejudice against 'mixed race people' were the Black/White and minority mixed groups, perhaps suggesting that these types of mixed people are more negatively racially targeted than others.

Respondents in the Black/White group (42%) and minority mixed (almost 43%) group most frequently indicated that they would describe

Table 5.3 Would you describe yourself as being a member of a group that is discriminated against in this country?

	Black/ White ($n = 157$)	E/SE Asian/ White ($n = 46$)	Arab/ White ($n = 29$)	S Asian/ White ($n = 50$)	minority mixed ($n = 40$)
Yes	66 (42.0%)	8 (17.4%)	10 (34.5%)	15 (30.0%)	17 (42.5%)
No	68 (43.3%)	31 (67.4%)	15 (51.7%)	29 (58.0%)	17 (42.5%)
Don't know	23 (14.6%)	7 (15.2%)	4 (13.8%)	6 (12.0%)	6 (15.0%)

Note: Percentages are column percentages; this sub-group analysis is based on 322 respondents as four subjects could not satisfactorily be assigned to one of the five main groups.
Source: Main student survey.

themselves as being a member of a group that is discriminated against in this country, higher than both South Asian/White (30%) and Arab/White (35%) mixes (see Table 5.3). This finding accords with the prior observation concerning perceived discrimination against mixed race people in Table 5.2. By comparison, just 17% of the East or SE Asian/White group reported that they belonged to a group which was discriminated against. This finding echoes a US-based study which found that part-Black biracial adolescents perceived more ethnic discrimination, in comparison with other biracial groups such as Asian/White and Hispanic/White (see Herman 2004).[4]

The proportion indicating that they did not know (whether they belonged to a group which suffered racial discrimination or not) was fairly consistent across the six different mixes (12–15%). Even though 42% of Black/White respondents saw themselves as part of a group which was discriminated against, it is equally interesting that slightly more Black/White respondents (43%) reported that they did *not* consider themselves to be a member of a group that was discriminated against in Britain. In fact, across all the mixed groups (with the exception of 'minority mixed' where the proportions were equal), more respondents replied negatively, than positively, to this question. But as discussed below, some respondents, including many non-Black respondents who reported (in the survey) that they did not consider themselves to be a member of a group that was discriminated against, revealed experiences from their childhoods and pasts which qualifies our interpretation of these seemingly straightforward responses.

Those who responded 'yes' to the question of whether they described themselves as a member of a group that was discriminated against were further asked: '*Which group is that?*' (open response). About half in the Black/White group who responded affirmatively indicated that the group was 'Black' or 'Black Caribbean', followed by a smaller number of respondents who wrote in 'mixed race', with some responses being more specific (e.g. *'mixed race Asian – I appear Asian to some'* and *'Mixed race and black'*).

By comparison, the relatively small number of East or SE Asian/White mix responses to this question (*'Which group is that?'*) were more heterogeneous, not always referring specifically to their ethnic or racial group (e.g. *'everyone is discriminated against by somebody'*, 'mixed race', 'Asian', 'Chinese', 'Muslim', 'Christian').[5]

The most direct survey question on discrimination asked about treatment by peers, teachers, and other adults (see Table 5.4, Figs. 5.1–5.3).

Table 5.4 How often peers, teachers, and other adults are unfair or negative to the respondent because of their race/ethnicity

	Black/White ($n=157$)	E/SE Asian/ White ($n=46$)	Arab/White ($n=29$)	South Asian/White ($n=50$)	minority mixed ($n=40$)
Your peer/fellow students					
1 (AN)	115 (73.2%)	43 (93.5%)	23 (79.3%)	42 (84.0%)	28 (70.0%)
2	28 (17.8%)	2 (4.3%)	4 (13.8%)	5 (10.0%)	7 (17.5%)
3	9 (5.7%)	1 (2.2%)	1 (3.4%)	2 (4.0%)	3 (7.5%)
4	3 (1.9%)	0	1 (3.4%)	1 (2.0%)	1 (2.5%)
5 (AA)	0	0	0	0	1 (2.5%)
No answer	2 (1.3%)	0	0	0	0
College lecturers					
1 (AN)	124 (79.0%)	43 (93.5%)	26 (89.7%)	48 (96.0%)	33 (82.5%)
2	17 (10.8%)	3 (6.5%)	2 (6.9%)	2 (4.0%)	4 (10.0%)
3	7 (4.5%)	0	1 (3.4%)	0	2 (5.0%)
4	5 (3.2%)	0	0	0	0
5 (AA)	1 (0.6%)	0	0	0	0
No answer	3 (1.9%)	0	0	0	1 (2.55)
Other adults					
1 (AN)	72 (45.9%)	31 (67.4%)	17 (58.6%)	32 (64.0%)	20 (50.0%)
2	36 (22.9%)	11 (23.9%)	7 (24.1%)	10 (20.0%)	9 (22.5%)
3	28 (17.8%)	3 (6.5%)	3 (10.3%)	6 (12.0%)	8 (20.0%)
4	13 (8.3%)	1 (2.2%)	2 (6.9%)	2 (4.0%)	3 (7.5%)
5 (AA)	6 (3.8%)	0	0	0	0
No answer	2 (1.3%)	0	0	0	0

Note: Percentages are column percentages; this sub-group analysis is based on 322 respondents as four subjects could not satisfactorily be assigned to one of the five main groups.
Source: Main student survey.

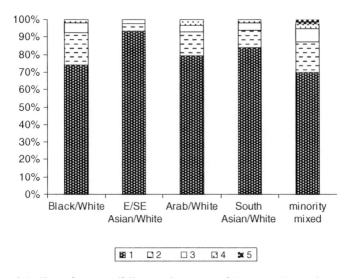

Figure 5.1 How often peers/fellow students are unfair or negative to the respondent because of their race/ethnicity

Note: 4 and 5 are worst scores; 3 middle of range.

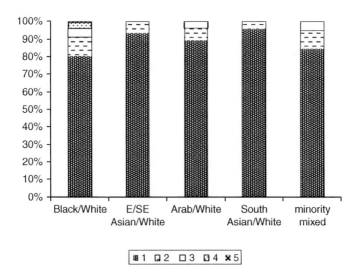

Figure 5.2 How often college lecturers are unfair or negative to the respondent because of their race/ethnicity

Note: 4 and 5 are worst scores; 3 middle of range.

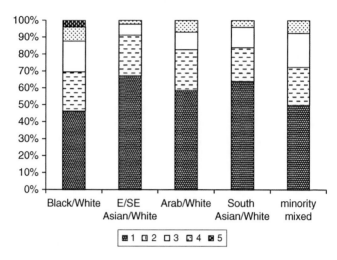

Figure 5.3   How often other adults are unfair or negative to the respondent because of their race/ethnicity

Note: 4 and 5 are the worst scores; 3 middle of range.

The question was: 'How often are the following people unfair or negative to you because of your race/ethnicity?', with the response formats (below):

		Please circle one number per line			
	Almost never				*Almost always*
Your peers/fellow students	1	2	3	4	5
University lecturers	1	2	3	4	5
Other adults	1	2	3	4	5

If one takes the worst scores – those to the right of the middle value (3), that is, 4 and 5, akin to frequently and almost always – interesting differences emerge across the mixed groups. With respect to *peers*, Black/White mixes are not markedly disadvantaged, with around only 2% scoring 4 or 5 – the same as the South Asian/White group and less than Arab/White and minority mixed groups (though all the counts comprise very small numbers). If we define frequency as all values excluding 'almost never', then the minority mixed and Black/White groups have the worst experience. Moreover, almost 4% of the Black/White group reported scores of 4 or 5 for *lecturers*, while none of the other groups scored within this range at all.

While all groups reported higher frequency scores (2 or above) with 'other adults' than for peers or lecturers, differences between the mixed groups were also most marked for *other adults* (that is, adults in the general population). Around 12% of the Black/White group had scores of 4 or 5, compared with 2.2% in the East or SE Asian/White group, and 4% in the South Asian/White group. Furthermore, a substantial proportion of 'minority mixed' (27.5%) respondents (some of whom were part-Black) also chose mid-level scores (3 or 4) for *other adults*. A small number of Black/White students (6 of 157) scored 5 (almost always) with 'other adults' – the only mixed group which scored 5 for 'other adults'.

So while very few respondents, overall, reported that either students/peers or lecturers treated them in a prejudicial or discriminatory way, part-Black respondents were more likely to report higher scores, especially in relation to 'other adults', and more likely to choose middle-level values on the numerical scale concerning their peers/fellow students, and also their lecturers. Although the survey did not explore further the nature of these interactions, the interview evidence indicates that many of the 'other adult' experiences were ones that were largely impersonal, in public spaces, and could include experiences such as feeling monitored suspiciously in stores, or not being treated well in service settings, such as in restaurants – findings which echo those reported by Feagin (1991) in his study of middle-class African Americans' experiences of racism in public settings.

But negative racial encounters with 'other adults' in public settings were also reported by non-Black mixed respondents (albeit with lower scores usually ranging between 2 and 3): For instance, David, who was East or SE Asian/White, described how racism from his childhood and teenage years had affected him: *'Direct racial abuse (verbal and physical) as a child and teenager; occasional ill-defined "attitude" from some people as an adult, on grounds of my race (rarer, but does still happen). This tends to make me naturally reserved and defensive in social situations. It has also led to my fostering a very individualistic approach in life.'* In the interview, David also spoke of how difficult it was to be racially marked: *'It's hard when you feel just like other people, and they regularly remind you, or treat you like you are not like them.'*

While the reports of negative racial encounters appear to be relatively modest across many of the survey questions, especially in university settings, we must note that (despite some variability in class background) this sample of mixed race young people in higher education constitutes a relatively privileged sector of the population. Given this bias, it may be that our findings under-report the extent and nature of racial prejudice and discrimination, as experienced not only by part-Black respondents, but other types of mixed individuals as well. Next, the sub-set of interviews enabled us to probe in more depth both across and within disparate mixed groups.

Perceptions of and responses to racial interactions

The sub-set of interviews allowed us to probe more deeply into respondents' perceptions and experiences of negative racial encounters, both past and present. In the in-depth interviews, respondents were asked if they experienced any forms of racial prejudice or discrimination, what they believed was the basis of this discrimination and whether they thought that they would be adversely affected by discrimination or prejudice in the future, including their work lives. One reason why these interviews are important is that we cannot assume that there is necessarily a shared understanding of what we mean by 'racism', given its multifarious manifestations and the wide usage of the term in social life.

Furthermore, the interview respondents were asked about how they responded to negative racialized encounters – revealing rather different modes of understanding and coping with racisms. These interviews also explored respondents' experiences of exclusion or hostility in relation to co-ethnic minority people and groups, in addition to White people. A number of respondents who did not report racism as an issue in the survey did talk about experiences of racial prejudice and racism in their interviews – though the meanings and significance of such experiences could vary across respondents.

Respondents often talked about racial incidents when they were at school (and see Tizard & Phoenix 1993; Ali 2004). While some of these incidents were regarded as intermittent and minor, others were reported as being very upsetting and traumatic. Such incidents in the past, however, could still colour their experiences. Children and young people who are not White, including multiracial young people, can be subject to various forms and messages of devaluation, so that they may unconsciously internalize negative meanings and messages (Ali 2003; Rockquemore & Laszloffy 2005; Katz 1996). While various authors, such as Rockquemore and Laszloffy (2005), have discussed the 'internalized oppression' (characterized by feelings of shame and the acceptance of negative stereotypes) experienced by Black and part-Black people, this argument can be extended, more generally, to other minority and multiracial people in contexts in which Whiteness is the norm and ideal (Frankenberg 1993).

For instance, Janine, who was Arab/White, recalled painful memories of how she was treated in her predominantly White neighbourhood during her childhood and adolescence: *I never used to talk to my [Iranian] dad about it, because I didn't want him to feel guilty, never used to talk to him about it. My mum was aware, but she would say just ignore it . . . . . It was very hard. I used to feel like a real outcaste, yeah.*

And Peter (East or SE Asian/White) reported that when he was growing up, he had felt racially marked and vulnerable: *'Yeah I was called gook because I'm like Asian.'* Like Janine, Peter never spoke to his parents about it, and tried to ignore such incidents. And while he no longer felt that racism was a major problem in his day-to-day life, he believed that such experiences had been formative for his personality and sense of belonging in Britain, reporting that he felt less socially confident as a result of such experiences.

While our survey data suggests that part-Black respondents (Black/ White and part-Black minority mixed) were more likely to report negative racial encounters than other types of mixed respondents more generally, these figures may obscure the disparate ways in which different types of mixed individuals could feel negatively racialized by others, as well as the varied experiences and perspectives found *within* each mixed group. For instance, interview respondents (across all the disparate types of mixed groups) could vary considerably in not only their perception and understanding (their 'reading') of a specific encounter, but also in their response to a racialized encounter.

Coping with racisms

There was no automatic or common mode of coping or responding to experiences of perceived racism (Lamont 1999; Collins 1990; Byng 1998). For instance, while some individuals seemed highly strung or upset by specific incidents, others were much more philosophical about how other people treated them. There were several ways in which our mixed young people responded – and these responses were not necessarily mutually exclusive: they could (a) minimize the negative interaction, so that it was viewed and understood as a 'non-event' (Byng 1998), even if they knew that they had been subject to a racist act or sentiment. In other words, some respondents were able to deny the significance of such an interaction for how they saw and felt about themselves; (b) distance themselves or remain cautious and reserved from members of the group with which they had experienced negative racial encounters or experiences of rejection, whether with White people or with co-ethnic minorities; (c) 'pass' as White, so that they could avoid the racial stigma of being 'different' – though this was rare, or at least very rarely admitted in the interviews.

For instance, George (Chinese/White), who was discussed in Chapter 4, was rather anxious about the possibility of a negative racial encounter, based upon how he had been treated, cumulatively, over the years, especially in less cosmopolitan areas. One reason George had moved to London was to live in a more multiethnic place, where he did not stand out as being 'different'. Nevertheless, some months after our interview, in an email communication, he revealed that he had just experienced racial abuse from some young men on the street, when he was visiting Essex.

When asked if the ways in which others saw and treated him affected the way he saw himself, George replied: '*Yes. The realisation that White British people – the group I was brought up on – will never fully accept me as one of them has made more accepting of my mixed race parentage.*'

Clearly, the cumulative effect of racialization as a 'Chinese' or foreign person, by others, made a big impact on George, who now saw himself partly in those terms. Given his numerous experiences of racial abuse, George was now primed to be wary of groups of White men, especially when he was outside of metropolitan areas. George's reactions to his negative experiences with White men in particular is reminiscent of Keith's (Chapter 4) reports of feeling uncomfortable and devalued (as a Black and White man) by White people in the wider society. Keith's experiences had led him to primarily associate with Black people and had reinforced his sense of being a disadvantaged minority.

By comparison, Danny (Black/White) reported that when their family moved into a predominantly White neighbourhood in his teens, some White men had threatened him with a knife and had suffered significant verbal abuse over the years. Danny described one incident: *I was walking to Tescos, I was with my 19-year-old brother, and someone wound down the window and said, 'fucking nigger'. My brother was in shock... the man that was at the bank, he was like 'I'm sorry about that'.* Nevertheless, Danny said: *I don't let what people think get to me... I don't feel stereotyped or anything like that... I just walk around normally like everyone else.*

It was clear from the interview that Danny felt very supported by both his White father and his Black mother and that they had taught him to be proud of who he was. Somehow, his sense of self-esteem and confidence appeared to be strong, and he adopted a rather philosophical attitude towards racist people and encounters, explaining that there was not much he could do about 'those people' (see Kuo 1995; Byng 1998). Like Danny, some respondents acknowledged the dynamics of racism, and the fact that they could even be subject to it. However, they claimed that they could ignore, disregard, or overcome it. For instance, Keisha (Black/White) did not feel racially targeted or disadvantaged:

> Keisha: *Sometimes I think you can be discriminated because of it [your race], but I don't think it really has an impact on my life, as long as I work hard and know where I want to go, I can do that on my own.*
>
> Interviewer: *So you don't think being mixed race will hold you back in the future in getting certain jobs or education?*
>
> Keisha: *I don't think so. I think a lot of Black people feel they get put down because of their colour or women feel that they get put down, but I think that once you work really hard, as long as you can get to it . . . . Ok, there's a lot of racism in the world today, but there's a lot of improvements being made to stop those kinds of things and I don't really think that can be something that can hold you back . . . . . . as long as you know what you want just try and achieve it.*

Perhaps not surprisingly, threats of violence or physical attacks, though relatively rare, were almost exclusively reported by our male respondents. In addition to overt racial hostility or prejudice, some respondents reported instances in which they realized that they were racially objectified by the wider public, and even, at times, by their friends, whom they did not consider to be racist, as such. For instance, Tara (who was minority mixed), said: '*Like I don't wake up feeling oh I'm mixed race. Like sometimes I'm shocked when my friends bring it up. Like the other day my friend, she's really naïve, she asked me what color my veins are.*' So even when respondents are not themselves aware of being or feeling in any way different from others, they inevitably encounter 'stupid questions' or remarks which make it all too clear that their friends and peers can see them as racial others. Nevertheless, Tara maintained that she did not consider her 'race' to be a major impediment in her life; nor did she feel racially disadvantaged.

These interviewees (Danny, Keisha, and Tara) all responded to potentially negative interactions by minimizing their significance, and/or by attributing bad or stupid behaviour onto others, thus deflecting negative meanings and emotions which could otherwise be directed towards themselves. Furthermore, some respondents invoked alternative measures of success or moral self-worth, to counteract their sense of being racially devalued by others, such as having a strong work ethic or loyal, interpersonal relationships with others (Lamont 1999; Byng 1998;

Crocker & Quinn 1998). It may also be that respondents who coped successfully with potentially upsetting racial encounters possessed a relatively 'integrated multiracial identity' (such that they perceived less distance and conflict among their disparate racial backgrounds) and/or were more able to code-switch and relate to disparate kinds of people (see Jackson et al. 2012).

A small number of respondents admitted that they dealt with perceived racism by 'passing'. This was clearly a strategy which could be adopted only by people who were seen as phenotypically White. As found in Table 5.2, many of our mixed race respondents believed that there was racial prejudice against South Asians and Muslims (though respondents could multi-tick and did not rank groups). This finding was also borne out in the interviews, across all the mixed types. For instance, Jane (South Asian/White) spoke about the intermittent ways in which she could feel negatively racialized, and why she identified as mostly 'White':

> *When I was younger, I would probably not have gone for White, I liked being different.... But I was actually discussing with my mum recently, I actually highlighted things like a lot of the racial tensions that have occurred because of 9/11 and 7/7, that I think there's a bit of stigma attached to being identified as Asian, which probably influences me, and I think in a way, people, and it's awful to say, but people would treat you differently if people would identify you as White rather than as Asian. This is a sad reflection of society.*

Jane took refuge in and embraced (albeit rather uncomfortably) her White identity and appearance. While she did not exactly hide the fact that her mother was South Asian, she did not volunteer this information either and knew that most people simply assumed that she was White. Because of her White physical appearance (and her Anglo surname), her claim to Whiteness was not challenged (see Edwards & Caballero 2008). Thus Jane was able to exercise an ethnic option which was not available to mixed individuals who did not look White by prevailing societal norms.

By comparison, Nat, who was also South Asian/White, spoke of the ways in which he was subject to racial othering as a Muslim, due to his appearance:

> *In [x], where I work on occasion, I work with some Turks, and a lot of people ask if I'm Turkish ... I had a beard earlier on in the year, and pretty*

much every day someone would ask if I was Muslim…pretty odd ones as well, they would say ,'Are you a non-drinking Muslim?', things like that. I politely said, 'no I'm not', took me ages to figure out, I thought 'hold on, I've got a beard and I've got quite dark skin'. But I don't think I'm particularly that dark, I'm not darker than an average person who's been on holiday for two weeks in Ibiza or….I've had a surprising number of racial incidents [in X, where he was in university].

When asked for examples of racial abuse, Nat reported: '*You're gonna have to excuse the language, but I've been called a black Afghan cunt, a black Muslim cunt, a fucking Afghan, a fucking Paki, a black twat, seriously*'.

Nat described the first of several racist incidents near his university, which took place at a kebab shop:

I think the guy called me a fucking Paki…I was just so shocked I couldn't believe it. I felt quite hurt by it. I was so taken aback by it, I couldn't believe that someone was so narrow minded to actually give that racial abuse. I never ever thought that sort of thing happened because I've never experienced it myself [where he had grown up]. To actually have it directed at me…one guy said it in front of a policeman. The PC said I can do him under section 4, I think it's called, I was like yeah go…I had him arrested, gave a statement, I dropped the charges at the end of the day. The guy's spent the night in a cell, hopefully would have thought about it….A drunken incident, I'm sure he's a nice bloke, he's just had a few too many…that's what you've got to think about it.

It's clear that both Jane and Nat were aware of the negative meanings associated with being Asian and Muslim in contemporary British society. But unlike Jane, Nat's physical appearance precluded the option to pass as White. Yet Nat was clearly surprised by the racial abuse he encountered when he moved to a predominantly White university 'up north', as he had not been subject to such incidents where he had grown up. What is also interesting is Nat's ultimate assessment (or rationalization) of his distressing experience in front of the kebab shop: rather than assume that the man who abused him is a terrible racist, he minimizes the significance of the abuse by reasoning that he is still probably '*a nice bloke*'.

In fact, Nat bends over backwards to emphasize his belief that people share much more in common with each other than they may think, on the basis of outward physical differences. Such thinking was extended to conclude that the man who abused him was probably quite an ordinary person, rather than some rabid xenophobe. Nevertheless, Nat was sufficiently shaken by the incident so that he turned to a trusted friend:

> *When I received racist abuse in X, the person I sought out was a friend called Sara who I knew was from Pakistan and was a Muslim, and she had had a bit of abuse. The first person I sought out to talk about it was her … Sara has had these experiences, she'll understand where I'm coming from, she's been brought up in I think West Yorkshire, I thought I'd talk to her about it.*

Some respondents, like James (who was South Asian/White), made a point of emphasizing their nationality and cultural belonging, as British or English, while minimizing the significance of ethnic or racial differences, which were characterized as largely superficial, background attributes: *'In order to counter accusations of foreignness, I often point out that I am probably no less English than someone who happens to be white but is Jewish, or half Polish, or something like that. Let's face it, it is the skin colour that causes the problems, most people never question a white person about their background unless they look different in some way'*. Thus there was no one mode of understanding or coping with negative racialized interactions across our interview subset.

Exclusion or prejudice from other minorities/co-ethnics

While our interview respondents talked in some depth about the ways in which some of them did or did not feel racially targeted and stigmatized by the wider society, and in particular by White people, some of our respondents also referred to feelings of marginalization or exclusion by their minority co-ethnics (see Mengel 2001). In fact, some studies argue that being *'both and neither of their heritages'* involves a distinctive standpoint or life experience for mixed people (Mengel 2001; Brackett et al. 2006). In one study of Black and biracial (Black/White) students at a predominantly White university in the United States, Smith and Moore (2000) found that biracial students, as well as Black students who had grown up in primarily White areas, were significantly less likely to feel close to other Black students on campus. Such biracial students who felt socially distant reported that they felt little in common, culturally and socially, with other Black students, and some also reported that they were racially excluded or marginalized by other Black students. Their sense of social distance was also *'in part a function of their need to embrace both the nonblack and black aspects of their racial identity, a choice that they feel creates tension between themselves and monoracial blacks'* (pp. 34–35).

One common theme reported among respondents was the theme of being subject to tests of ethnic and racial authenticity – though this could manifest in a variety of ways (Song 2003). For instance, Janine (discussed earlier, who was Arab/White) said that she sometimes felt low-level hostility from Iranian people, who made her feel bad about not speaking Farsi, or who would ask 'awkward questions' about her knowledge of Farsi or of Iranian cultural practices. The process of seeing mixed respondents as fractionated, marginal beings was not specific to any one type of mixed group. For instance, Carrie (discussed in Chapter 4) claimed that she encountered more negative racial experiences with Black, than White, people:

> Int: *What about children growing up at school? Did you get any racial abuse?*
> Carrie: *I got a bit from the Black community for some reason . . . like 'you're half-breed, I'm not gonna talk to you'. It was actually shocking, but it's always the Black community, never the White . . . . I think there's a stigma against the White, but Black people think it's OK, I'm half Black so they think they can say what they want to me.*

Junko, who had a Japanese mother and White English father, reported that her negative treatment by Japanese people in Japan was much more problematic than the way in which she was generally regarded by White people in Britain. Junko believed that Japanese people could see her as 'only' partly Japanese (and thus not really Japanese) and that Japanese people could subscribe to rigid notions of blood quantum and discourses of racial purity (see Spickard 1989).

> Int: *Have you ever felt racially discriminated against in Britain?*
> Junko: *I don't think so, I never really felt . . . not in England, not from British people or anything, but in Japan yeah. I think there's a lot of xenophobia. I would like to research that going there. You do feel that, even if you do have a Japanese passport that you're not one of them. You are foreign . . . and you're outside.*

When asked how other Chinese people reacted to the knowledge that Meghan, who was Irish and Chinese, had Chinese ancestry, she said:

> *No, they never recognize it. Like in my class at university, there were always the White people. Obviously people were friends, but the Chinese people stuck together. It wasn't until second year that they [the Chinese] realized*

that I was Chinese. When they realized I didn't speak Mandarin, it was almost even worse than being White. It was like you're Chinese but you haven't even acknowledged the culture.

Some respondents felt that they could be subject to forms of rejection from more than one group: For example, Natalie, who was Black Jamaican and English, regarded herself as 'mixed race', but felt marginalized by both White and Black people. Nevertheless, Natalie concluded that, while she remained rather marginal in relation to 'full' Black people, she felt even more rejected by White people, who did not acknowledge her White ancestry.

Natalie: *Say if I had to [say which group accepted her more], it would have to be black people, because being mixed race you really do see the negatives and positives of both sides. Like there's racism on both sides. Black people can be prejudiced against mixed race people, they don't see us as fully black, a full member.*

Int: *How did you get that ... somebody not giving you full recognition? They're not giving you the right amount of respect?*

Natalie: *Some people sometimes snigger, older black women. If we don't know something fully, because we've been raised by two different cultures, certain things we might need to be educated on because we're British and we don't live in Jamaica, there are certain things we might not know about food, culture ... if I went to a white group, I'd probably feel more rejected by them ... cos they really don't accept me, because they don't see my white side. Like I said they associate me to be black ... Black people would be more accepting because they've known oppression, rejection, so could relate to that a bit more.*

The dynamics of exclusion by co-ethnic minorities could be especially difficult if one was deemed to look White (see Chapter 4). Kathy (Black/White), who was usually seen as White, did not report any racism from White people in the interview. What bothered her more was her sense of being pointedly ignored or excluded by other Black people, even when she made a point of telling them that she had some Black ancestry:

Kathy: *'Well I would say it was from a Black person .... they didn't treat me the same as they treated my friends because they thought I was White and she was Black.'*

Interviewer: *So they didn't know that you were mixed?*

Kathy: *No, and it's this type of discrimination...It always happens. It's always like....sometimes you think like OK and you try to come into the conversation and then you just like....you just feel as if you're being pushed away from the conversation and you just have to leave it like that.*
Interviewer: *And what kinds of things would they talk about that would make you feel like you're being pushed away?*
Kathy: *Oh I don't know actually but I think it's just normal stuff. You're just not included.*

While Khanna (2011) found that Black/White biracial people in the United States could employ racial symbols to claim recognition of their mixed status (and thus membership in either White or Black groups), these interview excerpts suggest that some attempts to 'belong' or to gain recognition of a shared racial background could be rebuffed or entirely negated by others.

Thus a strong recurrent theme was a heightened awareness among some respondents that other monoracial minorities could subject them to rigid notions of blood quantum and racially authentic scripts of behaviour in assessing their membership within their group (Song 2003; Appiah 2005). Many of these respondents were aware of often unspoken discourses of racial authenticity in which certain markers of belonging, or being able to claim membership, could be stringently and negatively applied to them (Dyson 1994). Not surprisingly, ostracism and hostility from monoracial minority groups or individuals could highlight the social distance such mixed individuals could feel, in relation to those groups. And if they had had fewer negative experiences with their White peers, this could result in them feeling more comfortable and/or less judged with White people (such as Tara). The denial of group membership because they were deemed not sufficiently Black, or Asian, is thus the opposite of how the 'one drop rule' of hypodescent (and its inclusion of all people with some Black ancestry in the category Black) has operated for part-Black people, historically, in the United States (and to some extent, de facto, in Britain).

Discussion

The survey findings at the beginning of this chapter revealed that most of our mixed young people did not perceive racism from peers or their lecturers, but were more likely to report negative racial interactions with 'other adults' – especially part-Black students. This is not surprising, since university campuses are somewhat protected settings where there is a cultural and intellectual emphasis upon ethnic and racial diversity as a good in its own right, as something which can enhance people's learning more generally. However, probing in the interview sub-set revealed a more complex picture of how respondents perceived, understood, and coped with negative racial experiences and encounters.

While Black/White respondents were more likely (than any other group) to see themselves as members of a group that was discriminated against in Britain (almost 42%), slightly more of the Black/White respondents (43%) reported that they did *not* feel that they belonged to a group which was discriminated against. Findings for this question are difficult to interpret. Oudhof (2007) considers this measurement instrument of discrimination in the European Social Survey (ESS) question *'can be positioned somewhere between measuring discrimination experiences and attitude measurement'*, a measure of 'perceived discrimination' or 'assessed discrimination', referring to the own membership group of the respondent. The figure of 42% for the Black/White group is higher than that reported for the Black population in Britain (around 28%) reported in the ESS. In so far as the respondent's own experiences and those he perceives for his group are likely to be mutually entailed, the responses may have been influenced by a number of factors, including the differences in the respondents' ethnicity (our survey sub-group is mixed but the ESS sample is mono-racial), the survey context, and the characteristics of the respondents: those in our student survey were from relatively privileged backgrounds, with a significant proportion living in a highly diverse metropolitan setting.

As in the previous chapter concerning racial mismatch and misrecognition, one's physical appearance (along with other ethnic and racial markers, such as first and last names) was critical for how other people did or did not racialize them as 'other', as well as for how co-ethnic minority people did or did not recognize their membership within their group, based upon discourses of a shared ethnic or racial ancestry and/or shared culture. In this respect, this finding meshes with US studies which have emphasized the importance of 'colorism' and physical appearance in minority people's experiences of prejudice and discrimination. Nevertheless, one's physical appearance did not necessarily predict how our mixed race sample made sense of, and responded to, negative racialized interactions, such as being excluded or rejected by others. In comparison with the US studies discussed at the beginning of this chapter (many of which focused specifically on Black/White people or which did not differentiate among disparate types of mixed people), our study examined the experiences of a wide range of mixed people, which pointed to both inter- and intra-group differences among the mixed population – making it very difficult to generalize about whether 'multiracial' people can be said to be racially disadvantaged or subject to forms of racial prejudice and discrimination.

We found a considerable degree of variation within all the mixed groups concerning coping responses to perceived racism. A small number of respondents who looked White 'passed' to avoid the stigma of being a racialized other.

Some practised avoidance of certain groups or settings for fear of being racially abused or rejected, and/or gravitated more to one side of their heritage over another. Some respondents claimed that they were not subject to negative racial encounters at all, while others recognized that they were, but denied these interactions of any meaning or significance for them, via a number of different means. One not uncommon response to perceived racisms was to emphasize a moral scale of self-worth which was not dependent upon the approval of the wider society (Duneier 1992), and especially the approval of 'other adults'. While they acknowledged the continuing dynamics of racisms, these respondents refused to evaluate themselves in relation to the often prejudicial modes of assessment and social status attributed to them by the White mainstream (cf. Lamont 1999; Byng 1998).

Some, though not all, working-class respondents like Keith were more likely to feel vulnerable to prejudice than middle-class respondents who did not feel so conspicuously judged by others. Caballero et al.'s (2008) study of British couples with 'multiple mixing' found that middle-class households could command considerable economic and cultural resources in raising their children in particular ways. One reason for this may be that some middle-class respondents may have greater expectations of equal treatment than working-class respondents (Small 2001; Fhagen-Smith 2010); such individuals may also be more sensitized to perceived slights in their status. It is also possible that some individuals (whether working or middle class) may put voluntary boundaries on parts of their social lives which creates a social space that is relatively free of potentially negative encounters (Byng 1998:474).

In addition to negative interactions with White people, another key finding in this chapter was that we need to be much more specific about the dynamics concerning negative racialized interactions, as these may not always concern White people. As has been documented in a number of studies, mixed people can be subject to attributions of incompleteness, fractionated selves, and/or a lack of ethnic and racial authenticity; such attributions could be based upon an alleged shortcoming in terms of blood quantum or in mixed respondents' ability to demonstrate cultural practices and knowledge, such as fluency in another language. Although some mixed people were aware of their 'in-between' status, vis-à-vis monoracial groups, this did not necessarily result in feeling racially marginalized or excluded.

Based upon the diversity across our sample (including within specific mixed sub-groups), it would be difficult to conclude that multiracial people occupy a shared and specific standpoint which leads them to be especially aware of negative racialized encounters (as has been argued, e.g. by Brackett et al. 2006), in comparison, for example with 'non-mixed' monoracial minorities. Nor could we conclude, on the basis of our findings, that there is something inherently distinctive about the forms of racisms suffered by our respondents, at least in relation to the White population, in comparison with that suffered by non-mixed minorities (Thornton 1996).

In relation to those who experienced racism in interactions with White people, the basis of others' prejudicial or discriminatory behaviours towards them was not due to the fact that they were *mixed race* per se – but because these individuals were seen as non-White, for example as Black, or Asian, or somehow 'other'. As discussed in the last few chapters, mixed individuals who were seen as racially indeterminate could be subject to xenophobic attitudes and behaviours towards them. The annual British Social Attitudes survey found that in 2011 some 51% of those surveyed would like to see immigration levels *'reduce a lot'*, a figure which has risen from 39% in 1995. While NatCen notes that most of the increase in demand for reduction dates back to the late 1990s/early 2000s, showing that attitudes are impervious to changing migration levels, the statistics perhaps *'reflect a default preference for reduced migration in all circumstances'* which may be linked to exclusionary nationalist discourses (NatCen 2012).

In this respect, many mixed race people are subject to racist beliefs and behaviours, just as other monoracial minorities may be, and those who are engaging in such racist behaviour are probably unaware of their mixed status (or it would be inconsequential). In the case of the part-Black respondents who reported negative racial experiences, they were seen as Black, and thus attributed many of the negative stereotypical characteristics associated with Blackness. Thus our findings suggest that while the potential forms of racism suffered by mixed people vis-à-vis White people cannot be clearly differentiated from that suffered by other monoracial minorities, mixed people's experiences of being marginalized or rejected must include a consideration of their sense of belonging in relation to co-ethnic monoracial groups, not only Whites.

So, how should we interpret claims by some respondents that they have either not suffered racism (or were unaffected by racist incidents), since we are not privy to how much racial discrimination these respondents have actually experienced, or witnessed their reactions to such experiences? Some respondents, like Tara, were quite reflexive in talking about the fact that she did not feel racially 'different' or disadvantaged – though many people seemed to expect her to feel this way, being Black African and Malaysian. Tara said, '*Maybe I'm being naïve, but I don't think I've ever experienced any racism.*' Yet others, like Kareem, who clearly described incidents of racial abuse, reported that he '*could not care less*' and had successfully minimized such incidents in his everyday life.

It is of course possible that such respondents are entirely sincere in their claims about being unaffected by racism – even if they acknowledge that racisms still operate in a variety of ways. Some respondents, either consciously or unconsciously, may not want to see themselves as victims of racism (see Hall 1996). It may also be the case that some individuals are able to mediate or resist forms of discrimination by constructing a social reality in which they actively interpret the meanings of specific encounters in their lives (Byng 1998). That is, some individuals may resist forms of racism by employing self-definition and self-determination, rather than accept others' images and understandings of them (ibid.). This ability to 'mediate' forms of racial prejudice and discrimination may take a variety of forms and may include the refusal to recognize that an encounter was meaningful or racially discriminatory. Why and how specific individuals are able to engage in such forms of resistance, while others are not, requires further research and does not necessarily map neatly along class backgrounds.

6
How Central Is 'Race' to Mixed Race People?

Introduction

In the previous chapters, we have seen how our mixed race respondents exercised ethnic options over time and in a variety of contexts and how some of our sample were able to name just *one* racial/ethnic group that contributed most strongly to their identity. We have also examined the ways in which disparate mixed individuals can differently perceive, understand, and respond to other people's perceptions and treatment of them. In this chapter we explore the relative importance of various identity dimensions for different racial/ethnic groups, and we focus especially on the importance of ethnic and racial identities for our mixed respondents' sense of selves and their everyday lives.

A person's racial/ethnic identity may be only one strand or component of their identity, and in fact it may not be the most important of such strands. The meaning and significance of race and/or ethnicity may be shaped by many different factors, such as one's familial upbringing, the ethnic and racial composition of one's neighbourhood and social network, the proximity of relatives, and one's socioeconomic background.

What are the collective identities that we hold, value, and demand to be recognized and respected in our culture? Jenkins (1996) identifies a number of primary identities – selfhood, human-ness, gender, and, under some circumstances, kinship and ethnicity – that are more robust and resilient to change in later life than other identities. Similarly, Appiah (2005) argues that the major collective identities that demand recognition in North America are religion, gender, ethnicity (or nationality), race, and sexuality, and these identities all manifest themselves to their holders in different ways.[1] Indeed, it is now commonplace to

126

talk of such collective social identities as key features of people's lives. Many of these identities have been brought into the public domain by our invention of categories for them, for instance in the vocabulary of equality and diversity (see Aspinall & Mitton 2008).

How one or more bases of identification might combine and shape the experience of being 'mixed race' is therefore likely to be complex. We know very little about the variable strength of disparate identities, the extent to which they overlap, or the possibility that one identity might reinforce or weaken another, and/or resist the imposition of external, unwanted definitions.

Race as a master status

Such social identities were conceptualized in the disciplines of the social sciences in the mid-20th century. It was American sociologist Everett C. Hughes (1897–1983) who coined the term 'master status' in the 1940s (Hughes 1945), with special reference to race, and 'Race Relations and the Sociological Imagination' was the subject of his address as the 53rd president of the American Sociological Association. In the 1950s the idea of status positions rose to prominence in the field of social psychology in the work of Gouldner (1954) and Erikson (1959), with 'master statuses' being classified as either 'ascribed' (such as sex or race) or 'achieved' (such as educational level or occupation).

The enduring influence of Hughes' conceptualization of 'master status' has shaped much work on social status over the last half century or so. Becker's (1963:31–39) work on the sociology of deviance, for example, uses Hughes' term 'master status' as one to which most other identities are subordinate. Other candidates advanced as 'master statuses' (and frequently citing Hughes' original conceptualization) include religion (Bartkowski 2004), AIDS/HIV (Haas & Dur 1992), being overweight (Hiller 1982), gang membership (Miethe & McCorkle 1997; Brownfield et al. 2001), giftedness (in school) (Bryant 1990), infertility (Bryant 1990), homelessness (LaGory et al. 2005), and refugee status (Hein 1993).

The 'master status' of an individual was defined as one which, in most or all social situations, will overpower or dominate all other statuses. A master status has always been seen as important as it influences every other aspect of life, including personal identity and everyday practices and experiences. For instance, master statuses can entail dominant modes of behaviour which are prescribed either implicitly or explicitly by particular groups, and pressures to adhere to 'normal' behaviour (whatever this may be) may be quite significant – especially in relation to racialized scripts of behaviour (Song 2003:48). As discussed in Chapter 4, expectations concerning dominant modes of behaviour are also linked with groups' understandings of ethnic and racial authenticity (Taylor 1994). However, the influence of traditional master statuses, such as race, are subject to change, especially in contemporary periods of significant demographic change and diversification, such as found in Britain today (see Vertovec 2007).

It is not difficult to see why 'race' became a 'master status'. 'Race', as it is popularly understood, is likely to be 'visible' to others, in the form of phenotypical features as opposed to ethnicity, which is usually understood to be based primarily on cultural cues (van den Berghe 1978). Race is frequently established early on in life and is arguably less negotiable than ethnicity (Cornell & Hartmann 1998; Morning 2008). Because of race's visibility, the holding of a racial identity is distinctively tied to and interwoven with a collective racial identity, that is, being treated *as* an 'African-American', for example.

While Hughes saw 'master statuses' as social labels and not personally held identities, the consequence of which is that the individual has little control over his or her master status in any given social interaction, our social identities continue to be primarily constituted by social practices. However, the fact that we do make choices from this 'toolkit of options' (Appiah 2005:107) – that many labels are *self*-assigned – makes the use of the term 'master identities' more appropriate.

Another theoretical strand that informs our discussion in this chapter is that of 'intersectionality'. The main contribution of intersectionality theory has been to challenge the presumption that race/ethnicity, class, gender, nationality/national identity, sexuality, and others exist as discrete and independent identity strands and analytical categories (Hall & du Gay 1996; Collins 1990). Rather, intersectionality focuses on the simultaneous and interacting effects of these categories of difference and delineates the multiple layerings and combinations of gender, ethnicity, class, and nationality (Ali 2003; Anthias & Yuval-Davis 1992). The relevance of intersectionality here is that it challenges the singular status of any given status dimension or identity domain, such as race, gender, or socioeconomic position.

Amongst the different identity domains, we have placed emphasis upon race/ethnicity, both as an identity strand and as a key demographic characteristic of respondents, to maintain a focus on our mixed race respondents. More than a half century after Hughes first identified race as a 'master status', this chapter assesses whether race still occupies this primary position among our 'mixed race' respondents in an era in which this dimension of identity has been increasingly challenged. And if race is now a less salient master status, what other aspects of identification have come to the fore? Furthermore, we also explore the extent to which our mixed respondents place importance on not just 'race', but on their mixedness per se.

Background surveys: the Citizenship Survey and the Fourth National Survey

Before we examine the findings of our own survey of young mixed race people, we review the findings of two surveys from the United Kingdom, which provide a good point of comparison to our own survey. These include the results of the 2007 Citizenship Survey, a survey of adults (aged 16 and over) in England and Wales. This survey asks about *'how important various things are to your sense of who you are'*, measured in four response categories of importance (and a 'don't know' option). It then identifies *'the most important'* through a process of derivation or further questioning.[2] To a lesser extent, we review some of the findings of the 1994 Fourth National Survey (FNS), which poses the question: *'Suppose you were describing yourself on the phone to a new acquaintance of your own sex from a country you have never been to. Which of the following would tell them something important about you'*; it also asks for the 'two most important' things. This question removes gender from the list of possibly important identities, and this is arguably a key limitation; nevertheless the authors of the FNS decided not to list gender because gender was assumed to be a central identity for most people. We also make a brief reference to the 2006 Social Capital Community Survey in the United States, which used identical wording and similar response categories to that in the UK Citizenship Survey. While the original datasets for the 2007 Citizenship Survey and 1994 FNS were accessed, only aggregate findings were available for the US 2006 National Social Capital Community Survey for comparative purposes.

All of these surveys provide a measure of the salience of certain dimensions of identity and (in the UK surveys) the most important or 'master identities'. The number of dimensions asked about varies from 5 in the US Social Capital Survey to 17 in our own student survey (see Table 6.1). There is substantial equivalence across most dimensions.

Analyses were undertaken of the saliency of identity dimensions and of the 'master' identities by the demographic sub-group of ethnicity/race. None of the surveys explores the degree of mutual implication

Table 6.1 Identity attributes in UK and US surveys

UK: Main student survey (17 dimensions)	UK: Citizenship Survey (13 dimensions)	UK: Fourth National Survey (12 dimensions)	USA Social Capital Community Survey[1,2] (5 dimensions)
'The kind of study or work you do or did'	'Your occupation'	'Your job'	'Your occupation'
'Your ethnic group or cultural background'	'Your ethnic or racial background'	'Whether you are white, Black, Asian, Chinese or mixed'	'Your ethnic or racial background'
'Your religion'	'Your religion'	'Your religion'	'Your religion (if any)'
–	'Your national identity'	–	'Being an American'
'Your regional identity (Londoner, Geordie, etc.)'	'Where you live'	–	'Your place of residence'
–	'Your interests'	–	–
'Your family'	'Your family'	–	–
'Your social class (working class, middle class, etc.)'	'Your social class (working, middle)'	'Your father's job'	–
'The country your family came from originally'	'The country your family came from originally'	'The country(s) your family came from originally'	–
'Your gender'	'Your gender'	–	–
'Your age or life-stage'	'Your age and life stage'	'Your age'	–
'Your level of income'	'Your level of income'	'Your level of income'	–
'Your level of education'	'Your level of education'	'Your education'	–
'Your political beliefs'	–	–	–
'Your nationality'	–	'Your nationality'	–
–	–	'Your height'	–
–	–	'The colour of your hair and eyes'	–
'The colour of your skin'	–	'The colour of your skin'	–

'*Any disability you may have*'	–	–	–
'*Your sexuality/ sexual orientation*'	–	–	–
'*Something else (please write in)*'	–	–	–

Main student survey: Suppose you were describing yourself, which of the following things would say something important about you (tick all boxes that apply)? And which of the above would be the single most important and second most important thing that would say something important about you?

Citizenship Survey, 2007: We'd like to know how important various things are to your sense of who you are. Please think about each thing I mention, and tell me how important it is to your sense of who you are? Please choose your answer from the card. (Response options: Very important; Quite important; Not very important; Not at all important; Don't Know.) Which one of these would you say is the most important?

FNS, 1994: Now some questions about yourself. Suppose you were describing yourself on the phone to a new acquaintance of your own sex from a country you have never been to. Which of these would tell them something important about you ... (Response options: Important – Yes; Important – No.) And which of these would be the two most important things to say about yourself to this new acquaintance?

Social Capital & Community Survey, 2006: We'd like to know how important various things are to your sense of who you are. When you think about yourself, how important is (DIMENSION) to your sense of who you are? (Response options: Very important, Moderately important, Slightly important, or Not at all important.) [1]Social Capital Community Survey, 2006, National Sample, Kennedy School of Government, Harvard University; [2]Staten Island Social Capital Community Benchmark Study, 2007, College of Staten Island/CUNY.

or interaction between the different identity dimensions.[3] However, an attempt is made to explore this area through two approaches. First, we investigate the intersection of ethnicity and social class demographically in the Citizenship Survey by examining how different social class groups prioritize ethnicity. Second, the *potential* for interaction between different identity dimensions is investigated by identifying which sets of dimensions most frequently cluster together in our student survey. For these young mixed race adults, the sub-set of 65 in-depth interviews is then used to explore what their choices (including those who indicate that their ethnic/racial backgrounds are important and those who do not choose this basis of identification) may mean in their everyday lives and the interaction between identity categories such as race/ethnicity, class, gender, and nationality.

The 2007 Citizenship Survey

The 2007 Citizenship Survey (contemporaneous with our student survey) contained ethnic group data for 14,038 respondents on the

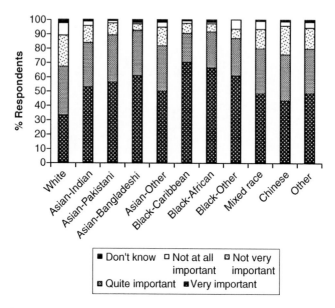

Figure 6.1 Importance of ethnic or racial background to respondents' sense of who they are, by 2001 census categorization (11 groups)
Source: 2007 Citizenship Survey (accessed via ESDS Data Archive).

question assessing the importance of ethnic or racial background for respondents' sense of who they are. Respondents were able to indicate a range from 'very important' to 'not at all important', with two middle values in between. Figure 6.1 shows the level of importance respondents attached to this dimension.

On the measure of 'very important', ethnic or racial background had the greatest saliency in the three black groups: Black-Caribbeans (70.2%), followed by Black-Africans (66.3%) and Black-Other (60.9%). It was also considered very important by over half the respondents in the main Asian categories: Bangladeshi (60.7%), Pakistani (56.1%), and Indian (52.7%). In all other categories a minority of respondents considered ethnic or racial background to be very important, varying from a third (33.0%) in the White group to 49.8% in the Asian-Other category. The 'Mixed' category occupied a similar position (48.2%) to Asian-Other and Other. Amongst minority ethnic groups saliency was lowest in the Chinese category, though still at 43.3%. When the 'very important' and 'quite important' categories are combined, the rank-order changes little, with the greatest saliency found in the

Bangladeshi category (92.4%), followed by Black-African (91.5%) and Black-Caribbean (90.3%), Chinese (75.6%), and White (67.0%) groups.

What, then, are the competing *salient* identities – that is, identities which are chosen with some frequency, but which don't quite meet the 10% cut-off, as with master identities (see Table 6.2)?[4] The Citizenship Survey contains a number which may be regarded as within the 'cultural' question set (religion, national identity, and the country your family came from originally) and other more general ascriptive categories (such as education, income, and social class). 'Family' was selected by three-quarters or more of respondents in all the ethnic groups. Religion was selected by half or more of respondents in the four Asian groups and the Caribbean and African groups. National identity was selected by between two- and three-fifths of respondents (with the exception of Chinese). Gender, occupation, and level of education were also important. Level of income, age/life-stage, and where you live, less so. Social class was chosen by around only a fifth in most groups, having the highest saliency in some of the most disadvantaged groups (Africans and Bangladeshis). For most identity attributes saliency was lowest in the Chinese group.

Perhaps not surprisingly, one *master identity* predominates in the 2007 Citizenship Survey, that of 'Your family' (Table 6.3). This was the most frequently selected dimension across *all* 16 census categories. If 'master identities' at the group level are defined as those selected by at least 10% of group members, then only one other 'master identity' emerges, that of religion, chosen, for example by 34.4% of Pakistanis, 19.1% of Black Africans, and 18.3% of Mixed White and Black Africans. The only other dimensions that came close to 'master identity' status were occupation amongst the Chinese (9.8%) and ethnic or racial background amongst Black Caribbeans (8.6%). 'Your social class', 'Your gender', and 'Where you live' mattered the least.

The Fourth National Survey

By comparison, in the 1994 Fourth National Survey (FNS), ethnicity attributes scored highly. A majority in the different groups chose ethnic/racial background (whether 'White, black, Asian, etc.') (ranging between 56% and 76%) as an attribute saying something important about them, the highest proportion being found in the Caribbean group – but with the Chinese almost as high at 74% – interestingly, much higher than they scored on ethnic or racial background in the

134

Table 6.2 Salient identities in the 2007 Citizenship Survey

	Occupation	Ethnic or racial background	Religion	National identity	Where you live	Interests	Family	Social class	Country origins	Gender	Age & life-stage	Level of income	Level of education
White British	39.5	32.8	19.9	47.6	30.4	41.7	87.9	16.3	40.0	46.1	29.0	29.1	32.4
White Irish	37.3	39.8	33.7	44.6	31.3	38.0	91.0	21.7	56.6	50.6	33.1	33.7	34.9
Any other White background	41.3	35.9	25.4	41.3	20.5	43.4	84.1	14.1	46.2	45.9	29.7	28.7	46.8
Mixed White & Black Caribbean	48.4	56.4	33.5	48.9	29.3	46.3	87.2	20.7	40.4	54.8	45.7	44.7	43.6
Mixed White & Black African	38.5	44.0	39.4	46.8	27.5	41.3	81.7	19.4	43.5	49.1	38.0	33.3	45.4
Mixed White & Asian	44.6	35.9	38.0	42.4	31.5	44.6	87.0	14.3	35.9	52.2	40.2	37.0	54.3
Any other Mixed background	44.7	48.9	36.2	44.7	30.9	55.3	87.2	19.1	45.7	47.9	38.3	39.4	46.8
Asian or Asian British – Indian	52.4	52.7	56.7	52.7	33.2	33.8	87.9	24.4	45.3	49.2	36.5	39.4	52.1
Asian or Asian British – Pakistani	38.0	56.1	77.2	52.1	29.8	29.2	88.4	20.3	43.6	50.7	33.9	34.3	48.3

Asian or Asian British – Bangladeshi	48.6	60.7	81.4	58.6	39.0	38.3	88.3	26.6	52.1	55.9	46.2	44.1	49.3
Any other Asian/Asian British background	52.7	49.8	50.9	46.3	29.7	39.2	86.9	23.0	45.2	47.7	39.2	46.6	57.2
Black or Black British – Caribbean	47.0	70.2	51.2	55.0	32.5	47.5	88.1	24.3	56.7	61.3	42.8	43.0	48.4
Black or Black British – African	54.2	66.3	71.7	59.7	39.1	47.7	90.5	30.4	61.9	63.1	49.6	48.1	59.0
Any other Black/Black British background	41.3	60.9	47.8	41.3	26.1	43.5	80.4	17.4	58.7	58.7	41.3	37.0	54.3
Chinese	44.5	43.3	14.6	34.1	12.8	25.6	74.4	14.0	34.1	36.6	23.8	22.6	39.0
Any other ethnic group	51.8	48.4	47.0	50.9	34.8	41.4	86.4	23.0	52.5	51.6	37.3	43.0	49.5
ALL GROUPS (unweighted data)	**43.1**	**42.5**	**35.2**	**49.4**	**31.1**	**40.7**	**87.7**	**19.2**	**44.1**	**49.1**	**33.3**	**33.8**	**40.1**

Source: Citizenship Survey, 2007.

Table 6.3 Master identities in the 2007 Citizenship Survey

	Occupation	Ethnic or racial background	Religion	National identity	Where you live	Interests	Family	Social class	Country origins	Gender	Age & life-stage	Level of income	Level of education
White British	3.0	0.9	3.2	5.0	1.2	3.5	75.4	0.3	1.4	1.0	1.7	1.5	2.0
White Irish	3.3	1.3	8.5	5.9	0.7	1.3	71.2	0.7	3.3	0.7	2.0	0.0	1.3
Any other White background	6.0	0.4	7.7	3.9	0.0	5.3	64.9	0.7	2.8	0.4	1.8	2.5	3.9
Mixed White and Black Caribbean	2.9	3.4	7.4	4.0	0.6	0.6	66.3	0.0	1.1	0.0	4.0	6.9	2.9
Mixed White & Black African	2.9	7.7	18.3	1.9	0.0	3.8	52.9	0.0	2.9	1.0	0.0	2.9	5.8
Mixed White & Asian	4.8	1.2	6.0	1.2	1.2	1.2	75.0	0.0	0.0	0.0	2.4	3.6	3.6
Any other mixed background	3.3	6.5	4.3	4.3	0.0	5.4	63.0	0.0	4.3	0.0	1.1	3.3	4.3
Asian or Asian British – Indian	5.8	3.4	12.0	4.3	1.2	1.5	60.5	0.5	1.8	0.5	1.2	2.2	5.3
Asian or Asian British – Pakistani	2.7	5.3	34.4	2.2	1.0	0.5	44.6	0.0	1.5	0.6	0.3	1.4	5.5

Asian or Asian British – Bangladeshi	2.2	4.0	**34.1**	1.8	1.1	0.7	**45.7**	0.0	1.4	1.4	2.5	1.4	3.6
Any other Asian/Asian British background	7.7	3.8	8.0	4.2	0.0	2.7	**61.3**	0.4	0.8	0.4	1.1	3.1	6.5
Black or Black British – Caribbean	3.1	8.6	**10.7**	4.2	0.8	0.8	**59.5**	0.1	3.5	0.8	2.7	2.0	3.1
Black or Black British – African	4.5	4.1	**19.1**	2.4	1.4	1.4	**55.3**	0.0	2.3	1.0	1.0	2.3	5.0
Any other Black/Black British background	2.4	4.9	7.3	0.0	2.4	2.4	**70.7**	0.0	0.0	2.4	2.4	4.9	0.0
Chinese	9.8	5.6	2.1	4.9	0.0	1.4	**62.9**	0.0	0.7	0.7	2.1	2.1	7.7
Any other ethnic group	6.2	2.7	9.2	2.2	2.0	1.0	**64.4**	0.2	3.2	1.0	0.5	1.0	6.2
ALL GROUPS (unweighted data)	**3.7**	**2.5**	**8.7**	**4.3**	**1.1**	**2.6**	**67.8**	**0.3**	**1.7**	**0.9**	**1.6**	**1.8**	**3.2**

Note: Master identities shown in bold (selected by 10% or more of group members).
Source: Citizenship Survey, 2007.

Table 6.4 Things that say something important about respondent (percentages)

Dimension	Caribbean	Indian	African Asian	Pakistani	Bangladeshi	Chinese
A. Nationality	81	78	69	74	63	77
B. White, Black, Asian, etc.	76	68	60	56	64	74
C. Country your family came from	63	67	62	67	76	65
D. Religion	44	73	68	83	75	25
E. Skin colour	61	37	29	31	21	15
F. Height	31	30	26	26	26	13
G. Colour of hair or eyes	30	25	24	26	19	13
H. Age	61	57	50	65	57	50
I. Job	56	57	65	64	54	61
J. Education	47	49	60	57	53	54
K. Level of income	16	19	17	19	14	6
L. Father's job	10	14	15	19	7	7
Weighted Count	765	606	290	397	141	183
Unweighted count	580	595	361	538	289	101

Source: 1994 Fourth National Survey of Ethnic Minorities (FNS).

Citizenship Survey (see Table 6.4). Across all groups under a fifth selected either level of income or father's job. This survey did not seek a single 'master identity' but rather asked for the 'two *most* important' attributes. Nationality was stressed but religion emerged as the 'master identity' amongst South Asians (but chosen by few Caribbeans and scarcely any Chinese). Skin colour was the third most important item for Caribbeans but inconsequential for the other groups.

Our 'ethnic options' main student survey

Our main student survey, which draws upon the Citizenship Survey categories, asked: '*Suppose you were describing yourself, which of the following things would say something important about you*' (multi-ticking from a list of 17 items). This survey also requested the first and second most important items.

The most salient identity attributes were '*the kind of study or work you do or did*', followed by '*your age or life-stage*', '*your family*', and (jointly) '*your level of education*' and '*your ethnic group or cultural background*' (see Table 6.5). '*Your gender*' was also amongst those things selected by more than half of the respondents. Of lesser importance

Table 6.5 Things respondents select as saying something important about themselves (percentages)

	Attributes selected	First choice	Second choice
A. Your age or life-stage	64.4	17.2	11.7
B. The kind of study or work you do or did	72.4	14.1	11.0
C. Your level of education	54.6	6.7	9.5
D. Your level of income	11.7	0.9	0.9
E. Your political beliefs	20.9	2.8	1.8
F. Your family	63.5	21.2	12.9
G. Your ethnic group or cultural background	54.6	9.2	12.3
H. The country your family came from originally	30.4	0.6	2.8
I. Your regional identity (Londoner, Geordie, etc.)	41.7	2.8	9.5
J. Your nationality	34.0	0.9	4.9
K. Your religion	23.6	4.9	4.6
L. The colour of your skin	16.6	3.7	2.8
M. Your social class (working class, middle class, etc.)	23.3	1.2	5.2
N. Your gender	52.1	5.8	6.1
O. Any disability you may have	4.9	0.6	0.0
P. Your sexuality/sexual orientation	10.7	0.0	0.9
Q. Something else	8.6	1.5	1.5

Notes: Examples of Q ('something else') attribute selected responses ($n = 28$): 'hobbies'/'interests', 'friends', 'beliefs & what they stand for', 'illness', 'ethnic outlook', 'what you do for fun, for example 'transport/going out', 'personality', 'musical taste', 'I am a whole person, none of these by themselves define me completely', 'my accent', 'my approach to life', 'my personality and who I am', 'relationship status with friends', 'the languages I speak', 'the relationships I have with family (mother) partner and friends', 'the university I went to', 'Your spirituality (also where is language)', 'sports i.e. basketball', 'to know who I am in life, the days have gone where people's backgrounds are judged, it's not about colour of the skin but on the content of your character'. Examples of Q (first choice): 'Be free, before you're consumed by the majority', 'I don't think that any of the above are important when describing yourself [sic] things like hobbies and interests say'.
Source: Main student survey.

were 'your nationality', 'your religion', and 'country of family origins' (selected by between a quarter and third of respondents). A person's 'regional identity' was, perhaps surprisingly, more important (at 42%) than all of the latter. One reason for this was that many respondents from London (or now studying in London) professed a strong sense of being a 'Londoner'; furthermore, a minority of respondents also talked of being proud to be 'Northern'. 'Social class' was mentioned by under a quarter (23%) and 'your political beliefs' by somewhat fewer. Less than a fifth of respondents selected 'skin colour' and around only one in ten respondents or fewer mentioned 'your level of income', 'any disability', 'your sexuality/sexual orientation', or 'something else'.

In this survey the *most important* (first choice) item respondents selected as saying something important about themselves was, again, 'family', but this dimension was less dominant than in the Citizenship Survey (see Fig. 6.2 on the following page.). Over 10% of respondents also selected 'age or life-stage' and 'kind of study or work' as 'master identities': ethnic group or cultural background almost scraped over the threshold at 9.2%. If one takes first *and* second choices combined, this rank-order is broadly maintained: ethnic group or cultural background, level of education, regional identity, and gender are selected by 10% or more as first and second choices. Around only 6% or less each selected level of income, political beliefs, family origins, nationality, skin colour, social class, disability, and sexuality. These findings show that ethnicity is a *salient identity* (selected by 55% of respondents) but only one of several of a list of broad, ascriptive identities chosen by a majority of respondents. However, it did not emerge as a '*master identity*' based on the 10% threshold.

Interpreting the choice of ethnicity/race as important

As discussed above, while ethnic and racial background was often a salient identity for our mixed race respondents, they were not necessarily of importance to all of our respondents, as we discuss below. In fact, an analysis of our interview sub-set shows that the survey choices of ethnicity and race as 'very important' could also mean that their race/ethnicity could be meaningful or important in a variety of ways, not just one uniform way. Furthermore, the interviews revealed that while some respondents found one or both of their parents' 'races' (and/or cultural backgrounds) to be important to them, it did not necessarily mean that they found their mixedness to be important. Yet others could be attached to the idea of being mixed per se. Thus it is important to distinguish analytically between an attachment to one's ethnic and racial ancestry and culture, from an attachment to the idea of being a 'mixed' person.

For instance, one Black/White respondent, Sandy (see Chapter 3), indicated that her specific ethnic group and cultural background (her father was Black Barbadian and her mother was White English) was

141

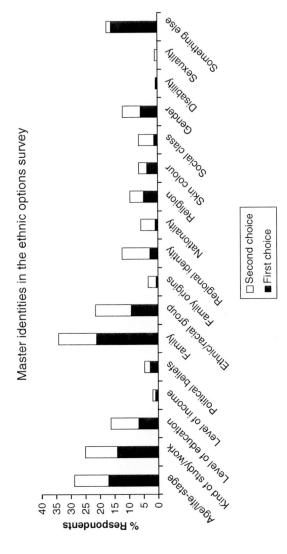

Figure 6.2 The first and second most important identity attributes
Source: Main student survey.

something which would say something important about her (it was her second choice). But when asked about whether being mixed per se was of importance to her, she did not regard this attribute to be an important part of how she saw herself, or how others saw her: '*I don't think they [teachers or other people] treat me differently because I'm mixed. They might treat me differently because I'm a girl or because I know stuff....I think they treat me different for other reasons but I don't think they treat me different because everyone is so mixed....*'

In fact, some of our respondents revealed in their interviews that neither their parents' backgrounds nor their mixedness were particularly central to their sense of selves. For instance, Richard (19), who was Portuguese/Pakistani, indicated that he did not really identify with any ethnic or racial groups (as his sense of being from London and British identity were primary). When asked how his parents' backgrounds and his mixedness influenced his day-to-day life in multiethnic London, where he had grown up, Richard replied: '*I just don't let it affect me....I wouldn't really say that it's that much of a hindrance or help at all...It's something that's neutral, it has no bearing on my life really.*'

Interestingly, he differentiated his being mixed race from his interest in his parents' cultural backgrounds, though even his interest in the latter was relatively limited. While Richard was fairly interested in Portuguese culture (in particular), his attachment was largely symbolic; he reported that he did not speak the language, and that he mostly felt British – a term of national belonging which he considered to be race neutral. By comparison, being mixed, per se, was no basis of identification for Richard. Richard's emphasis upon how little his parents' ancestries and his mixed status shaped his sense of self or daily life must be understood within the context of his upbringing in a city as cosmopolitan as London – one's mixedness in London would be regarded as relatively ordinary but it would be of much more prominence if one grew up in a White village in the Cotswolds.

Yet others highlighted their mixedness above any one ethnic or racial background. For instance, Carrie, who had a Black mother and White father, wished to be seen, first and foremost, as a 'mixed race' person with both Black and White ancestry. As discussed in Chapter 3, Carrie's strong sense of being mixed was based upon her view that being mixed race was a distinctive status (and 'race') in itself. Like Carrie, Sara (who was Arab and White) strongly identified as someone who was 'mixed', evoking notions of a hybrid, border identity which transcended attachment to any one ethnic or racial ancestry. Sara reportedly felt extremely attached to both sides of her family: '*Yeah I just feel very, very half.*'

While some respondents' main basis of identification was their regional identity (e.g. sense of being a Londoner, and British, like Richard above), some respondents identified a religious affiliation as primary, superseding ethnicity and race. For instance, Samuel, who had an Iranian mother and White British father, said that he did not identify in racial terms, and he had refused to choose one 'race' in the forced choice question. Instead, he reported that his Jewishness was the most important part of who he was, along with his nationality (his Britishness), the kind of study or work, and his family. He explained that the fact that his parents were of different backgrounds did not matter very much because of their shared commitment to Judaism, which effectively formed the 'glue' to their family: *'Yeah. We're kosher. And it's just second nature. It's just a natural part of family life . . . . It's just who you are.'* In fact, for Samuel, his Jewish and British identities trumped any other identities that he possessed.

Thus the interface between race and culture (and or religion, or sense of national belonging) also makes discussions about the assumed primacy of racial difference (between the parents) problematic (Katz & Treacher 2005). A child may be from two different 'races' but her parents may have grown up in the same community sharing the same culture, values, and lifestyle (e.g. grown up as Londoners in the same neighbourhood) (ibid.). At the same time, another child may be a 'pure' black or white child but have parents who come from quite different cultural and religious backgrounds (e.g. White Jewish and White Protestant backgrounds) – see Caballero et al. (2007). The potential ways in which race intersects with nationality, ethnicity, religion, and so on can be rather unpredictable and variable.

In comparison with Samuel, whose Jewishness was central to his sense of self (and his sense of distinctiveness, in relation to the British mainstream), Ellie, who was 'Burmese' (the term she used) and English, and who grew up in a primarily White town northwest of London, emphasized her sexuality more than any other identity attribute. In the survey, she had indicated that her parents' and their ancestors' race/ethnicity were relatively unimportant and had ticked 'sexuality' and *'your age or life stage'* as the two most important items. Ellie revealed that being lesbian was central to who she was – though this was unusual in our sample. When queried about her parents' ancestry in the interview, she responded: *'It's never really been discussed . . . it's only maybe recently that stories of our ancestors have actually been mentioned. I mean it was never something that was considered important to be part of.'* Later in the interview, when Ellie was asked how central her mixed heritage was to her sense of self, she replied, '*Not really at all to be honest. I mean, I kind of identify really with White anyway... just in the sort of interests I have, sort of culturally.*' Although many respondents reported that either one or both parents had made some attempt to introduce their cultural backgrounds into family life, Ellie's exposure to Burmese culture had been very limited, as her mother had stressed the importance of fitting into mainstream White British culture.

Interestingly, while 'the colour of your skin' was selected by just 17% of respondents, almost two-thirds – 63% – of these respondents were either Black Caribbean/Black African/Other Black and White. In comparison with Richard, Samuel, and Ellie, above, part-Black respondents were more definitive about how they were seen by others (see Chapter 4), as 'Black' (as opposed to mixed), and those who ticked 'colour of your skin' also often ticked 'ethnic group or cultural background' as well. For instance, Natalie, who described herself as White British and Black Jamaican, chose 'the colour of your skin' as first choice, then 'family' as her second choice. In her interview, she spoke of how other people saw her: '*It's just everywhere. Definitely at university, they'd say "the black girl", unless I've actually had to say to people, actually I'm mixed race....So I prefer to be mixed race. Through my experiences in life people have said black girl....because the colour of [my] skin.*' Thus, throughout Natalie's life, she had been constantly reminded of her Blackness; as such, she possessed a heightened awareness of how visible her skin colour was to others. Her blackness had therefore become central to her sense of self and her daily interactions, including her attempts to correct people who saw her as Black, as opposed to 'mixed race'. While many Black/White respondents did not choose 'the colour of your skin', this group was more likely to do so than other types of mixed people in our sample. This meshes with the finding (see Chapters 3 and 4) that part-Black people felt more consistently racially assigned, as Black, than other mixed individuals (in relation to their minority ancestries).

Although in the minority, some interview respondents actually privileged their mixed status above other attributes, including their specific 'ethnic group or cultural background(s)'. For instance, Valerie, who had a Chinese mother and Indian father, chose 'your level of education' and 'your age or life-stage' as the two most important bases of identification in the survey; she did not tick 'your ethnic group or cultural background'. Nevertheless, the interview revealed that she was attached to her mother's Chinese heritage, and that she possessed a very strong sense of being a 'mixed' person in cosmopolitan London. As a mixed person, Valerie felt that she somehow embodied the multiethnic spirit and feel of London: '*I think I'm a citizen of the future and one day every-body will be like this.*' At the same time, she was constantly aware of (and enjoying) the fact that other people saw her as hybrid, and difficult to categorize, thus reinforcing her sense of being a mixed person:

It's not a bad thing. I love curiosities. I love them. Maybe I don't want to be an object but it's like something that people ... I feel I've got something that people lack in a way, like quite like being half this, half that and being able to have both. I think ... I think people are curious because they ... I think people are curious because they're like 'wow'!

Thus these interview excerpts provided more detail concerning the many different ways in which 'race', ethnicity, and cultural background, and a mixed status, might or might not be central to mixed young peoples' sense of selves. Interviews also revealed the ways in which a variety of attributes could intersect with one another, in ways which were not always easily ranked in a top-down fashion.

How identities in the population intersect and cluster

In Table 6.5 (earlier in the chapter) we see how the different identity attributes listed attracted varying levels of support, with 'age or life-stage', 'kind of study or work', 'level of education', 'family', 'ethnic group or cultural background', and 'gender' being selected by more than half of our respondents. However, this does not tell us about the strength of associations between the attributes and how (or if) they shape or modify each other through processes of intersection.

As direct survey evidence on such matters is limited, two approaches are used to investigate intersectionality: first, rather than focus on the mutual implication of identity attributes that are selected as 'important', the relationship is examined between one of these attributes (ethnic-ity/race) and social class as defined as a characteristic of the population sample. Second, in our own 'mixed race' dataset, a statistical technique (Jaccard Similarity Coefficients) was used to look at patterns in the selection of identity attributes (see Table 6.6).

The 2007 Citizenship Survey does not ask respondents about the rela-tionships between the identities they select. Ethnic/racial background has, therefore, been examined in terms of the social class of respon-dents who indicated that it was very important (see Table 6.7). This data indicates that a person's social class (whether manual or non-manual[5]) only made a statistically significant difference to whether they identified

146

Table 6.6 Jaccard Similarity Coefficient Matrix[1]

	A	B	C	D	E	F	G	H	I	J	K	L	M	N	O	P
A	0	0.59	0.49	0.12	0.21	0.48	0.48	0.27	0.43	0.32	0.23	0.16	0.24	0.53	0.04	0.12
B	0.59	0	0.52	0.11	0.20	0.52	0.46	0.27	0.42	0.32	0.23	0.15	0.21	0.46	0.06	0.10
C	0.49	0.52	0	0.19	0.19	0.45	0.40	0.29	0.37	0.31	0.17	0.20	0.30	0.41	0.07	0.14
D	0.12	0.11	0.19	0	0.12	0.12	0.09	0.10	0.07	0.13	0.11	0.16	0.18	0.09	0.15	0.12
E	0.21	0.20	0.19	0.12	0	0.18	0.21	0.15	0.18	0.15	0.14	0.10	0.20	0.17	0.06	0.11
F	0.48	0.52	0.45	0.12	0.18	0	0.49	0.32	0.31	0.31	0.25	0.14	0.20	0.42	0.05	0.11
G	0.48	0.46	0.40	0.09	0.21	0.49	0	0.39	0.37	0.35	0.31	0.17	0.25	0.43	0.04	0.12
H	0.27	0.27	0.29	0.10	0.15	0.32	0.39	0	0.24	0.27	0.27	0.15	0.15	0.28	0.05	0.10
I	0.43	0.42	0.37	0.07	0.18	0.31	0.37	0.24	0	0.29	0.22	0.15	0.25	0.35	0.05	0.13
J	0.32	0.32	0.31	0.13	0.15	0.31	0.35	0.27	0.29	0	0.21	0.16	0.25	0.28	0.07	0.10
K	0.23	0.23	0.17	0.11	0.14	0.25	0.31	0.27	0.22	0.21	0	0.16	0.16	0.19	0.04	0.12
L	0.16	0.15	0.20	0.16	0.10	0.14	0.17	0.15	0.15	0.16	0.16	0	0.24	0.19	0.08	0.09
M	0.24	0.21	0.30	0.18	0.20	0.20	0.25	0.15	0.25	0.25	0.16	0.24	0	0.22	0.08	0.10
N	0.53	0.46	0.41	0.09	0.17	0.42	0.43	0.28	0.35	0.28	0.19	0.19	0.22	0	0.04	0.14
O	0.04	0.06	0.07	0.15	0.06	0.05	0.04	0.05	0.05	0.07	0.04	0.08	0.08	0.04	0	0.16
P	0.12	0.10	0.14	0.12	0.11	0.11	0.12	0.10	0.13	0.10	0.12	0.09	0.10	0.14	0.16	0

Notes: [1]This technique provides some measure of similarity between any two of our identity attributes in the matrix of the full 16 attributes, the Jaccard Coefficient measuring the number of individuals who ticked both attributes as a proportion of the number that ticked at least one. The procedure was undertaken in MATLAB using the procedure: >> Y = 1-pdist(X,'jaccard'); >> squareform(Y).

Key: Where A – Your age or life-stage; B – The kind of study or work you do or did; C – Your level of education; D – Your level of income; E – Your political beliefs; F – Your family; G – Your ethnic group or cultural background; H – The country your family came from originally; I – Your regional identity (Londoner, Geordie, etc.); J – Your nationality; K – Your religion; L – The colour of your skin; M – Your social class (working class, middle class, etc.); N – Your gender; O – Any disability you may have; P – Your sexuality/sexual orientation.

Source: Main student survey.

Table 6.7 The effect of respondents' social class on selection of the ethnic/racial background identity attribute as 'very important'

Ethnic/Racial background of respondent	Social class group[2]	'Ethnic/racial background' as identity attribute		Manual vs. Non-Manual: odds ratio (OR) (95% confidence interval)
	N = non-manual M = manual	'Very important' (n)	Not very important[1] (n)	
White British	N	1,424	3,046	1.21 (1.09 to 1.33)*
	M	1,058	1,875	
White Irish	N	31	62	2.00 (1.03 to 3.88)*
	M	30	30	
Any other White background	N	61	129	1.75 (1.07 to 2.85)*
	M	48	58	
Mixed White & Black Caribbean	N	41	36	1.25 (0.66 to 2.36)
	M	44	31	
Mixed White & Black African	N	23	28	0.88 (0.36 to 2.15)
	M	13	18	
Mixed White & Asian	N	15	39	3.47 (1.24 to 9.74)*
	M	12	9	
Any other mixed background	N	29	25	0.65 (0.26 to 1.61)
	M	12	16	
Asian/Asian British – Indian	N	381	362	1.15 (0.90 to 1.47)
	M	215	178	
Asian/Asian British – Pakistani	N	185	134	0.76 (0.52 to 1.10)
	M	89	85	
Asian or Asian British – Bangladeshi	N	65	32	0.63 (0.35 to 1.13)
	M	51	40	
Any other Asian/Asian British background	N	73	65	0.79 (0.47 to 1.36)
	M	41	46	
Black or Black British – Caribbean	N	294	115	0.92 (0.66 to 1.26)
	M	227	97	
Black or Black British – African	N	227	118	1.15 (0.81 to 1.62)
	M	172	78	
Any other Black/Black British background	N	15	13	1.30 (0.32 to 5.29)
	M	6	4	

Table 6.7   (Continued)

Ethnic/Racial background of respondent	Social class group[2]	'Ethnic/racial background' as identity attribute		Manual vs. Non-Manual: odds ratio (OR) (95% confidence interval)
	N = non-manual	'Very important' (*n*)	Not very important[1] (*n*)	
Chinese	N	45	48	0.75 (0.34 to 1.64)
	M	14	20	
Any other ethnic group	N	87	101	1.33 (0.87 to 2.03)
	M	86	75	

Notes: [1]The response categories for the 'ethnic or racial background' identity attribute were dichotomized into 'very important' and not very important (encompassing 'quite important', 'not very important', and 'not at all important'). [2]The social class variable used was 'Social Class (Old Scheme)' (known as Registrar General's Social Class Scheme) (variable 915): Response categories were dichotomized as Non-manual (I Professional etc. occupations; II Managerial and technical occupations; III(i) Skilled occupations N – non-manual) and Manual (III(ii) Skilled occupations M – manual; IV Partly skilled occupations; and V Unskilled occupations). *Statistically significant difference for the OR (manual vs. non-manual).
Source: 2007 Citizenship Survey.

ethnic/racial background as 'very important' in the three White groups and the Mixed White and Asian group (although it is possible that confounders might have influenced this outcome and, also, an occupationally based measure of social class may provide a more limited and less nuanced approach than, say, education or living standards). One could, therefore, hypothesize that there is only weak intersectionality between social class and ethnicity identity attributes amongst minority ethnic groups.

The Citizenship Survey provides just one direct measure of intersectionality: respondents who said that their national identity *and* religion were (very or quite) important to them were asked if they ever felt that there was a conflict between these (a question redolent of the literature on conflictual master statuses). Under 5% of respondents in the three White groups indicated that there was a conflict all or most of the time, but 5–9% in the White and Asian, Chinese, Other Black, Black Caribbean, Indian, Other Asian, and Black African groups, and 10.7% for the Any Other, 12.3% for Bangladeshi, 12.7% for Pakistani, 13.1% for White and Black Caribbean, 13.7% for Other Mixed, and 16.4% for

White and Black African groups did report this to be the case. The higher proportion of three of the mixed groups responding affirmatively to this question is notable.

To investigate intersectionality in our student survey, the strength of association between any 2 of the 16 identity attributes was investigated statistically using the *Jaccard Similarity Coefficient Matrix* (see Table 6.6). 'Ethnic group or cultural background' had strong similarity in pairs with other high frequency attributes, notably, 'age/life stage', 'kind of study/work', 'level of education', 'your family', and 'gender'. Perhaps not surprisingly, a number of respondents in the in-depth interviews who nominated the importance of 'ethnic group or cultural background' also chose 'your family'. Leo, who had an Iranian mother and English father, chose these two attributes as the two most important to him. In Leo's case, his attachment to 'family' was primarily about his interest and attachment to his mother's Iranian culture and extended family in Iran: '*I mean obviously I go to Iran and I'm Muslim...I have a lot of contact with the Iranian side and that's family for me. Like my mum's family is my family really. I don't know anyone on my father's side...*' Thus, for Leo, 'family' and 'ethnic group or cultural background' were effectively intertwined, but applied to only one side of his family. An asymmetry in attachment and/or contact with each side of the family was not unusual among our respondents, although Leo's case may have been more pronounced than in most cases.

Regional identity also has reasonably strong associations with age/life stage, kind of study/work, level of education, and ethnic group or cultural background. Country the family came from, religion, and nationality all have the strongest association with ethnic group or cultural background. While skin colour was an infrequently selected attribute that has weak associations with most others, its strongest association is with social class, perhaps suggesting that those from lower social classes more strongly experience the burden associated with discrimination based on skin colour (see Herring et al. 2004; Rondilla & Spickard 2007). This was evident in the case of Keith, who felt like a racialized and disadvantaged minority, due to his Blackness, and his working-class background (discussed in previous chapters). Social class was most strongly associated with level of education.

Clearly, pairs with strong similarity can be regarded as approximating intersectionality. However, we are not able to *systematically* assess whether there is intersectionality operating – in terms of 'the co-constitution of identities' (Grabham et al. 2009:2) – and not just incidental co-selection in these pairs; if there is intersectionality, we don't

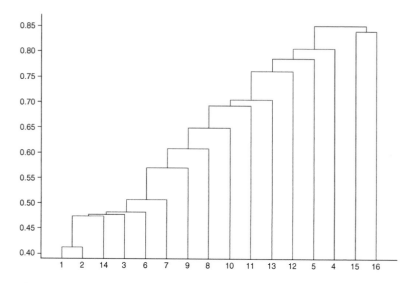

Figure 6.3   Hierarchical clustering of identity attributes
Notes: This procedure was undertaken in MATLAB: >> Y = pdist(X,'jaccard');
>> Z = linkage(Y); >> dendogram (Z). Key: See Table 5.
Source: Main student survey.

know how strong it is and what form it takes. Perhaps intersectionality is easier to assess where few respondents select the pairs as such 'exceptionality' may be more likely to be commented on.

These pairings across the 16 identity attributes do cluster together (see Fig. 6.3). A hierarchical clustering algorithm is used which groups data over a variety of scales by creating a cluster tree or dendogram. The tree is not a single set of clusters, but rather a multilevel hierarchy, where clusters at one level are joined as clusters at the next level. Clearly, most frequently selected attributes dominate the clustering, ethnic or cultural background (7) being seen to cluster with other frequently selected variables, such as gender (14), kind of study/work (2), level of education (3), and family (6). However, more powerful analytical tools are needed to identify *actual* intersectionality and the form it takes. This may, in turn, give rise to a more penetrating theorization of the concept and a better understanding of the processes contributing to intersectionality. While intersectionality 'puts complexity centre-stage', Grabham et al. (2009) state a truism: *'Intersectionality requires vectors and identities that exist apart from each other. Acting like a fastener, or zip, intersectionality presumes the gaps that it attempts to close. This raises the question of whether there are, in fact, any areas of the social that exist apart from the meeting point, or overlap, that intersectionality describes'*. The challenge becomes one of identifying analytically just how pairs of identity attributes feedback upon each other or are routed through one another.

Discussion

We began this chapter with a review of some large-scale surveys, which provide a novel source that can be exploited to measure salient and master identities across an array of identity attributes. Our focus was on a few UK surveys which provided access to a dozen or more attributes – which helps us to identify salient identities. In the case of master identities, however, all identities compete for this position so there is a process of displacement.

While some studies may question the view that race/ethnicity continues to be a person's 'master identity' amongst respondents from minority ethnic groups, most of the survey data, including our survey of mixed race young people, show it to be a 'salient identity'. The 2007 Citizenship Survey revealed 'family' and 'religion' to be 'master identities' (defined as an identity selected by 10% or more of people in that group). 'Ethnic group or cultural background' came close to attaining 'master identity' status in the Caribbean group and 'occupation' in the Chinese group.

The 1994 Fourth National Survey omitted 'gender' from its elements of self-description as *'it was assumed that nearly everybody would in fact regard their sex as something important about themselves'* (Modood et al. 1997). The omission of 'Your family' (in the FNS) raises similar concerns. 'Family' is so self-evidently important to most people so that its likelihood of selection is high. Jenkins (2006:64), for example, describes kin group as *' . . . an obvious source of enduring individual primary identity. No matter the time, place or culture, one of the most important elements in individual identification, by self and others, is kinship'*. Moreover, the ways in which 'family' is seen as important are so multifarious that it does raise the question: what does it mean for 'family' to be selected? Indeed, in the context of master identities, 'family' trumps – and so displaces – most other attributes.

Given the questionable efficacy of the category 'family', as such a broad term that can mean so many different things, we examined the second choices of respondents in the 'mixed race' survey who identified 'family' as first choice. Around 14.5% selected 'ethnic or cultural background': omitting 'family' and redistributing these second choices would still have put ethnic/cultural background in third position (after age and study/work) amongst master identities. Interestingly, 'family' has remarkably consistent *saliency* across the categories. In the case of master identities it is often claimed that a strong value is placed on family relationships amongst South Asians (see Modood et al. 1997:15), yet the proportions are lowest in these and the African and Caribbean categories simply because for some respondents 'religion' is even more important: such is the nature of 'master identities' and the displacement of close competitors.

Nevertheless, some interesting findings are revealed with respect to particular ethnicities, especially for the black groups. In the Citizenship Survey, 'ethnic or racial background' had the greatest saliency (on the measure of 'very important') in the three black groups. In the FNS, a majority in the different groups (including the Chinese) chose 'White, black, Asian, etc.' (ranging from 56–76%) as an attribute saying something important about them but the highest proportion was found in the Caribbean group. Skin colour, too, had the greatest saliency amongst Caribbeans in the FNS and amongst Black/White mixes in our student survey. These data point to the continuing importance of broader social practices ('identification as' or societal perceptions) in shaping ethnic/racial identifications, as well as the persistence of societal discourses around Blackness, including both positive and, more commonly, negative, values attached to Blackness (Alexander 1996; Hall 1997).

A number of factors may account for the relatively modest position of race/ethnic background as a master identity in Britain. With respect to *race*, the concept of ethnicity or ethnic group has been in the ascendancy in the last two or three decades (Jenkins 1997; Hickman 1998). There is also some emergent evidence that being mixed, especially in large metropolitan areas, is regarded as increasingly ordinary (Caballero et al. 2008). A new generation of British-born young people in multiethnic Britain, including many White, minority, and mixed individuals, may conceive of ethnic and racial backgrounds as much less meaningful than in the past, though this is likely to be influenced by the geographical context and the ethnic and racial composition found in specific areas.

In our survey of mixed race young adults, family, age/life-stage, and kind of study/work emerge as 'master identities'; omitting 'family' and redistributing the second choice responses takes ethnicity just above the threshold. In this sample age and kind of study/work are likely to be very prominent as the study sample is comprised of young people in higher education, at a key transitional life stage, and often living away from home and from direct parental influence for the first time (and more subject to new peer influences).

Other factors include the rise of religious identities at the expense of racial/ethnic ones, particularly the increasing prominence attached to Muslim identity. Most of the survey data shows the importance of religion in the South Asian and some Black groups. Indeed, religion was the only other master identity in the Citizenship Survey, being chosen by around a third of Pakistanis and Bangladeshis, a fifth of Black Africans and Mixed White and Black Africans, and a tenth or so of Indians and Black Caribbeans. While the survey respondents were able to prioritize religion as an identity dimension, the interview data and a growing number of qualitative studies indicate that second-generation British Muslims value both their religion and their nationality (as Britons), in addition to various other attributes, and do not regard the two as somehow inherently in tension with each other (see Song 2012; Edmunds 2009). Indeed, the Citizenship Survey data reveal that around only 12% of Pakistanis and Bangladeshis who said that their national identity *and* religion were (very or quite) important to them felt that there was a conflict all or most of the time between these dimensions.

While the survey data tell us which of the identity attributes are salient, prioritized, and co-selected, the interview data enable us to explore how specifically these dimensions shape our respondents' everyday lives and actions. Indeed, the co-dependency or intersectionality of identities based on race, national identity, and religion may have weakened the position of any one of these identities on their own. The interviews demonstrated the variable ways in which specific attributes (whether one's 'race', religion, sexuality, or mixedness) did or did not matter, and the particular ways in which specific attributes were meaningful or important. Being mixed, per se, was absolutely central to some respondents, while it was reportedly inconsequential to others – but what that reported centrality meant in their day-to-day lives could vary considerably. The salience of one's mixed status, or of one's ethnic group and cultural background, could vary both across and within the different mixed groups.

The survey found a strong measure of similarity between family origins, religion, nationality, and ethnic group/cultural background and also between the latter and other collective identities such as gender. While these dimensions remain distinct analytical categories necessary for empirical enquiry, it is clear that many are so consequential for identity that they are frequently mutually entailed in each other. For example, religious and ethnic identifications can be blurred for many second-generation Asian Muslims in particular, whose consciousness of being Muslim constitutes an assertion of 'public ethnicity' (Modood 1996; Jacobson 1997). Similarly, ethnic identifications and national identity have become implicated in each other with terms such as British and English being frequently used in self-descriptions. It is now common to talk of fragmented identities and multiple allegiances rather than discrete identity categories.

There is relatively little comparable data from other countries with which to assess wider, cross-national and cross-cultural trends. The only such source we identified is the 2006 US Social Capital Survey which shows ethnic or racial background to be the least important identity attribute in the population as a whole (see Fig. 6.4), compared with occupation, place of residence, religion, and being an American – a rather surprising finding for a country so conscious of its racial divides. However, there are interesting differences between the white and 'non-white' groups (Fig. 6.5).

What is notable in Figure 6.4 is that each identity attribute (besides 'being an American') attracts a higher proportion of 'very important' responses amongst the non-white compared with white respondents. Perhaps many identity dimensions can be hypothesized as being more important amongst the non-white population when its members are confronted by societal norms based on white standards and culture. However, the growth in interracial partnering and the mixed population in Britain, and even in the United States, is likely to deepen the already complex and multiple layerings and combinations of identification.

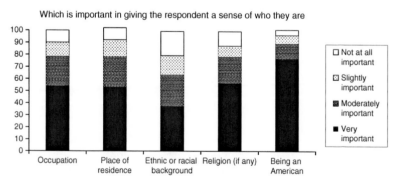

Figure 6.4 'Salient identities' in the 2006 US Social Capital Community Survey
Note: Unweighted number of national respondents: 2,741.
Source: 2006 US Social Capital Community Survey. Cambridge, MA: University of Harvard. Available at: http://www.hks.harvard.edu/saguaro/communitysurvey/.

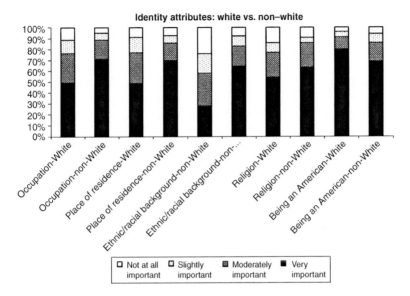

Figure 6.5 'Salient identities' in the 2006 US Social Capital Survey: white vs. 'non-white' respondents
Note: Unweighted number of national respondents: 2741.
Source: 2006 US Social Capital Community Survey. Cambridge, MA: University of Harvard. Available at: http://www.hks.harvard.edu/saguaro/communitysurvey/.

There is now growing policy interest by bodies such as Britain's Equality and Human Rights Commission in how various ascribed identities interact and contribute to multiple forms of disadvantage. The fact that one's race (or mixedness) is not necessarily most central (or even that salient, in the case of some), or only meaningful in specific ways and contexts, points to the need for nuanced policies which account for the possibility of the ways in which ethnic and racial identities combine with many other status dimensions such as gender, class, religion, age, and region – thus rethinking, rather than assuming, the automatic salience of certain identities over others.

This study has shown that, while ethnic/racial background are salient identities, their position as 'master identities' has been challenged by other identity attributes, notably, the family, religion, age/life stage, and work/study, at least for this young, relatively privileged sample of students in higher education. Given the key transitional moment at which we found our respondents (in higher education), it is also of course possible that the relative importance of specific identity attributes could shift over time. Perhaps only in the Black-Caribbean group does ethnic/racial background constitute a 'master identity'. Moreover, social class, which has occupied such a prominent position in patterning identity in the past, does not figure centrally in the choices made by our survey respondents – though, again, it is important to caution that this sample is a relatively privileged one in higher education, and not representative of mixed young people throughout Britain.

It is clear that the multidimensional nature of identification and the extent to which the different attributes are implicated in each other are likely to further challenge the position of race/ethnicity as other dimensions like religion and national identity fold into or fragment this attribute. The growth in interracial partnering and the mixed population in Britain is likely to further weaken the practice of a single racial affiliation. While continuing, albeit changing, patterns of social inequality and disadvantage will surely mediate the relative positionings of various identity attributes, 'race' as a master, or as the surveys show, salient identity, appears to be of less obvious importance to many younger minority and mixed peoples' lives in Britain today – especially for those in urban, cosmopolitan contexts.

7
Rethinking Ethnic and Racial Classifications

Introduction

One of the key research questions investigated in our study concerns the ability of official classifications to capture the racial/ethnic identifications of young 'mixed race' people, such as in the Census or other ethnic monitoring forms which are now rife in contemporary life. In Chapter 2 we explored respondents' mostly unprompted self-descriptions of themselves and in Chapter 3 how they would respond if they had to choose just one racial/ethnic group in which they felt they belonged. As we found in both these chapters, official forms of data collection on ethnicity are often reductionist, whereby respondents are asked to shoehorn their choices into pre-designated categories on a 'best fit' basis.

While many scholars of ethnicity have argued for its fluid, multidimensional and socially constructed nature (see Nagel 1994; Song 2003; Cornell & Hartmann 1998), measures of ethnicity used in large-scale surveys, such as decennial censuses, typically treat ethnicity as if it is a mutually exclusive, stable and uni-dimensional attribute (Burton et al. 2010). This disjuncture between theories of ethnicity and measures of ethnicity used to map and document forms of demographic change in the wider society is perhaps not surprising, but it makes the study of a population (which is differentiated into ethnic and racial categories – such as 'mixed race') fraught with difficulties. As aptly put by Burton et al. (2010):

> Finding a simple way of meaningfully summarizing ethnic group therefore invites problems, as there are no 'essential' components and there is no continuous concept of single groups. It is

virtually impossible to create single, mutually exclusive categories for ethnicity measures which are both conceptually coherent and which invite recognition and identification from respondents. (1335)

A critical examination of official classification systems is important for various reasons, but the growing diversity of the British population makes this issue especially pressing. What we now see emerging is an increasing number of country origin groups not captured by the census classifications. The ONS estimates that in 2010–2011 there were 56 foreign country of birth groups each comprising 25,000 or more people in the United Kingdom, some of which conceal multiple ethnicities, such as South Africa, Kenya, Zimbabwe, and Uganda.[1] Just five of these groups had matching census ethnic labels. Some foreign country of birth groups have grown dramatically in just over half a decade: for example, in 2004–2011, Poland, from 95,000 to 587,000 (518%); Lithuania, from 22,000 to 107,000 (386%); Philippines, from 62,000 to 124,000 (100%); Sri Lanka, from 71,000 to 129,000 (82%); and Somalia, from 76,000 to 112,000 (47%). Many groups (such as Somali, Filipino, and Sri Lankan, to name a few) are currently hidden and invisible in 'Other' categories attached to the 'White', 'Asian', 'Black', and 'Chinese/other ethnic groups' headings.

Such diversity is now a product of not just those ethnic groups that have a link to Britain's colonial past but what Kymlicka (1995) calls 'polyethnic minorities'. Indeed, Hollinger talks of a 'diversification of diversity' and Baumann (1996:10) of 'communities within communities, as well as cultures across communities'. Vertovec (2007:3) has coined the term 'superdiversity' to describe this complex mix, '...*a term intended to underline a level and kind of complexity surpassing anything the country has previously experienced*'. While he indicates that such superdiversity is largely conditioned by immigration dynamics, the term is used to describe the dynamic interplay of many variables: country of origin, ethnicity, languages, religion, regional and local identities, cultural values, migration channels, legal status, and the processes and practices of transnationalism.

Official bodies, such as Britain's Office for National Statistics (ONS), are fully aware of Britain's growing diversity. Census development programmes are now comprehensive exercises that encompass several years of cognitive research, small-scale tests, and large-scale, population-level trials, all of which endeavour to ensure that the ethnic categories used in Census classifications are 'locally grounded' and acceptable to the communities they describe and to capture this growing ethnic diversity. The latter has been achieved by increasing the number of ethnic categories on the form (from 9 in 1991 to 18 in 2011) and by adding additional dimensions to the cultural question set (religion in 2001 and national identity and main language in 2011).

The argument that terminology should be sensitive to, and reflect, the ways in which people and groups express their identities is articulated by the ONS, which has argued that *'categories should be used . . . that reflect people's own preferred ethnic descriptions of themselves'* (ONS 2003). The US Census Bureau, too, has emphasized that the terms used to identify population groups should be familiar and acceptable to the people described *'if the principle of self-identification is to be honored'* (Office of Management and Budget 1997; and see Nobles 2000; Roth 2010).

In fact, we know from our research that some respondents choose to identify in non-standard and sometimes unique ways. There is now ample provision in official ethnicity classifications to give an open response if none of the categories are suitable, and we know from census findings that significant proportions of respondents reject a pre-given category and opt for a write-in description: 2.8% of the 'White', 23.6% of the 'Mixed', 10.6% of the 'Asian', and 8.4% of the 'Black' pan-ethnicities in the 2001 England and Wales Census utilized the free-text provision. However, one of the drawbacks of ethnicity data collection through only unprompted open response (not embedded in a classification) is the high proportion of unusable data including non-response, sometimes exceeding 20% (Aspinall 2012). So for reasons of utility, Census data collection has eschewed this method. Nor can the classification be extended to encompass numerous country/national origin categories to cater for all needs as respondent burden (associated with selecting a category) and administrative burden (the resources needed to process the data) impose limits.

Thus, multiethnic states such as Britain do not have an easy task: Ethnicity classifications count populations as well as individuals and the categorization has to include everyone. Moreover, it has to meet a range of validity and utility criteria, including, for example, the use of categories that are robust and reliable (that is, that have validity on re-test). One key and controversial issue underlying Census and other official classification systems is that of terminology.

Our student survey included question sets on both terminology and classifications to help rethink how 'mixed race' might be captured in

ethnic/racial classifications and to inform the 2011 Census development programmes in Britain. In this chapter, we first explore how
our respondents view various forms of terminology used in relation to
mixed people. We then focus upon the ways in which mixed young
people responded to a longer and more detailed set of classifications in
describing themselves, followed by a discussion of whether the umbrella
term 'mixed race' suggests a shared set of experiences or a growing
consciousness of commonalities with other mixed people.

Preferences in terminology

Both the 2001 England and Wales Census, and the Scotland Census,
used the overarching label 'Mixed' (the 2011 England and Wales Census
used 'Mixed/Multiple ethnic groups'), a decision made late in the 2001
Census development programme without exploration of the saliency
of such generic terms amongst the mixed population. We wished to
establish preferences for such terms, to identify those which mixed
people objected to on official forms, and to explore respondents'
understandings of the various terms applied to mixed people.

A review of the policy literature to identify the range of generic terms
that have been proposed, debated, and used for the 'mixed race' population found no consensus on what constitutes appropriate terminology.
Clearly, terminology that is unfamiliar to, or poorly understood by, the
members of a group that it purports to describe will be of questionable validity and utility, especially if such terminology is used in data
collection.

'Mixed race', the most widely used term in Britain, colloquially and
in scholarship, has been contested on the grounds that it embodies the
word 'race', a discredited concept that carries much historical baggage.
This dissatisfaction has led to the search for an alternative. Advocacy
of the term 'mixed origins' dates from 1994 when the Royal Anthropo-
logical Institute of Great Britain and Ireland unanimously carried the
resolution, proposed by Michael Banton, that: '*The Council ... expresses
concern at the increased use in Britain of the expression "mixed race" since
this implies that there are pure races. The Council believes that the expression "mixed origin", though not ideal, would be preferable*' (Anon 1994; and
see Banton 1999). Similarly, the British Sociological Association (BSA)
uses arguments to claim that 'mixed race' '*... is a misleading term since it
implies that a "pure race" exists*' (BSA 2005):

> It should be recognised that the idea of race mixture or being
> 'mixed race' is informed by a racial discourse that privileges the

notion of essential races. Some social scientists aim to establish a new vocabulary other than the highly contentious notion of 'race'.

The BSA's statement also suggests that emerging identities, often described in terms of hybridity, borderlands, shifting boundaries, and multiplicity, produce new cultural forms and practices that cannot satisfactorily be defined by race and/or ethnicity. However, the BSA does not endorse 'Mixed-Cultural', pointing to the criticism that the term assumes that ' *... all cultures are equal and overlooks relations of power and domination that rank cultures differentially'*.

A strong rationale for the use of 'mixed origin' is its resonance with the popular companion term 'ethnic origin' and the use of 'origin' in the law. The Race Relations Acts of 1965, 1968, and 1976 all used the term 'race or ethnic or national origins' and this (or similar) wording has been recapitulated in subsequent statutes, including the Race Relations (Amendment) Act 2000 and Nationality, Immigration and Asylum Act 2002 ('nationality or ethnic or national origins'). It was, no doubt, adopted to be consistent with the wording of the 1965 International Convention on the Elimination of All Forms of Racial Discrimination which defined discrimination in terms of any distinction, exclusion, or preference based on 'race, colour, descent, or national or ethnic origin'. Given the extent to which this nomenclature has become embedded in UK and international statutes, the argument from the viewpoint of legal usage is a powerful one.

However, support for terms using 'origin' has gained little momentum in other areas. One difficulty is the term's face validity as it lacks reference to ethnicity and race. This term is 'implicitly ambiguous' and one *'which could describe any individual with a diverse background – i.e. English and Scottish – and not solely individuals who stem from a mixture of so-called different races'* (Ifekwunigwe 1997:128). The distinction between mixed race and multiethnicity was one that concerned the US Census Bureau in its development of terminology for the 'two or more races population' in the lead up to the 2000 Census and continues to be the subject of wide debate amongst anthropologists and sociologists (see Azoulay 2003).

In addition, there are those 'politically correct' terms that encompass the word 'heritage', such as 'dual...', 'mixed...', and 'multiple heritage'. These are relatively recent arrivals whose wider usage has been catalysed by officialdom. They have been adopted by some government departments, especially the Department for Children, Schools and

Table 7.1   Terms used on the main government websites

Term	Dept of Health	Dept for Children, Schools & Families	Home Office	Dept of Communities & Local Govt
Mixed parentage	1	9	13	6
Mixed race	1	22	28	67
Mixed origins	0	5	1	2
Dual heritage	0	29	5	6
Mixed heritage	0	49	3	16

Note: Searches undertaken on main government department websites, accessed 1 October 2008: www.dh.gov.uk/, www.dcsf.gov.uk/, www.homeoffice.gov.uk/, www.communities.gov .uk/. Terms entered as 'exact phrase'. See Aspinall (2009).

Families, as a strategy to avoid the use of the contested term 'mixed race' (Table 7.1). For example, Tikly et al. (2004:17) state that:

> ... we use the term 'mixed heritage' rather than the more commonly used term 'mixed race' to refer to those pupils and people who iden-tify themselves, or are identified, as having a distinct sense of a dual or mixed, rather than 'mono heritage' ... The decision to use 'mixed heritage' instead of 'mixed race' was adopted in order to ensure con-sistency of terminology on DfES literature. However, it was apparent in interviews that the majority of pupil and parent respondents used 'mixed race', whilst some were content to use 'half caste'. For most pupils and parents, 'mixed heritage' was not a term that they were familiar with and were less comfortable with its initial use in the interview.

The lack of acceptance of these terms amongst 'mixed race' people, and the view of some that they are externally imposed terms, weaken their legitimacy. They also suffer the same drawback as 'mixed ori-gins' in that *heritage* is non-specific with respect to the implied referent of inherited characteristics. While Ifekwunigwe (1997:128) sees some merit in 'dual heritage' as it *'pinpoints the convergence of different cul-tures and ethnicities'* and *'the fact that it is de-racialized also broadens its potential relevance'*, the term could, again, equally describe people who are mixes of different White groups. Moreover, as with 'mixed parentage', a term popularized in the 1990s as another alternative to 'mixed race', 'dual heritage' limits a person's mixed background to just two groups. The census agencies in the United Kingdom side-stepped this controversy over terminology by avoiding all these terms in favour of 'Mixed' (a usage that spawned the term 'mixedness' (Runnymede Trust 2007)).

In an attempt to throw some light on these debates about terminology, we asked respondents in both the pilot survey and the main student survey about their preferences regarding terminology. Respondents were asked which of a list of *general terms for mixed race* they preferred and in both surveys they were invited to multi-tick.

The general term of choice amongst respondents in these surveys was 'mixed race' (Table 7.2), with just over half the respondents in the student survey selecting this. Other terms that attracted much less support amongst students were 'mixed heritage' (18%), 'mixed origins' (16%), and 'mixed parentage' (13%). Indeed, terms indicating only two groups, 'mixed parentage', 'dual heritage' (12%), and 'biracial' (4%), were amongst the least popular for students, as was 'multiethnic' (7%). Interestingly, a significant number of students reported 'no preference' or 'never thought about it', and comprised a fifth of the sample (in each case). This latter finding meshes with some of the interview data from previous chapters, in which some of our respondents reported that being mixed, per se, was not of particular importance or a central basis of identification for them.

Table 7.2   Respondents' preferences for general terms for mixed race

General terms	Pilot survey ($n = 47$)	Student survey ($n = 326$)
I do not identify as mixed race	1	15
I identify as mixed race & prefer the terms ...		
Mixed parentage	10	42
Mixed race	32	176
Dual heritage	5	38
Mixed heritage	11	58
Multiracial	2	32
Biracial[1]	–	13
Multiethnic[1]	–	23
Mixed origins	4	51
Some other term	4	16
No preference	4	60
I never think about it	3	62

Note: [1]Not included in the pilot survey.
Sources: (i) Pilot survey: see Aspinall et al. (2006). http://www.pih.org.uk/images/documents/ mixedraceinbritain_report2.pdf; (ii) Main student survey: Aspinall et al. (2008).

Table 7.3 Terms respondents found offensive or would not like to see on official forms

Terms	Pilot survey	Student survey
'Half-caste'	7	60
'Biracial'	0	19
'Coloured'	0	11
'Half breed'/'half bred'	2	10
'Dual heritage'	8	9
'Multiracial'	3	7
'Multiethnic'	0	7
'Mixed parentage'	2	7
'Mixed race'	0	6
'Mixed heritage'	3	4
'Mongrel'	0	5
'Mixed origins'	5	3

Sources: 'Mixed race in Britain' pilot survey; Main student survey.

Our respondents were also asked if there were any terms (including any of those listed in Table 7.2) that they found offensive (or did not want to see on forms). If they responded 'yes' to this question, they were asked to write in the term(s). Around a third of respondents in the two surveys said that there were objectionable terms, and a dozen different terms were identified (Table 7.3).

The most frequently mentioned offensive term was 'half-caste', while others included 'biracial', 'dual heritage', 'coloured', and 'half breed/bred'. Our mixed respondents gave a range of reasons why they found these terms offensive or inappropriate. In the pilot survey, dislike of 'dual heritage' focused on its limitation to two groups, for example: *'Many of us are more than dual!'* Also, terms like 'dual heritage' and 'mixed origins' were seen as attempts to disregard race. Others regarded 'mixed origins' and 'mixed heritage' unfavourably as they '*...do not accurately represent "Mixed Race" as they are too general*' and 'sound negative'. 'Half-caste' was regarded as pejorative by several respondents, on the grounds that it suggested only partial recognition and negative historical connotations:

' "half-caste" is terrible! Makes you sound as though you're "half a person"'; 'They [including words like half and semi] suggest I am less than whole and have historical meanings & usage which demean us'; 'I am not "dual"/two of/half of even though PC social workers "adopt" this term'; 'It was formally used in a prejudiced/ignorant way'; 'sounds derogatory', and 'Because it portrays the notion that I am only half a person'.

Like 'half-caste', 'half breed', too, was regarded as 'very negative' or with *'negative connotations, linked to racist ideology & slavery'*. Any terms encompassing race were felt to be inappropriate by another respondent: *'I think of having "origins", but I have always felt that the only "race" is the human race and as a result do not believe there are "different" types of human beings.'*

In the student survey, similar objections were voiced. With respect to the term 'half-caste', respondents stated:

> *'Degrading and unnecessary'*; *'Half-caste has negative historical origins'*; *'Makes you sound incomplete'*; *'Because it dates back to the slave trade & what caste you belong to'*; *'I don't see different races as castes (as in levers of class). We are all equal'*.

In general, 'half-caste' was regarded as both derogatory and antiquated. 'Biracial' was disliked for a range of reasons: *'Has an element of sexual orientation'*; *'biracial is too categorical (i.e. just not 2 races)'*; *'These (dual heritage, biracial) do not apply to those with more than two racial backgrounds, so may be inaccurate for some people.'*

Nevertheless, some respondents reported that they did not care about, or think much about, terminology, especially in relation to official forms. For example, Valerie, who was Chinese and Indian, articulated the view that it did not really matter which terms one used to describe being mixed, despite the fact that (as discussed in Chapter 6) her mixedness was very central to her sense of self. For example, when asked about which general terms she preferred to refer to mixture, she ticked several, including 'mixed race', but then added: *'Yeah but...mixed race – nice and simple and quick and life goes on'*. Later in the survey, she also wrote: *'Life is too short to worry about definitions. I am mixed-race and currently in the process of defining my own lifestyle to have, therefore, no time for race issues. Maybe later (retirement?).'* For Valerie, more important than debates about terminology was the unique way in which she lived her life, which implied many modes and bases for association and networking.

Some respondents, like Kareem, who was Pakistani and Yemeni, reported that he did not care about how other people labelled him and did not give much thought to terminology: *'If you go to me, "oh Pakistani guy or Arab guy", I wouldn't really give a damn because it doesn't really have that big an effect on me....I couldn't care less.'* When asked if he thought he had anything in common with other mixed people, he responded, *'...Everyone's just the same, just normal. Just because of your race, it doesn't make you more compatible with a certain group. I'm just like normal.'*

Finally, respondents in the pilot and student surveys were asked who they thought terms like 'mixed race' and 'mixed parentage' should refer to (with the option to multi-tick across four options).

The largest number of counts in both surveys was recorded for *'people who are mixes of white and any minority racial/ethnic group'* (Table 7.4). However, significant numbers also felt that the terms should refer to *'people who are mixes of minority racial/ethnic groups'* and *'people of disparate ethnic origins'* (one respondent adding: *'I think that the categories should not be entirely based on racialisation but should reflect white ethnicities & cultures'*). There was least support for limiting the term to *'people who are mixes of white and black groups only'*, although this description is probably the dominant societal understanding of the term 'mixed race' in Britain.

These findings may suggest a contrast between how 'mixed race' is conceptualized in Britain and in the United States – though the term 'multiracial' is more commonly used in the United States. In the Current Population Survey Supplement's exploration of 'preferred racial

Table 7.4 The group terms should refer to

Group terms should refer to	Pilot study	Main study
'People who are mixes of white and black groups only'		
Yes	12	80
[†]*'Absolutely not exclusively'*	1	
'People who are mixes of white & any minority racial/ethnic group'		
Yes	24	211
'People who are mixes of minority racial/ethnic groups excluding white (for example, 'Black and Asian')		
Yes	16	128
[†]*'Racial – what do you mean'*	1	
'People of disparate ethnic origins (e.g. "Welsh & Polish")'		
Yes	14	127
[†]*'People of any racial mix'*	1	
[†]Other annotated responses (in substitution of above):	4	
'Any body who feels it reflects who they are'; 'Mixes of ethnic groups whose physical make-up varies significantly'; 'None of above – people who are mixes of any group'; 'People of any mix'.		

Sources: 'Mixed Race in Britain' pilot survey ([†]annotated on the questionnaire); Main student survey.

terms', 28% selected 'multiracial' and 16% 'mixed race'. While 'mixed race' is almost invariably used to indicate colour-based racial identities (for example where one parent is 'White' and one 'Black') in the United States, in Britain a more nuanced usage has emerged in which some see the term as also encompassing mixed minority and even multiethnic (as opposed to multiracial) identities (see Parker & Song 2001). The different processes of ethnogenesis (not to mention very different histories) go some way to explaining the differences between the two countries. Also, these findings lend support to the official use in Britain of 'Mixed', which challenges the automatic racial basis of mixed status, and opens the door to a wider interpretation of 'mixedness'. We now turn to an examination of how our mixed race young people responded to an extended list of classifications to describe themselves.

Classifications

The 2001 (and 2011) Census posed the question: '*What is your ethnic group?*' While Scotland offered a single 'Any Mixed background' write-in option on its 2001 Census, England and Wales offered an overarching 'Mixed' category in the Census ethnicity question, with a set of four sub-categories (three pre-designated and one open response). This English and Welsh schema has been subsequently widely adopted across government and statutory bodies for ethnicity data collection. No other official categorization has been developed, besides some attempts to add additional 'mixed' codes in *extended* classifications.

The write-in options in the 2001 and 2011 Census may have gone some way to addressing the criticism levelled at census ethnicity classifications that '*the very process of compelling people to assign themselves to one of a small number of racial or ethnic "boxes" is, at best, essentialist and, at worst, racist*' (Bonnett & Carrington 2000:488). Yet we do not know how satisfactory and valid the pre-designated categories were for those who *did* assign their ethnicity by using them – though the interview data in the preceding chapters has shown that the terms that mixed individuals choose require interpretation and do not necessarily tell us very much about what respondents mean by such choices. In our discussion below, we first examine responses from respondents in our initial pilot survey concerning their views of the 'Mixed' sub-categories used in the 2001 England and Wales Census. Second, we discuss findings of an extended version of the 2001 Census 'mixed' categorization used in our main student survey.

The 2001 and 2011 Census categorizations

In the 2001 England and Wales Census, respondents were asked, *'What is your ethnic group?'*, and were invited to tick the appropriate box amongst 16 categories listed, including four 'Mixed' options:

Mixed

- White and Black Caribbean
- White and Black African
- White and Asian
- Any other Mixed background, *please write in* _____

In addition to concerns about the face validity of the 'Mixed' heading (and subcategories), the conceptual base underlying the 'Mixed' section heading was unclear. While the question was labelled *ethnic group* and the tick boxes *cultural background*, the options were clearly '... *countries or regions of family origin*' (Finney & Simpson 2009). Moreover, the pre-designated 'mixed' categories align more strongly with conventionally defined 'mixed race' than 'cultural background': they all include 'White' as the first named of the two groups and the 'White and Asian' option uses the pan-ethnic or racial 'Asian' label rather than the cultural background designations.

Further, the 2001 Census findings indicate that some who ticked the 'White and Asian' category interpreted 'Asian' as continental Asian, as their countries of birth were in SE Asia and West Asia rather than South Asia (Indian subcontinent) as the Office of National Statistics had intended. The 'Any other Mixed background' open response option was poorly answered: 59% of records contained no information about ethnic background in the write-in section. Finally, there was evidence of 'mixedness' *within* each of the pan-ethnicities. For example, in the 'Black or Black British' section (which was one of 5 possible headings in the 2001 Census ethnicity question), 84% of those who selected the 'Other Black' group gave a description; 13% were coded to a 'Black Mixed' group, indicating mixed ethnicity where both or all ethnicities described are from different black groups. Thus, the census 'mixed' categorization was unlikely to accurately capture those of minority mixed identities, many of whom would be concealed in the 'Other' write-in categories in the Asian/Asian British, Black/Black British, and Chinese/other ethnic group sections.

The heading 'Mixed' in the 2001 England and Wales Census was changed to 'Mixed/Multiple ethnic groups' in the 2011 England and Wales Census (Fig. 7.1). This change appears to signal the recognition

---

What is your ethnic group?

→ Choose **one** section from A to E, then tick **one** box to best describe your ethnic group or background

A White

☐ English/Welsh/Scottish/Northern Irish/British
☐ Irish
☐ Gypsy or Irish Traveller
☐ Any other White background, write in:

_____

B Mixed/multiple ethnic groups

☐ White and Black Caribbean
☐ White and Black African
☐ White and Asian
☐ Any other Mixed/multiple ethnic background, write in:

_____

C Asian/Asian British

☐ Indian
☐ Pakistani
☐ Bangladeshi
☐ Chinese
☐ Any other Asian background, write in:

_____

D Black/African/Caribbean/Black British

☐ African
☐ Caribbean
☐ Any other Black/African/Caribbean background, write in:

_____

E Other ethnic group

☐ Arab
☐ Any other ethnic group, write in:

_____

Figure 7.1   England and Wales 2011 Census: ethnic group question

of people with more than dual heritages. Some notable additions and changes were also made to the 2011 ethnicity question, which was expanded from 16 tick boxes to 18, to include (for the first time) 'Gypsy or Irish Traveller' under the 'White' heading and 'Arab' under the heading 'Other ethnic group', reflecting the lobbying efforts of British Arab organizations. While 'Chinese' was previously listed under the heading 'Chinese or Other ethnic group' in the 2001 Census, in 2011, it was listed under the 'Asian/Asian British' category, along with South Asian ethnic groups such as Indian, Pakistani, and Bangladeshi. Thus, in the

2011 Census respondents may interpret the 'White and Asian' option to also include those with Chinese origins, disrupting comparability with the 2001 data.

Additional evidence suggests that some mixed respondents object to an overly narrow understanding of who is mixed, and an overly limited set of Census categories. For example, there is no 'mixed minority' option in the 2001 or 2011 England and Wales Censuses (Aspinall 2009), and this was commented upon. In the pilot (but not main) study, a general population 'mixed' sample was asked if there was anything they particularly liked or disliked about the census categorization. Of those who responded to this question, just over half (55%) referred to aspects of the Census categorization which they disliked. Some responses concerned the fact that the three pre-designated categories were all mixes that included 'White':

> *Because it insinuates that you are white & another race'; 'It doesn't cater for nearly all the mixed race population – focuses ultimately white and minority mixes plus excludes dual minority'; 'What about mixed not including white'; and 'They all include White, whereas there are no other given categories for people who are mixed but not part white.*

Other pilot respondents felt the choice was too limited or lumped together people as 'other':

> *'It's too restrictive and doesn't include other mixes'; 'The question singles out Caribbeans, Africans and Asians. What if you are mixed French or any other race for that matter although you can write in'; 'There are more mixes than listed above! Some people have more than two'; and 'I dislike being described as "other"'; 'Not dislike but wonder if the white category could be more detailed e.g. Polish-Indian?'*

There were also a few comments about the conceptual base of the question, and objections to the way in which 'White' was presented as a self-evident, homogeneous category which did not seem to require specification:

> *'If the question were to be asked, I'm not sure what is being asked. What colour skin are you, and what black-ness are you or where do you come from/origins, in which case the word "black" is irrelevant. The fact that we categorize colours (skin tones) makes us feel, I believe, that we must be more segregated and that we truly belong to a category, which I disagree with';*

*'Why is "white" a pure term that needs no other definition when black
needs to be explained'; and 'I really dislike the use of the term "White" in
the census identity classification because it presumes that people who are
white are similar enough not to need to be identified whereas the non-whites
all have to be categorised'.*

These criticisms chime with some of the findings discussed in Chapter 2
and underline the view held by some that Census (and other official)
classifications are often limited, arbitrary, and opaque. Yet as many people in the pilot survey indicated positive things about the census 'mixed'
categorization as those who named things which they disliked. Most of
these respondents indicated that it was easy to complete or simple (*'easy
to fill in forms'*, *'simple – good for statistics'*, *'easy to complete [tick box]'*,
etc.). A significant number liked the fact that it catered for their specific
mix (*'I like it because my situation is described so there is a box for me'*;
'There's options to be specific'; *'It allows me to accurately describe my ethnic
origin'*; and *'Makes you feel like you belong, i.e., not just other…'*). Other
respondents specifically mentioned the open response option amongst
the four categories (*'the fact that there was room for me to write in'*; *'It allows
scope for weird & wonderful combinations in the free text bit'*). Respondents also acknowledged the more general benefit of the categorization
(*'It made Mixed race a recognised grouping in the UK'*; *'it moves "mixed" from
a general term that may not fully identify your racial identity'*).

Extended 'mixed' categorization

A more detailed classification of 'mixture' (than in the Census ethnicity question) was developed in the pilot phase through an evidence
synthesis (including analysis of findings of the pilot survey) to provide
more finely granulated categorization for use in the main student survey. In this extended classification respondents could choose from 12
options, 5 of which had write-in options. Respondents were asked (see
Table 7.5): *'Which of the following groups do you feel best describes you?
[Please tick one box only]'*

In Table 7.5, the 11 'mixed' groups map back to the Census categorization. Because Black and White individuals were dominant in our sample
(157 of 326), it is not surprising that relatively large numbers chose
'Black Caribbean and White' and 'Black African and White'. We found
that 'Chinese and White', 'Other E/SE Asian and White', 'Arab and
White', and mixed minority categories emerged as important – even
though none of these subcategories are used under the 'Mixed' heading
in either the 2001 or 2011 Censuses. 'Any other mix' remained large,

Table 7.5   Responses to 2001 extended classification for the 'mixed' group[6]

Classification	Count
1. Black Caribbean and White	96
2. Black African and White	36
3. Other Black (*please write in*[1]:..............................) and White	5
4. Indian and White	25
5. Pakistani and White	7
6. Bangladeshi and White	1
7. Chinese and White	14
8. Other East or SE Asian (*please write in*[2]:..................) and White	21
9. Arab (or Middle Eastern or North African) and White	24
10. A mix of two groups other than White (e.g. 'Black and Chinese'): *please write in*[3]:...	13
11. Any other mix: *please write in*[4]:.............................	75
12. A single racial/ethnic group only: *please write in*[5]	9

Notes: [1] Examples of free-text responses: 'Native South American Indian'; 'Asian'. [2] 'Japanese'; 'Filipino'; 'Indonesian'; 'Malaysian'; 'Vietnamese'. [3] 'South American & Mauritian'; 'Black & Venezuelan'; 'Black & SE Asian'. [4] 'Black, White, and Asian'; 'Sri Lankan & White'; 'Half Indian, Quarter Russian, quarter Dutch'; 'Black Caribbean, Mauritian and European White-English and Spanish'; 'Asian/African'. [5] This category was included for those with a mixed heritage – as captured in other questions on respondents' racial/ethnic identity – who wished to identify with a single group, for example 'Black'. [6] Mapping to 2001 Census categories: White & Black Caribbean (1); White and Black African (2); White & Asian (4, 5, 6); Any other Mixed background (3, 7, 8, 9, 10, 11).
Source: Main student survey (*n* = 326).

in part catering for those whose ancestries comprised more than two groups: 20% of the main study sample named more than two groups in free text. These research findings show that Census categorization for 'mixed' considerably simplifies the complexity of those who have mixed heritage.

Thus, a more refined classification of the 'Mixed' group is feasible in those circumstances where it is needed but would clearly need further testing in general population samples before it can be recommended for wider adoption. Clearly, the strength of this approach lies in the fact that, in this relatively young, educated structured sample, the current census classification misses the complexity and diversity of those with mixed heritage. Moreover, further testing may reveal that intra-group heterogeneity correlates with outcomes important in policy-making, such as health and educational attainment. As the suggested extended classification maps back to the census 'mixed' categories, analyses examining changes in these populations over time should not be affected.

Multi-ticking and other options

A key objective of the study was to investigate whether there were better ways to capture the 'mixed' population than the categorization used in the 2001 England and Wales Census and to inform the census agencies of these findings as part of their 2011 Census Development Programmes. Three census ethnic group questions were evaluated: that asked in 2001 in England and Wales; a version of this in which the four 'mixed' categories were replaced by a 'mixed' open response option; and a 'mixed' option to multi-tick across the other 12 categories (multi-ticking was adopted in the 2000 US Census race question and in the 2001 Canadian Census on population groups) (Aspinall 2003). Respondents were asked which of the three variants was easiest and most difficult to complete and which best enabled them to describe their racial/ethnic identity, by actually completing the three questions. Respondents in the main student survey reported that they found the 2001 Census question easiest to complete and the multi-ticking option most difficult and that the open response question best enabled respondents to describe their ethnic or racial identity (followed by the census question).

In addition, two quality measures were derived. Respondents' *understanding* of the question (using a rule-based method incorporating non-response, misreporting, etc.) was best for the census question, followed by open response. However, the *information content* yielded by the question (again, using a rule-based method that measured the accuracy, precision, and completeness with which the multiple groups were described) was highest for open response, followed by the census question. These findings – which indicate that multi-ticking is not currently a recommended option for the UK – were submitted to ONS and the General Register Office[2] (Scotland). After reviewing this evidence and further evaluation, both census agencies decided not to utilize this approach to capture the 'mixed' group in the 2011 Census (ONS 2008; Scottish Government and General Register Office for Scotland 2008).

Respondents were also asked to complete a further question promoted by Berthoud (1998) – asking for their 'family's ethnic origins' (mother's family and father's family) – though this was not further evaluated as ONS had ruled out the use of a status measure rather than a self-identity question in the 2001 Census Development Programme. Although 'White' was broken down and 'Mixed' added to Berthoud's list of ethnic origins, this question yielded the highest information content of all the classification options. However, it proved complex to code given the range of permutations of selected categories that included free text, again reducing its attractiveness as a census question.

Is there a growing sense of a 'mixed' group in Britain?

The Census (and now many other official bodies) employs the overarching term 'mixed' in its ethnicity question, thus suggesting that there is a 'mixed' demographic segment or sub group in the population who may share something in common – but if so, what, exactly, is shared? This question has not yet been investigated in the United Kingdom. As Jenkins (1996) reminds us, ' . . . *group membership is a relationship between members . . . they can recognise each other as members. Membership of a category is not a relationship between members*' (and see Brubaker 2004). The ONS is careful to refer to the 2001 Census tick box options as 'categories' rather than groups, these 'mixed' options being decided by the categoriser. Yet in the 1991 Census 230,000 persons eschewed the predesignated options and wrote in a 'mixed' description. This was the product of collective internal definition even if it did not come about through mixed race persons 'co-actively' seeking this outcome or the self-conscious mobilization of such identities though group processes. It does suggest the mutual acceptance of a need for official recognition and perhaps a first step towards group identification. That process has no doubt been catalysed by the 'mixed' categorization in the 2001 and 2011 Censuses.

Unlike the United States, where there is now a significant 'multiracial movement', much of which emerged from university campuses, in which disparate types of mixed people came together to lobby for recognition as 'multiracial', such sentiments and mobilizations are yet nascent in the United Kingdom (Song 2012). When our interview respondents were queried about whether they felt they belonged to a 'mixed race' group, or whether they believed they shared any commonalities with other mixed people more generally, relatively few respondents responded affirmatively to these questions. It will be recalled, too, that only 16% of respondents in the main student survey had selected the option '*it is the group I feel I belong to*' when asked to choose reasons for the particular free-text description they had given.

Overall, when asked if they felt anything in common with other mixed people in Britain, the majority of our interview respondents reported that they did not, or that being mixed would not be a sufficient (or necessarily primary) basis of identification with others. For instance, Paul (Chinese and Irish) talked about the fact that being mixed was absolutely central to how he saw himself, but when he was asked about whether he felt a sense of commonality with other mixed people, he replied:

> *No. The problem is that there's no clear dividing line. I think generally speaking I'd feel commonality with ... it depends on a lot of factors. I might feel a closer sense of identity with a British born Chinese person, than a half British, half Chinese person who was born in Malaysia. It really depends on the person's character and their identity too.*

Interestingly, Paul notes that he would feel more sense of commonality with someone who was Chinese and British, given their shared upbringing in Britain, than with a mixed person who did not share a British sensibility. So while in other parts of the interview, he talked about how being Eurasian, and mixed, was central to his sense of self, he eschewed any automatic or easy sense of commonality with others who also happened to be mixed. Furthermore, Paul reported that he felt more kinship with other Eurasian mixed people, such as himself, than, for example, with a Black and White mixed person, since he believed that the wider society's treatment of him and other Eurasian individuals would be relatively similar. He also believed that he would have experienced a more similar cultural upbringing with someone who had a Chinese (or other East Asian) parent than with a mixed person who did not have East Asian ancestry. So he did not think that a broad 'mixed' category – irrespective of specific ethnic and racial ancestries – resonated for him, or for other mixed people.

Like Paul, Nada (Arab and White) claimed that she would not necessarily feel a sense of commonality with another mixed person: '*I once heard a program on Radio 4 of people complaining that they felt really alienated by being a mixture of races, that they feel really alone and they have no identity ... But I never felt that. I just thought, 'God, do you have to base your identity on your race, you have choices you make in life ....'* But later, she acknowledged that: '*If you've had racial discrimination, say, then that feels like a real barrier imposed by someone else, whereas if you don't feel actually discriminated against by other people, then a lot more is up to you.*' In Nada's case, her lack of commonality with other mixed people corresponded with the fact that she had not been subject to forms of racism and the fact that her racial identity was relatively unimportant to her – though she did profess to a strong interest in her father's Lebanese background and culture. Rather than an attachment to and identification with a generic notion of mixedness, Nada reported that she was more likely to feel some sense of commonality with individuals who shared her Lebanese ancestry.

Like Nada, above, Stephanie (White and Black African) objected to the idea that mixed people in general would share something in common:

> *I don't think I would consider joining a group because I've not felt marginalised. Also it would be strange. I would more likely join a group to do with art because that's had more of an effect on me ....I don't know if I'd join a group of mixed race people, what we'd sit around talking about, because I'm not angry about anything or feel that's an overriding factor in my life ... unless I had lots of friends who were part of that group and do lots of nice things.*

Stephanie's emphasis upon her particular interests, such as art, as a basis for identification and social networking, meshes with our findings in Chapter 6 – that one's ethnic/racial background (or one's mixedness) was not necessarily an important attribute in describing themselves. Stephanie went on to explain:

> *...I think it depends on the person. I don't define myself by my race. I think it depends what their interests are, what their upbringing was like, if their upbringing affected them in the same way as mine, then maybe we'd have something in common, but other than that it depends on who they are as a person.*

It is very clear from Stephanie's interview that being mixed, per se, would not be a sufficient basis for feeling a sense of kinship with that person. However, there were some respondents who saw themselves as mixed race and reported that they felt a sense of kinship with other mixed people, more generally. For instance, Lori, who was Filipino and British, spoke of how being mixed was quite central to who she was:

> Int: *Well you call yourself mixed race but would you say that your sense of being mixed race is a really central part of your identity or not?*
> Lori: *It probably makes quite a large part of my identity.*

Int: *Yeah. In what way do you think?*

Lori: *I think it sort of broadens my cultural awareness of different people. I'm quite interested in sort of racial issues because I'm mixed.*

Int: *Do you feel in any way that you... Do you feel any sense of kind of commonality or connection to other mixed race people?*

Lori: *I think I do actually because like I'm quite close to 'R' (who is mixed) and one of my friends who is half Algerian. She is like my best friend and we talk about sort of... We have talked about being mixed race a lot. And like... Yeah I think it makes us easier to understand sort of like what... and with 'R' as well, both her parents are divorced as well and so we kind of have a similar like... And 'R' lives with her mum who is her white parent as well so we've sort of been raised in a similar way.*

A number of Lori's friends were also mixed, and while they were not Filipino and British, she and her friends related to each other as people who had a number of similar experiences in common – for instance, the ways in which other people saw them as racially ambiguous and the fact that they typically grew up relating to two quite distinct family cultures and sets of relatives. Lori also articulated the view that mixed people tended to be more culturally aware and cosmopolitan.

While a general sense of commonality with other mixed people was relatively rare among our interviewees, it was not uncommon for respondents to show curiosity about other people of the same 'mix' in the study. For instance, Samira, who was Portuguese and Pakistani, asked if there was anyone else like her in the study (there was), and asked if she could be put in touch with the other respondent. However, she did not demonstrate a more general curiosity about other mixed people. In London, where she had grown up, she reported that being mixed, per se, was not that unusual and would therefore not be an automatic basis for a shared sense of identification.

Nevertheless, many of these interview respondents shared a similar attitude towards the idea of being mixed (or the idea of people mixing more generally): that mixing was a good thing, and that to be mixed entailed the transgressing of unwarranted barriers. In this sense, many respondents saw themselves as part of a demographic vanguard, though they could have had very different experiences of being mixed. Furthermore, a number of respondents observed that, *in conjunction with* other important attributes, such as shared interests, they could relate well to other mixed individuals, especially if they were of the same or similar 'mix'.

The future of ethnic and racial classification

Will the growth and diversification of the mixed population threaten to undermine and/or destabilize the whole issue of ethnic and racial classification? How can multiethnic states, such as Britain, cope with growing complexity and diversity? Ethnic and racial classifications have to be responsive to the needs of their populations, including shifts in preferred terminology arising from new patterns of population mixing, changes in fashion, and political influences (Song 2012).

Categorizers must also be vigilant against the perceived reification of categories through repeated usage and the belief that ethnic identity has an underlying and unchanging 'essence' (Song 2003). A now familiar criticism of ethnic and racial classification systems and anti-discrimination legislation which employs such classifications is that they paradoxically reinforce notions of common sense understandings of ethnic and racial difference (Rattansi 2007). Yet if policy makers and researchers are to identify and monitor forms of ethnic and racial discrimination at a population level or in organizational settings, we need a set of terms with which we categorize specific 'classes' of people – just as we may name 'women' or 'lesbian', 'bisexual' and 'gay' people to identify the particular forms of discrimination they may experience.

How well the 2001 and, more recently, the 2011 Census 'mixed' categories capture the ethnic diversity of Britain now (and in the future) is debatable, depending on both the changing overall size of the mixed group and its composition. The major challenge is that migrants to Britain are coming from an ever-widening range of countries and entering into interracial/ethnic unions, bringing into question the utility of the current options. As noted earlier, while there is a real likelihood of under-reporting, by either parents (of mixed children) or of mixed individuals who may not have designated themselves as mixed, the Census is seeking to capture *a measure of self-ascribed identity rather than an operational definition of ethnicity (based upon actual mixed ancestry)*. If, as some of our evidence suggests, mixed individuals do not feel that the Census offers categories which match their own sense of selves, their choices may be arbitrary. However, datasets like the Annual School Census do currently indicate an acceptable degree of stability in the 'mixed' categorization over the short term and the 2011 Census findings will provide evidence of change over the longer term.

With respect to overall size, the 2011 England and Wales Census indicated a 'Mixed' population of 1,224,400, an 85.2% increase on the 2001 Census figure of 661,034. In addition there have been two sets of population projections by teams at the Universities of Leeds and Oxford undertaken in the last half dozen years. According to Rees' projections, the United Kingdom's 'mixed' group will grow from 676,000 in 2001 (1.1% share) to 1,306,000 by 2020 (2.0% share), representing a growth rate of 93% for 2001–2020 (Rees 2008). This projection already looks questionable given the 2011 Census findings. A more recent projection indicates a 'mixed' group of 1.6 million by 2031.[3] Coleman and Scherbov (2005) predict that the 'mixed' population will grow at 156% over the 20 years 2001–2020; in the longer term, they see the proportion of the population that has mixed origins rising rapidly from 1% in 2001 to 8% in 2050, becoming the most numerous minority group well before 2100. These projections for the mixed group are much more conservative than frequent pronouncements by the press that the mixed group will be the largest minority ethnic group by 2020. According to Rees (2008), the mixed group will still be smaller than the Asian (3,479,000) and Black (1,593,000) groups. Clearly, debates about the projected growth and size of the mixed population also depend greatly upon how, exactly, we count who is and is not mixed in the future (Song 2009). And as illustrated by some of the interview excerpts above, in what sense can we say that mixed people comprise a group, especially given the very many different types of mixed people in British society?

The efficacy of current (2011 Census) categorization is likely to be most strongly challenged by changes in the diversity of the UK population arising from international migration inflows, notably from countries which were not part of Britain's colonial project. This impact has been particularly prominent since the mid-90s. International migration inflows show a progressive rise from around 300,000 in 1995 to almost 600,000 in 2004. Migrants from New Commonwealth countries rose from around 60,000 in 1995 to 150,000 in 2004; however, inflows from other foreign countries (besides the Old Commonwealth) showed a much more marked upward trend, reaching a peak of around 200,000 in 2002 and driven mainly by waves of asylum seekers from failing and failed states. Thereafter, inflows have receded following the implementation of tighter controls. Such inflows *directly* contribute in only a limited way to the growth in the mixed population: Rather, this population will mainly grow through mixed unions – cohabitations and marriages – giving rise to mixed offspring. As international migration drives greater diversity in the population, this in turn will drive diversity in inter-ethnic union formation.

New migrants, especially those from non-Commonwealth countries, may find that the current 'mixed' categories have only limited meaning for them, given that the terminology (such as 'Black African' and 'Black Caribbean') strongly reflects Britain's colonial past. But as these groups increase in numbers and size, the lack of an obvious location in official classification may become a policy issue and possibly a political one if such groups gain a voice. Further, 'superdiversity' may drive up the proportion of the mixed population utilizing the *'Any other Mixed/multiple ethnic background'* write-in category as the option that would seem to best cater for those who are the offspring of parents of diverse ethnic origins. This trend is already apparent in many London boroughs that have been amongst the main recipients of international migrants, with the 'Any other mixed' category exceeding 50% of the 'mixed' group in annual School Census data in a number of these areas.

In spite of the current evidence indicating difficulties with multi-ticking, this format may prove in the longer term to be the best solution, especially given the finding that around a fifth of young people name three or more groups in unprompted response (see Chapter 2). Indeed, an ONS 2011 Census stakeholders' consultation argued:

> *Multiple ticking would give a much better breakdown of the 'Mixed' group than the current pre-designated categories. The 2001 Census (by its use of dual options and a duplex free text box under 'Mixed') assumed mixed parentage; some respondents may wish to identify more than two groups, for example, those who have Mixed parentage parent(s). In addition, the 'Other Mixed background' category is very large (the second largest in many administrative datasets) and conceals a significant number who identified in free text as mixed: 'Black and White'. Multiple ticking is an elegant solution to this problem of concealed diversity and has been handled satisfactorily in the USA with respect to reporting.*

The alternative of adding more 'mixed' categories to the Census ethnicity question (or an ethnicity question on another official survey) – such as 'White and Chinese' or a 'minority mixed' open response option – would be problematic, as the ethnicity question is already the longest question in the Census (and respondents may balk at an even longer list of options beyond the current 18 choices provided in the 2011 England and Wales Census ethnicity question).

Who should be considered 'mixed race' anyway? During the upcoming decade the current census 'mixed' categories may come to be seen as out of tune with the emerging complexity of mixedness which is likely to be increasingly characterized by diverse mixes at the national origin level that do not easily map into the four categories defined largely at the pan-ethnicity level. Indeed, the concept of multiethnicity may begin to look more appealing. Yet the state must decide who is 'mixed' and who isn't as this collectivity (however defined) is rapidly growing in size and mixedness is now an important component of the ethnic/racial diversity of Britain (and see Bratter 2007; Roth 2010 for discussions of the multiracial classification in the US).

There is a need for fresh thinking on these matters. With respect to conceptual base, census and other official categorization are likely to continue to favour a measure of self-ascribed identity. However, whether this is achieved in the case of the 'mixed' group through specifying exact combinations of interest (as in the 2011 Census) or through multi-ticking or, even, advocacy of an entirely open response option requires much more extensive exploration and testing than has hitherto taken place. The increasing prevalence and complexity of mixedness would appear to favour methods that capture multiplicity, that is, multi-ticking.[4]

Additionally, the pattern of migration dynamics over the last decade or so has strengthened the case for an additional question on ethnic origin/ancestry. US and Canadian Census data show that such questions capture a substantially higher percentage of 'multiple groups' reporting than mixing at the level of 'race' or 'population group' because such questions propel respondents to report at the national origin or specific socio-cultural group level. They are also straightforward, leaving it up to respondents to decide how far back they might wish to go with respect to their forebears (the evidence in Chapter 2 pointed to declining saliency the further back one goes). Moreover, such questions avoid the 'operational' approach of defining a person by asking about specific ancestors (as in Berthoud's (1998) proposed question on the respondent's mother's and father's family ethnic origins). The discourse on hybridity in this country is likely to remain focused on how individuals identify themselves and not on how they are defined by their forebears, an approach redolent of the fractionation processes and one drop rule of the first half of the last century.

8
Conclusion: What Is the Future of 'Mixed Race' Britain?

Key findings

Is the growth of mixed race people evidence of blurring racial boundaries and major structural change? The findings of this book suggest that the answer to this is yes, but with some major qualifications. As we have discussed throughout this book, there is evidence of race losing its fixity, especially in urban cosmopolitan areas where being mixed appears to be regarded as more ordinary than in the past. However, we must not overlook the ways in which 'race' continues to be real as a structuring force, both ideologically and materially (Bonilla-Silva 2003). Furthermore, what it means to be mixed remains highly variable, depending on multiple factors, including the specific ethnic and racial ancestries, socioeconomic background, as well as the locality of mixed individuals. So while significant changes are afoot, there is little doubt that 'old' polarities and cleavages also persist.

As we have shown in this book, young mixed people could exhibit quite varied identifications, experiences, and outlooks, especially in relation to multiple (not just dual) racial and ethnic identifications. Our respondents could vary considerably in terms of (a) the relative centrality of race or mixedness to their sense of selves and their everyday lives; (b) their interest and attachment to a minority and/or White heritage; (c) their sense of belonging and experiences of racism and exclusion, in relation to both White and co-ethnic people; (d) their phenotype and the degree to which others did or did not validate their asserted identities. Furthermore, our mixed young people's sense of selves and their expressed identifications could be changeable, both across time and disparate contexts, especially in terms of their expressed identities.

Our study has, in some respects, reinforced findings about different types of mixed people in the United States. On the one hand, we found that, as in the United States, Black/White people were more likely to be consistently racially assigned to their minority status (Black) than were other types of mixed people, such as South Asian/White and East or SE Asian/White individuals. In this respect, part Black people can be said to possess limited (albeit some) ethnic options. However, our part-South Asian and part-East/SE Asian respondents did not possess as much latitude in their ethnic options as is often suggested in US studies. Depending upon their physical appearance (which could be quite variable), they could be racialized as foreigners, or racially ambiguous, so that their claims to Britishness could be regularly challenged. Based on this study, it seems that the public's racial imaginary is still pretty limited, if we consider the ways in which Black/White people continue to be seen, or people's narrow understandings of what someone of a particular ancestry is supposed to look like.

And despite a growing intellectual awareness of the socially and historically constructed basis of 'race' and racial differences, ordinary members of 'the public' still subscribe to notions of clear racial boundaries and memberships, so that they may regard racially ambiguous individuals as inherently 'other'. In fact, not all of our respondents refuted the belief that distinct races actually exist. While some respondents explicitly asserted a mixed identity (or reportedly transcended racial thinking) as a means of conveying their rejection of exclusive, biological understandings of 'race', others did not necessarily reject the underlying premise of racial difference (that people can be divided into groups called 'races'), even if they believed that they should have *the right* to claim membership in more than one 'race', or that 'mixing' among monoracial people was a progressive trend.

Despite the fact that it was not uncommon for respondents to report a mismatch between how they saw themselves with how others saw them in racial terms, one rather surprising result was the substantial number of interview respondents (across all the mixed groups) who claimed to be indifferent to how others saw them. Our findings support a conclusion that there is a plurality of ways in which racial mismatch can be experienced, as opposed to the prevailing view that any disjuncture between expressed and observed identifications is somehow problematic – indeed, there were disparate bases upon which interviewees could feel misrecognized. There was no uniform desire among mixed people for identity validation, and this may also apply for other monoracial minorities more generally. Importantly, claims to indifference were not devoid of a recognition of continuing forms of racial prejudice and disadvantage, especially in certain institutional contexts; so these claims should not be interpreted as naïve denials of the existence of 'color-blind' racism. Rather, these respondents tended to articulate the view that they refused to take racial thinking and ideologies seriously and/or that they were able to deflect such thinking and prejudice in their everyday lives.

Nevertheless, there is little doubt, confirming prior studies in the United States, that phenotype, and how one is seen by others (and how one thinks one is seen by others), is central to the many interactions mixed individuals encounter throughout their lives – experiences which importantly shape (though not necessarily determine) their identities and identifications throughout their lives. As shown in our study of mixed young people in higher education, identity formation is subject to change over the life course, especially at key transitional moments in their lives (Doyle & Kao 2007), such as leaving home and entrance into a disparate social setting, where they may perceive different identity options around people who have not previously known them.

Experiences of racism were primarily reported in relation to our respondents' formative years at school, though for some respondents, concerns about racial prejudice were still ongoing. And while most respondents felt much less comfortable in less cosmopolitan towns and villages throughout the country (outside of 'their comfort zone'), reports of racism in cities were not unheard of. Nevertheless, our respondents, who were in higher or further education, and thus relatively privileged, reported relatively little prejudice or discrimination in their experiences in such education, though part-Black respondents reported more negative racialized experiences than other types of respondents.

This study also found that many respondents pointed to the importance of national and regional modes of belonging, and the intersection of racial, ethnic, regional, national, and religious attachments. Thus racial identity was not straightforwardly a master identity (though it remained a salient one) among our sample. While understandings of attributions of 'race' and racial difference could arise in specific ways and contexts, many of our respondents did not necessarily consider their race or even ethnic ancestry to be of particular importance – though our part-Black respondents were more likely to note the significance of their 'colour' and their negative racialization as Black people in many social interactions in public settings.

In Britain, it appears that, at least for this predominantly middle-class, metropolitan sample, an increasingly inclusive and race-neutral nationality, as British, is a central part of the experiences of many (though not all) younger mixed Britons day. If race is not always regarded as an important dimension of self-identity, then racial assignment by others may be divested of some of its potency and consequences.

Based upon our findings, current census classifications are clearly not adequate to capture the complexity of the growing mixed population. Agreement on measures of growing diversity and forms of demographic change in the wider society is increasingly challenging. There is also reason to be concerned about whether respondents who fill in survey forms are doing so accurately and consistently, especially given the jaded attitude of some people towards routine form-filling in contemporary life. Furthermore, we must remember that official terms, such as 'White' or 'Asian', do not speak for themselves, and actually require 'unpacking' and interpretation. All of these factors makes the study of a population (which is differentiated into ethnic and racial categories – such as 'mixed race') fraught with difficulties.

Thus there are some important methodological and theoretical implications of our study. Interpreting the racial identifications of respondents (especially those who are adolescents and young adults, at key developmental and transitional stages in their lives), based on one or several survey measures, courts the real danger of getting an incomplete and distorted picture of how mixed people conceive of themselves and experience their day-to-day lives. Interviews were crucial in being able to probe the meanings of the terms people used, and the role that 'race' and mixedness played in their daily lives.

As a comparative study into 'the' mixed population in Britain, this research has pointed to the great diversity found among mixed people and points to the need to continue research on this emergent sector of the population. In doing so, we need to avoid normative judgements about the growth of 'mixing' and mixed people as either good or bad for society. It is all too easy to over-simplify a complex array of evidence and concerns which don't easily boil down to a clear-cut conclusion about what the growth of mixed people portends (Silva & Reis 2012). In fact, while some people have celebrated the growth of mixed people, several concerns have also been registered regarding the official recognition of mixed people, as a separate entity, especially in relation to other ethnic minority groups.

The implications of the recognition of 'mixed' people

There is growing evidence that mixed people (and people in mixed families) are demanding the *public* recognition of being mixed per se (Taylor 1994; Kymlicka 1995) – as indicated in the provision of a 'mixed' category in officialdom, or the political mobilization of mixed people and families (DaCosta 2007). Increasingly, as evidenced through their visibility in popular culture and in 'serious' discussions of change in contemporary society (e.g. in contemporary society in the growth of websites addressing mixed young people or mixed couples and families), mixed people are achieving a degree of recognition as part of the British population, and not just as an outlier group.

One objection to the official recognition of multiracial people articulated by US commentators is that this category may reinforce top-down racial hierarchies in which mixed people will be regarded as an intermediate category 'above' Black in particular, as Rainier Spencer (2006) has argued:

> Instead of multiraciality being used in an abstract sense to discredit the idea of race, it is deployed in such a way that it reinforces racial boundaries. The assertion of a multiracial class as the product of mixture between whites and African-Americans creates the theoretical space for whiteness to maintain its mythical purity and for blackness to retain its essentially impure quality. (p. 86)

Furthermore, it has been argued that the creation of such a category would be invidious and would effectively result in people who are Black and White 'leaving' the Black community for the more favoured status of being a mixed or multiracial person (Spencer 1997); such 'racial re-districting' (Gallagher 2004) could then result in significantly smaller numbers of African Americans (or other monoracial minority groups) in various forms of official enumeration.

A second objection to the recognition (and thus institutionalization) of a mixed group is that some analysts, especially some in the United States, argue that this recognition can bolster a neo-conservative agenda which supports the idea of colour-blindness, in which racial boundaries and racisms are treated as misguided relics from the past (see Appiah & Gutmann 1996). Critics have pointed out that some neo-conservative support for the multiracial category in the United States (e.g. by Newt Gingrich) is fuelled by the hope that this category will help to dilute racial consciousness, identity politics, and thus a step towards dismantling affirmative action and other race conscious policies (Daniel & Casteñeda-Liles 2006:133). Civil rights leaders in the United States have also tended to oppose a 'multiracial' box in national surveys because, according to Kweisi Mfumi of the NAACP, the introduction of a multiracial box makes it more difficult to measure the effects of discrimination among Black people (which is currently understood as including mixed Black/White individuals) and further endanger affirmative action (Younge 2010).

Some critics in the United States accuse the multiracial movement (though it is not entirely homogeneous) of lacking an antiracist agenda, especially one that continues to address structural inequalities. However, in their defence, Daniel and Casteñeda-Liles (2006) note that *'[multiracial activists] have nevertheless highlighted how traditional civil rights organizations, leaders, and intellectuals may uncritically embrace identities and politics that have essentialist underpinnings (such as the one-drop rule)'* (141). In Britain, where policies to redress racism and discrimination have not been as constrained to rigid racial/ethnic typologies as in the United States, our agendas of equality, human rights, and diversity (as something to be valued in itself) – in which race/ethnicity is but one strand amongst seven equality groups – have created a strong civil apparatus for the recognition of difference.

A third, and now familiar, criticism (about the official recognition of mixed people) concerns many studies of ethnic and racial groups which employ racial classification more generally: that these studies paradoxically reinforce notions of common sense and essentialist understandings of ethnic and racial difference (Rattansi 2007). While the census and government have adopted the term 'mixed' as the overarching label for this group, its very use in a wider context of terms such as 'mixed race' is said by some to be problematic as it implicitly legitimizes the existence of 'pure races' (see Banton 1997; Rattansi 2007; Ali 2003; Small 2001). Yet there is, too, a recognition that the terminology we use needs to be sensitive to the preferences of those whom it describes, 'mixed race' having a saliency amongst this population (Aspinall 2009).

Paul Gilroy (2000:250–251) puts the challenge ahead of us well:

> The main problem we face in making sense of these and more recent developments is the lack of a means of adequately describing, let alone theorizing, intermixture, fusion, and syncretism without suggesting the existence of anterior 'uncontaminated' purities.... Whether the process of mixture is presented as fatal or

redemptive, we must be prepared to give up the illusions that cultural and ethnic purity has ever existed, let alone provided a foundation for civil society.[1]

Historically, beliefs and ideologies concerning notions of ethnic and racial purity *have*, in fact, been foundational for many societies. There have also been efforts in the 21st century by bioscientists and geneticists to reclaim 'race' as a term to describe distinctive genetic clusters at a population level (see Skinner 2007). To use Bruno Latour's phrase, there is strong evidence that the bioscientists' view is 'gaining in reality' over that of the social constructionists (see Hartigan 2008).

Rather than asking whether we should (and can) be post-race or not, we need to ask to what degree our interactions and conflicts with one another as individuals, groups, and societies *are less racialized than they have been in the past* (Rattansi 2007). While the language and concepts of race are still with us (in its various permutations, especially in relation to 'new racism' or 'cultural racism', which adroitly avoids the language of race), we still need a language with which to discuss both asserted and attributed forms of difference and disadvantage – whether imagined or real.

Thus the criticism that researchers who study 'mixed race' people are simply reifying race is a rather simplistic and unfair allegation, especially in relation to a number of scholars who clearly use the terms 'mixed' and 'mixed race' with conceptual disclaimers. It becomes tiresome to continually hark back to this debate about terminology – when in fact there is broad agreement among many analysts of 'race' that there are no real or meaningful biological or genetic differences among people of so-called disparate 'races' and that the creation and continuing justification of race ideologies and practices are socially and historically constructed and mediated.

In fact, the very critics who chastise others for using the terms 'race' or 'mixed race' are unable to employ language which is entirely untainted with racial inflections – and the simple and disingenuous replacement of one seemingly less problematic term for another does not take us any further in our attempts to understand how and why human beings continue to demarcate, identify, and attribute forms of ethnic and racial difference onto ourselves and others. Despite concerns about the reification of race, and debates about terminology, real changes are occurring, including evidence that some people are increasingly critical and reflexive about notions of racial difference.

The future of 'mixed race'

While mixed people have gained official recognition, at least in particular ways, what will be politically contested in the coming years are the terms of this recognition, including debates about what, if anything, mixed people's interests may be (Gallagher 2006). Since there is growing evidence of their highly diverse experiences, especially in metropolitan areas such as London, analysts and policymakers need to be careful about making assumptions about what being mixed means (Song 2010).

For instance, as discussed in Chapter 5, should we regard mixed people as a disadvantaged minority group? Do they suffer racism? Such questions are only now being broached in studies in the United States, where the multiracial category does not denote a protected class under the law (Daniel & Castañeda-Liles 2006:133). Some analysts, such as Daniel and Castañeda-Liles (2006), observe that interracial couples and multiracial individuals still encounter forms of discrimination based upon 'essentialist' understandings of race. By comparison, in Britain, there has been widespread governmental recognition of mixed status since 2001, based upon research on the educational attainment and the experiences of mixed children in the care and youth justice systems – though most of this research pertains specifically to Black/White people and not mixed people more generally.[2]

In an increasingly multiethnic society in which being mixed is likely to be less and less uncommon, and where 'super-diversity' is evident (Vertovec 2007), it is important that public policy is informed by research which captures the complexity and variability among multiracial individuals who may use a variety of ethnic, national, and racial terms to describe themselves. Ethnic and racial labels in common usage, of course, still carry a lot of weight in many contexts, but the heretofore dominant meanings which are associated with particular terms and categories are not impervious to change.

States will have to think hard about using the category 'mixed' – as we don't yet know whether this category actually corresponds to a real group of people who mobilize or see themselves as sharing common experiences and objectives. If one looks at the growth of various Internet websites aimed at multiracial people in Britain, such as People in Harmony, Intermix, and Mix-d, it is clear that some mixed people are beginning to see themselves as a part of a distinct group with particular concerns and issues which they wish to address in the public realm.

Furthermore, the pre-emption of the term 'mixed' by officialdom to delineate those who are mixes of pan-ethnic groups or socially constructed 'races' leaves other kinds of mixedness in an equivocal position with respect to recognition and enumeration. The 2001 Census showed that significant numbers indicated their mixedness *within* the pan-ethnicities through free-text descriptions. Clearly, there is now a much more prevalent mixed population that is not currently captured, if one defines mixedness as people who have multiple socio-cultural or national origins or affiliations that encompass ethnic, religion, and national identity groups that may be mutually entailed in each other. As population mixing begins to encompass a growing level of diversity in a country that is substantially driven by migration dynamics, the utility of the conceptual distinction we currently maintain between 'mixed race' and 'multiethnicity' may begin to diminish.

In our efforts to explore and investigate 'the' mixed population in Britain, we must not end up reifying their groupness, when our study suggests that there is no unitary or shared set of experiences which speak to all types of mixed people in Britain. Whether the multiracial population in the United States can be said to possess a coherent sense of a shared group membership is also in question. Unlike the experiences of 'coloured' people in South Africa, who had (and have) a clear sense of who they are as a group, with a distinctive history and status based upon the former Apartheid regime, Gary Younge (2010) has recently argued that multiracial people in the United States (in all their diversity) do not comprise a genuinely coherent group as such.

It is likely, in fact, that many mixed people share a great deal in common with other people in society, according to a variety of indicators – whether these be monoracial minority people or White people and so on. Even the most systematic attempts at (accurately) counting the mixed population in Britain (as in the census) are significantly limited by processes which government and researchers are unable to control. For example, when the US government disseminated trial questionnaires with a 'multiracial' box, one problem which arose was that people could have very different understandings of what 'multiracial' meant (Younge 2010:78). As Younge argues: *'But for a social identity (as opposed to a personal identity) to be viable it cannot be so porous that large numbers of those whom it should include fail to recognize it as meaningful while large numbers whom it should not include believe they are part of it'* (78). Indeed, the lack of stability of the *'two or more races'* population has been accurately demonstrated by the US Census Bureau. In a post-census validation survey, of non-Hispanic panel respondents reporting two or more races in the US 2000 Census, only 40% (724,686/1,814,610) also reported two or more races in the Census Quality Survey initial contact (60% switched to reporting a single race) (Bentley et al. 2003).

While we did not examine specific influences on identity choices, such as social class and contextual factors like the ethnic composition of respondents' neighbourhoods and the schools they attended, future studies of mixed race people need to probe the role of social class and these other factors in shaping how mixed race individuals perceive and negotiate their identity options (Caballero et al. 2008; Faghen-Smith 2010). In the United States, Brunsma and Rockquemore (2001) and Yancey (2006) found that the higher one's social class, the less likely the multiracial individual is to relate to their minority status, or identify with the 'lower status' racial identity (but see Roth 2005 and Xie & Goyette 1997 for slightly different findings). Coming from a relatively privileged background by virtue of being in higher or further education, many of our respondents may have been insulated from the harshest manifestations of racism and the full force of negative racial assignments by others. So we need to know more about the ways in which disparate types of mixed people fare socioeconomically, and how such patterns may vary regionally. In addition to histories of working-class White and Black people in interracial relationships (see Benson 1981), there is growing evidence of middle-class mixed relationships in Britain (see Caballero et al. 2007; and see Panico & Nazroo 2011).

In most studies of the 'second generation' and 'race relations', it is largely assumed that intermarriage is the ultimate litmus test of integration – so that analysts may assume that those who intermarry (with Whites) will automatically enjoy both economic and social mobility (see Gordon 1964; Alba & Nee 2003). If most mixed people in Britain partner with White individuals (as is currently the case), does this suggest a linear receding of racial identity and consciousness for mixed people, or is the picture likely to be more complicated? In fact, in Britain, very little is actually known about the racial consciousness of mixed people, or how mixed offspring actually fare in such interracial households in the contemporary context. In the increasingly complex landscape of many multiethnic societies, we must critically examine what we mean by 'integration', including forms of both economic and social integration (Song 2009). While intermarriage may be said to herald a form of structural assimilation (or 'integration' to use the British term) (see Gordon 1964), in terms of one's formal inclusion in certain families, social networks, and social institutions, we cannot assume that multiracial offspring of such unions straightforwardly 'belong' in mainstream settings or are necessarily more privileged than non-mixed minority individuals. Given the very substantial heterogeneity of the mixed population in Britain, it is imperative that we disaggregate the social and economic experiences of disparate mixed people.

Another area for future research is an examination of how mixed people as parents (and grandparents) think about the intergenerational transmission of racial identities, including their attitudes towards 'race' and racial difference, and the idea of being a mixed person. As discussed throughout this book, having mixed ancestry does not necessarily translate into someone ticking a 'Mixed' box in the Census (or any other general survey). And since many parents are likely to fill in the forms on behalf of their younger, co-resident children, the census may provide a parent's preferred classification of their child, which may not necessarily mesh with how the child sees herself, or will see herself as she matures. The ability to track individuals in longitudinal data, such as the census-based Longitudinal Study, will provide a point of access to such issues as age-specific racial assignment. The specific sex and ethnic/racial ancestry of the parent (of a mixed child) may be influential in shaping the ways in which they classify their children (as has been shown in the US – Qian 2004; Xi & Goyette 1997) – but this is still largely unknown in Britain (though the CCSR did some tabulations for the 1991 Census).

Do people who have one mixed parent (or a mixed grandparent) count themselves as being mixed or not? That is, how much of contemporary mixedness is related to a person's immediate ancestry or their more distant forebears? Furthermore, how should we define inter-ethnic/interracial marriages? ONS has reported measures at the pan-ethnic (or aggregate ethnic group) level and at the level of the full classification (16-categories). Again, this links to debates about terminology of the children of such unions, notably that of 'mixed race' vs. 'multiethnicity'. Perhaps, too, it is timely to argue for a stronger focus on inter-ethnic cohabiting unions and the extent to which they might provide evidence of changing patterns of population mixing.

Furthermore, while our study found that some of our respondents 'played down' the significance of ethnic and racial awareness and boundaries, we must not overlook the ways in which people and groups may still engage in forms of disapproval and intra-racial harassment of co-ethnics who dare to be-friend or enter into an intimate relationship with someone from another 'race'. Some US academics, for instance, have explored the dynamics around 'border patrolling' (Smith & Jones 2011) on multiethnic university campuses: '*As a form of borderism (Dalmage 2000), intraracial harassment is both a preventative measure, warning those who might cross ethnoracial boundaries about the sanctions they would suffer if they did, and a penalty, sanctioning those who do'* (Smith & Jones 2011:1568). While this phenomenon has not received much academic attention in Britain, there is no doubt that such warnings and sanctions effectively rearticulate and reinforce notions of racial difference and racial boundaries. It is likely that while attitudes towards interracial partnering are unquestionably now more relaxed, it still constitutes a 'bright' boundary transgression (Alba 2005) in many situations and places.

Increasingly, it is clear that there is no one mixed population or experience in Britain. Mixed experiences can differ across disparate types of mixed people, but we would also stress that there is considerable variation *within* specific mixed groups. However, the fact that there is currently no clear or coherent sense of a mixed identity or group in Britain does not mean that such an identity or sense of collectivity will not emerge in the future, especially if significant numbers of mixed people mobilize socially and politically around the idea of being mixed. But what such a mixed identity and interests portend will remain highly contested for years to come.

Notes

1 Exploring 'Mixed Race' in Britain

1. Platt's analysis of the Labour Force Survey notes that '*inter-ethnic partnerships are defined as those where one partner regards themselves as belonging to a different one of the 15 ethnic group categories to that claimed by the other partner*' (p. 13). Given the wide range of 15 ethnic groups (such as Mixed White and Asian, Black African, White Other, Other Asian, to name only a few), interethnic unions were not necessarily ones involving a White partner, though many of them probably do. Note, too, that only a third of Black Caribbean women and just over half of Black Caribbean men are married or cohabiting (Platt 2009).
2. The differential sizes of these mixed groups are notable: In the 2001 Census those with either Black Caribbean or Black African (and White) heritage constituted almost 47.9% of the total mixed population, rising to 48.4% in 2011, whilst almost 28.6% were Asian and White, falling to 27.9% in 2011. Many of the Chinese/White (and other East Asian/White individuals), and individuals with two disparate non-White parents, ticked the 'Any other mixed background' box in 2001. The 2011 Census data show that the mixed groups have grown at varying rates over the 2001–11 decade: the mixed 'White and Black African' group has grown the fastest, by 110.3%, followed by the 'Other Mixed' group (86.3%), 'White and Asian' (80.8%), and 'White and Black Caribbean' (79.7%). One commonly shared characteristic across the four subcategories is their youth: Owen (2007) showed that over 17% were children aged under 5, and almost half (47.5%) of the mixed population were children aged under 15 in 2001.
3. This ESRC project (RES-000-23-1507) was conducted by Peter Aspinall, Miri Song, and Ferhana Hashem from March 2006 to July 2008.
4. For more information, see Aspinall, P.J., Song, M., and Hashem, F. (2008). *The Ethnic Options of Mixed Race People in Britain Survey: Full Research Report (for ESRC Research Grant RES-000-23-1507).* (Swindon: Economic and Social Research Council). (see Awards and Outputs). http://www.esrcsocietytoday.ac .uk/ESRCInfoCentre/.

2 Racial Identification: Multiplicity and Fluidity

1. Thus at times we employ this differentiation between 'internal', 'expressed', and 'observed' identities in this book (though for a fuller discussion of the interactions of these aspects of identification, see Chapter 4).
2. All the ethnic questions for 'ethnic self-identification' in Canada's Ethnic Diversity Survey (Statistics Canada 2003) were open response and did not provide examples of ethnic or cultural groups (unlike the 2001 Canadian Census ethnic question). Race and ethnicity categorization examined in 37 US State

Medicaid Programs and 45 State Children's Health Insurance Programs in 2009 found that four and seven States, respectively, used only free text (Ulmer et al. 2009). In fact, a former director of the US Bureau of the Census has long advocated free-text data collection for race/ethnicity on the grounds of the growing diversity of the US population, a format virtually unused in Britain – see Prewitt (2005).

3. Our wider research indicated, for example, increasing use of the 'Any Other Mixed background' category (one of the four mixed categories offered in the England and Wales Census) in official datasets in a number of London boroughs that had experienced high levels of settlement of new migrants.

4. For example, in the 1998 Canadian National Census Test the non-response rate (6.5%) to the question on birthplace of parents was higher than that for similar questions such as birthplace of respondents (1.6%). However, the non-response rate for birthplace of grandparents was even higher, at about 11.5%.

5. While this was relatively rare, interpreting the cases in which respondents multi-ticked '5' (non-racial/ethnic) with '3' (mixed race), or '5' with other multiple options, is less than straightforward.

6. While it is possible that the interview sub-sample somehow differed from the survey sample from which it was drawn, one reason why so many interviewees revealed examples of shifting identifications (though of varying nature and degree) could be that interviews involved much more probing and allowed for fuller, more complex responses than did the surveys.

3   Differential Ethnic Options?

1. Some recent US studies have tended to suggest that parents of multiracial (White/non-White) children are likely to identify their children *'away from the minority designation and toward the multiracial and/or White designation'* (Brunsma 2005:1135) – that is, identify their children in relation to the more privileged group in society, and away from the more racially stigmatized group in society (especially among more socioeconomically privileged parents of Hispanic/White and Asian/White children – though class did not affect parental racial labelling among Black/White mixed children).

2. This was similar to the question asked in the 2011 England and Wales Census: How would you describe your national identity? *Tick all that apply* ('English', 'Welsh', 'Scottish', 'Northern Irish', 'British', 'Other, write in). The use of examples for the 'Other' category in the main survey question may have increased its usage compared with government social survey findings.

4   Does Racial Mismatch in Identification Matter?

1. In one American study concerning Black men and women, Hunter (2007) argues that skin colour has a greater impact upon the lives of Black women, than men; she finds that Black women with lighter skin are advantaged in comparison with those with darker skin.

5   Are Mixed Race People Racially Disadvantaged?

1. This question was adapted from one in the 2005 Home Office Citizenship (People, Families and Communities) Survey which asked: '*What groups do you think there is now more [less] racial prejudice against, compared with five years ago*', the same response categories being used (with the exception of 'Eastern Europeans'): 'Asian people (Indian, Pakistani, Bangladeshi); Black people (Caribbean, African); Chinese people; White people; Mixed race people; Buddhists; Hindus; Jews; Muslims; Sikhs; Asylum seekers/Refugees; New immigrants; Eastern Europeans; Other (specify)'. (See http://surveynet.ac.uk/sqb/surveys/citizenship.asp.)
2. This question was drawn from the European Social Survey (ESS).
3. This question was asked in a survey of the impact of racial-categorization, ancestry, and racial heterogeneity of contexts on measures of depressive symptoms and self-esteem among 781 multiracial and 4,333 monoracial American youth (Herman 2006).
4. Herman's (2006) study also compared multiracial students with their monoracial counterparts. Interestingly, though, monoracial Asians perceived almost as much discrimination as monoracial Blacks (p. 738).
5. As in the ESS, respondents were then asked: '*On what grounds is your group discriminated against?*' Of 'Black/White' respondents, 56 (88%) selected 'colour or race', 25 (39%) 'ethnic group', 14 (22%) 'nationality', 14 (22%) 'gender', 10 (16%) 'religion', 6 'age', and just 3 'language'. 'Colour or race' ($n=5$) and 'ethnic group' ($n=5$) were also important in the East or SE Asian/White group. 'Religion' ($n=8$) was the most important basis for discrimination reported in the Arab/White group. 'Colour or race' ($n=12$), 'religion' ($n=10$), and 'nationality' ($n=9$) were the grounds most frequently mentioned by the South Asian/White group.

6   How Central Is 'Race' to Mixed Race People?

1. There are, of course, other collective identities. Disability/impairment is an embodied identity, the bearers of which '...*have sought recognition, modelling themselves sometimes on racial minorities (with whom they share the experience of discrimination and insult), or (as with deaf people) on ethnic groups*' (Appiah 2005:304). Age may also be construed as an identity strand, manifested in such ceremonies/rituals as coming of age and retirement, and family or kin may also be important strands (Jenkins 1996). Social class is still pervasive, differentially driven by class-consciousness. Appiah (2005) also mentions caste (for those of South Asian descent) and clans.
2. Each wave surveys around 10,000 adults with an additional boost of 5,000 people from minority ethnic groups. The response rate for the 2007 Citizenship Survey varied from 49% to 59% across the three constituent samples including ethnic boost.
3. With the exception of one question in the Citizenship Survey exploring whether a conflict exists between religion and national identity for those identifying these strands as important.

4. Table 6.2 ('Salient identities in the 2007 Citizenship Survey') gives percentages of respondents saying whether a particular attribute is 'very important'. Master identity status is based on the question about which is 'the most important' (where it's necessary to achieve the 10% threshold). By comparison, Table 6.2 gives a measure of the magnitude of importance.
5. Collapsed from the full six categories so providing a sensitive measure: see footnote to Table 6.6.

7 Rethinking Ethnic and Racial Classifications

1. See Table 1.3. Estimated overseas-born population resident in the UK, by country of birth. July 2010 to June 2011: http://www.ons.gov.uk/ons/taxonomy/index.html?nscl=Population + by +Nationality + and + Country + of + Birth.
2. Submission by PJA. See Office for National Statistics. *Ethnic Group, National Identity, Religion and Language Consultation. Experts, Community and Special Interest Group Responses to the 2011 Census Stakeholders Consultation 2006/07* (London: Office for National Statistics, 2007) (October).
3. ETHPOP Database, accessed 28 March 2013: http://www.ethpop.org/.
4. Multi-ticking also skirts the political controversy over choosing one 'mixed' categorization. In the United States, some analysts and activists (especially among the African American population) have opposed the choose one box rule, and favoured a multi-ticking 'choose all that apply' approach, for some feared that the provision of a 'mixed race' box would result in Black/White mixed people (who are currently seen as Black) 'leaving' the Black community (see Spencer 1997; Gallagher 2006; among others). Such critics have argued that the creation of a mixed race category can create an intermediate category in the existing racial hierarchy and reinforce White supremacy (and further denigrate the status of non-mixed Black people) (see Daniel & Castañeda 2006 for a good discussion). By comparison, such objections to a mixed category were rare in the UK context; for instance, the late MP, Bernie Grant, argued that a mixed category would be meaningless and divisive for Black/White individuals.

8 Conclusion: What Is the Future of 'Mixed Race' Britain?

1. And as Rattansi (2007) elegantly puts it: '*In thinking about the potential for a post-racial future, we have to be aware that what we are contemplating are the chances that the distinctive and lethal combination of science, physiological classification and cultural evaluation that came into being in the late 18th century will no longer exercise the power it has had in the 19th and 20th centuries*' (162).
2. According to some commentators such as the journalist Laura Smith, the social disadvantage of mixed children can be overlooked, since in many contexts, mixed children are not considered to be a minority in the way that Black or Asian children are (Smith 2006).

References

Alba, R. (2005) 'Bright versus blurred boundaries: second-generation assimilation and exclusion in France, Germany, and the United States', *Ethnic and Racial Studies* 28(1), 20–49.

Alba, R. and V. Nee (2003) *Remaking of Mainstream America: Assimilation and Contemporary Immigration* (Cambridge: Harvard University Press).

Alexander, C. (1996) *The Art of Being Black* (Oxford: Clarendon Press).

Alexander, C. (2000) *The Asian Gang* (Oxford: Berg).

Ali, S. (2003) *Mixed-Race, Post-Race: Gender, New Ethnicities and Cultural Practices* (London: Berg).

Alibhai-Brown, Y. (2001) *Mixed Feelings* (London: The Women's Press).

Alibhai-Brown, Y. and A. Montagu (1992) *The Colour of Love* (London: Virago).

Anthias, F. and N. Yuval-Davis (1992) *Racialized Boundaries* (London: Routledge).

Anon. (2005) 'Master status', in J. Scott & G. Marshall (eds.) *Oxford Dictionary of Sociology* (third edition) (Oxford: Oxford University Press), p. 394.

Appiah, A.K. (2005) *The Ethics of Identity* (Princeton: Princeton University Press).

Appiah, A.K. and A. Gutmann (1996) *Color Conscious* (Princeton: Princeton University Press).

Aspinall, P.J. (2001) 'Operationalising the collection of ethnicity data in studies of the sociology of health and illness', *Sociology of Health and Illness* 23(6), 829–862.

Aspinall, P.J. (2003) 'The conceptualisation and categorisation of mixed race/ethnicity in Britain and North America', *International Journal of Intercultural Relations* 27(3), 269–296.

Aspinall, P.J. and L. Mitton (2008) ' "Kinds of people" and equality monitoring in the UK', *Policy and Politics* 36(1), 55–74.

Aspinall, P.J., M. Song, and F. Hashem (2008) *The Ethnic Options of Mixed Race People in Britain Survey: Full Research Report (for ESRC Research Grant RES-000-23-1507)* (Swindon: Economic and Social Research Council). Available at: http://www.esrcsocietytoday.ac.uk/ESRCInfoCentre/ (see Awards and Outputs). Last accessed 1 April 2010.

Aspinall, P.J. (2009) 'The future of ethnicity classifications', *Journal of Ethnic and Migration Studies*, 35(9), 1417–1435.

Aspinall, P.J. (2012) 'Answer formats in British census and survey ethnicity questions: does open response better capture "Superdiversity"?' *Sociology* 46(2), 354–364.

Aspinall, P.J. et al. (2006) *Mixed Race in Britain: A Survey of the Preferences of Mixed Race People for Terminology and Classifications. Interim Report* (Canterbury: University of Kent). Available at: http://www.pih.org.uk/images/documents/mixedraceinbritain_report2.pdf.

Azoulay, G.K. (2003) 'Rethinking "mixed race" ', *Research in African Literatures* 34(2), 233–235.

Back, L. (1995) *New Ethnicities* (London: UCL Press).

Ballard, R. (ed.) (1994) *Desh Pardesh* (London: Hurst & Company).

Banton, M. (1999) 'Reporting on race', *Anthropology Today* 15(3), 1–3.

Banton, M. (1997) *Ethnic and Racial Consciousness*, 2nd edition (Harlow: Addison Wesley Longman).

Banton, M. (2008) 'Problem-finding in ethnic and racial studies', in J. Eade, M. Barrett, C. Floud, & R. Race (eds.) *Advancing Multiculturalism, Post 7/7* (Newcastle: Cambridge Scholars Publishing), pp. 42–57.

Barn, R. (1999) 'White mothers, mixed parentage children and child welfare', *British Journal of Social Work* 29(2), 269–284.

Barn, R. and V. Harman (2006) 'A contested identity: an exploration of the competing social and political discourse concerning the identification and positioning of young people of inter-racial parentage', *British Journal of Social Work* 36(8), 1309–1324.

Barth, F. (1969) *Ethnic Groups and Boundaries: The Social Organisation of Culture Difference* (Oslo: Universitetsforlaget).

Bartkowski, P.J. (2004) *The Promise Keepers: Servants, Soldiers, and Godly Men* (New Brunswick, NJ: Rutgers University Press).

Bashi, V. and A. McDaniel (1996) 'A theory of immigration and racial stratification', *Journal of Black Studies* 27(5), 668–682.

Baumann, G. (1996) *Contesting Culture* (Cambridge: Cambridge University Press).

BBC News Online, 'UK attitudes on immigration and welfare "toughening"', Available at: http://www.bbc.co.uk/news/uk-19621020, downloaded 17 September 2012.

Becker, H. (1963) *Outsiders: Studies in the Sociology of Deviance* (New York: Free Press).

Benson, S. (1981) *Ambiguous Ethnicity* (Cambridge: Cambridge University Press).

Bentley, M., T. Mattingly, C. Hough, and C. Bennett (2003) *Census Quality Survey to Evaluate Responses to the Census 2000 Question on Race: An Introduction to the Data. Census 2000 Evaluation B.3* (Washington, DC: US Census Bureau).

Berthoud, R. (1998) 'Defining ethnic groups: origin or identity?' *Patterns of Prejudice* 32(2), 53–63.

Bonilla-Silva, E. (2003) *Racism Without Racists: Color-Blind Racism and the Persistence of Racial Inequality in the United States* (New York: Rowman and Littlefield).

Bonilla-Silva, E. (2004) 'From bi-racial to tri-racial: towards a new system of racial stratification in the USA', *Ethnic and Racial Studies* 27(6), 931–950.

Bonnett, A. and B. Carrington (2000) 'Fitting into categories or falling between them? rethinking ethnic classification', *British Journal of Sociology of Education* 21(4), 487–500.

Brackett, K. et al. (2006) 'The effects of multiracial identification on students' perceptions of racism', *Social Science Journal* 43(3), 437–444.

Bradford, B. (2006) *Who Are the 'Mixed' Ethnic Group?* (London: Office for National Statistics).

Bratter, J. (2007) 'Will "multiracial" survive to the next generation? The racial classification of children of multiracial parents', *Social Forces* 86(2), 821–849.

British Sociological Association (BSA) (2005) 'Equality and diversity: language and the BSA – ethnicity and race', Available at: http://www.britsoc.co.uk/equality/ (accessed 11 June 2012).

Brownfield, D., A.M. Sorenson, and K.M. Thompson (2001) 'Gang membership, race, and social class: a test of the group hazard and master status hypotheses', *Deviant Behaviour* 22(1), 73–90.

Brubaker, R. (2004) *Ethnicity Without Groups* (Cambridge: Harvard University Press).

Brunsma, D. (ed.) (2006) *Mixed Messages: Multiracial Identities in the 'Color-Blind' Era* (Boulder: Lynne Rienner Publishers).

Brunsma, D. (2005) 'Interracial families and the racial identification of mixed-race children', *Social Forces* 84(2), 1129–1155.

Brunsma, D. and K. Rockquemore (2001) 'The new color complex: appearances and biracial identity', *Identity* 1(3), 225–246.

Bryant, C.D. (ed.) (1990) *Deviant Behaviour: Readings in the Sociology of Norm Violations* (New York: Hemisphere Publishing).

Bulmer, M. (1986) 'Ethnicity and race', in R. Burgess (ed.) *Key Variables in Social Investigation* (London: Routledge).

Burton, J., A. Nandi, and L. Platt (2010) 'Measuring ethnicity: challenges and opportunities for survey research', *Ethnic and Racial Studies* 33(8), 1332–1349.

Byng, M. (1998) 'Mediating discrimination: resisting oppression among African American muslim women', *Social Problems* 45(4), 473–487.

Caballero, C. (2005) 'Mixed Race Projects': Perceptions, Constructions and Implications of Mixed Race in the UK and USA'. PhD Thesis, University of Bristol.

Caballero, C., R. Edwards, and D. Smith (2008) 'Cultures of mixing: understanding partnerships across ethnicity', *Twenty-First Century Society* 3(1), 49–63.

Caballero, C., J. Haynes, and L. Tikly (2007) 'Researching mixed race in education: perceptions, policies and practices', *Race, Ethnicity and Education* 10(3), 345–362.

Campbell, M. (2003) The 'One-Drop Rule': How Salient Is Hypodescent for Multiracial Americans with African American Ancestry? CDE Working Paper No. 2003–11 (Madison, WI: Center for Demography and Ecology, University of Wisconsin).

Campbell, M. (2007) 'Thinking outside the (black) box: measuring black and multiracial identification on surveys', *Social Science Research* 36, 921–944.

Campbell, M. and M. Herman (2010) 'Politics and policies: attitudes toward multiracial Americans', *Ethnic and Racial Studies* 33(9), 1511–1536.

Campbell, M. and L. Troyer (2007) 'The implications of racial misclassification by observers', *American Sociological Review* 72, 750–765.

Cashmore, E. (2008) 'Tiger Woods and the new racial order', *Current Sociology* 56(4): 621–634.

Cheng, C. and F. Lee (2009) 'Multiracial identity integration: perceptions of conflict and distance among multiracial individuals', *Journal of Social Issues* 65, 51–68.

Cheryan, S. and B. Monin (2005) 'Where are you really from?: Asian Americans and identity denial', *Journal of Personality and Social Psychology* 89, 717–730.

Coleman, D. (2010) 'Projections of the ethnic minority populations of the United Kingdom 2006–2056', *Population and Development Review* 36(3), 441–486.

Coleman, D. and S. Scherbov (2005) Immigration and ethnic change in low-fertility countries – towards a new demographic transition? Paper

Presented at the Population Association of America Annual Conference, Philadelphia.

Collins, Patricia Hill. (1990) *Black Feminist Thought: Knowledge,Consciousness, and the Politics of Empowerment* (Boston: UnwinHyman).

Cornell, S. and D. Hartmann (1998) *Ethnicity and Race: Making Identities in a Changing World* (Thousand Oaks, CA: Pine Forge Press).

Crocker, J. and D.M. Quinn (1998) 'Racism and self-esteem', in J. Eberhart & S.T. Fiske (eds.) *Confronting Racism: The Problem and the Response* (Thousand Oaks, CA: Sage. Crocker and Quinn), pp. 169–187.

DaCosta, K. (2007) *Making Multiracials* (Stanford: Stanford University Press).

Dalmage, H. (2000) *Tripping the Color Line* (New Brunswick, NJ: Rutgers University Press).

Daniel, G.R. (1996) 'Black and White identity in the new millennium,' in M. Root (ed.) *The Multiracial Experience* (Thousand Oaks: Sage), pp. 121–139.

Daniel, G.R. and J.M. Castañeda-Liles (2006) 'Race, multiraciality, and the neoconservative agenda', in D. Brunsma (ed.) *Mixed Messages* (Boulder, CO: Lynne Reinner Publishers).

Davies, M. (2007) 'Unity and diversity in feminist legal theory', *Philosophy Compass* 2(4), 650–664.

Davis, F. (1991) *Who Is Black?* (University Park: Pennsylvania State University Press).

Davis, K. (2008) 'Intersectionality as buzzword', *Feminist Theory* 9(1), 67–85.

Dawkins R. (2004) 'Race and creation', *Prospect Magazine*, October 23, 2004, Available at http://www.prospectmagazine.co.uk/magazine/richard-dawkins-race-evolution-in-group/

Doyle, J. and G. Kao (2007) 'Are racial identities of multiracials stable?' *Social Psychology Quarterly* 70(4), 405–423.

Duneier, M. (1992) *Slim's Table: Race, Respectability, and Masculinity* (Chicago: University of Chicago Press).

Dyson, M.E. (1994) 'Essentialism and the complexities of racial identity', in D.T. Goldberg (ed.) *Multiculturalism: A Reader* (Cambridge: Blackwell Publishers), pp. 218–229.

Earle, R. and C. Phillips (2009) 'Con-viviality and beyond: identity dynamics in a young mens prison', in M. Wetherell (ed.) *Identity in the 21st Century* (London: Palgrave Macmillan).

Edmunds, J. (2009) ' "Elite" young Muslims in Britain', *Contemporary Islam*, published online 22 December 2009.

Edwards, R. and C. Caballero (2008) 'What's in a name? An exploration of the significance of personal naming of 'mixed' children for parents from different racial, ethnic and faith backgrounds', *Sociological Review* 56(1), 39–60.

Edwards, R., S. Ali, C. Caballero, and M. Song (eds.) (2012) *International Perspectives on Racial and Ethnic Mixedness and Mixing* (London: Routledge).

Elster, J. (1993) *Political Psychology* (Cambridge: Cambridge University Press).

Erikson, E. (1959) 'Identity and the life cycle', *Psychological Issues* 1(1) (monograph).

Espino, R. and M. Franz (2002) 'Latino phenotypic discrimination revisited: the impact of skin color on occupational status', *Social Science Quarterly* 83, 612–623.

Feagin, J. (1991) 'The continuing significance of race: antiblack discrimination in public places', *American Sociological Review* 56, 101–116.

Feng, Z., M. Van Ham, P. Boyle, and G. Raab (2012) *A Longitudinal Study of Migration Propensities for Mixed Ethnic Unions in England and Wales*. IZA Discussion Paper No. 6394. Available at SSRN, http://ssrn.com/abstract=2019446.

Ferguson, C., S. Finch, and O. Turczuk (2007–08) *Citizenship Survey. Race, Religion and Equalities Topic Report* (London: Department for Communities and Local Government), December 2009.

Fhagen-Smith, P. (2010) 'Social class, racial/ethnic identity, and the psychology of "choice"', in K. Korgen (ed.) *Multiracial Americans and Social Class* (London: Routledge), pp. 30–38.

Finney, N. and L. Simpson (2009) *Sleepwalking to Segregation?* (Bristol: Policy Press).

Ford, R., R. Jolley, S. Katwala, and B. Mehta (2012) *The Melting Pot Generation. How Britain Became More Relaxed on Race* (London: British Future).

Frankenberg, R. (1993) *White Women, Race Matters: The Social Construction of Whiteness* (Minneapolis: University of Minnesota Press).

Funderburg, L. (1994) *Black, White, Other* (New York: Morrow).

Furedi, F. (2001) 'How sociology imagined race mixing', in D. Parker & M. Song (eds.) *Rethinking 'Mixed Race'* (London: Pluto Press).

Gallagher, C.A. (2004) 'Racial redistricting: expanding the boundaries of whiteness', in H. Dalmage (ed.) *The Politics of Multiculturalism: Challenging Racial Thinking* (New York: State University of New York Press), pp. 59–76.

Gallagher, C.A. (2006) 'Color blindness: an obstacle to racial justice?' in D. Brunsma (ed.) *Mixed Messages* (Boulder, CO: Lynne Reinner Publishers), pp. 103–116.

Gans, H. (1979) 'Symbolic ethnicity: the future of ethnic groups and cultures in America', *Ethnic and Racial Studies* 2(1), 1–19.

Gilroy, P. (1987) *There Ain't No Black in the Union Jack* (London: Routledge).

Gilroy, P. (2000) *Between Camps* (London: Penguin).

Gilroy, P. (2004) *After Empire: Melancholia or Convivial Culture?* (London: Routledge).

Goffman, E. (1968) *Stigma: Notes on the Management of Spoiled Identity* (Harmondsworth: Pelican).

Goldstein, J. and A. Morning (2002) 'Back in the box: the dilemma of using multiple-race data for single-race laws', in Joel Perlmann et al. (eds.) *The New Race Question: How the Census Counts Multiracial Individuals* (New York: Russell Sage), pp. 119–136.

Gordon, M. (1964) *Assimilation in American Life* (New York: Oxford University Press).

Gould, S.J. (1996) *The Mismeasure of Man* (Cambridge: Harvard University Press).

Gouldner, A.W. (1954) *Patterns of Industrial Bureaucracy* (New York: Free Press).

Grabham, E., D. Cooper, J. Krishnadas, and D. Herman (2009) *Intersectionality and Beyond: Law, Power and the Politics of Location* (Abingdon: Routledge-Cavendish).

Haas, S. and W. Dur (1992) 'Care of PLW HIV/AIDS between HIV-master-status and autonomy of patients. Results of a Viennese study'. International Conference AIDS D519 (abstract no. PoD 5784).

Hacking, I. (1986) 'Making up people', in T.C. Heller, M. Sosna, & D.E. Wellbery (eds.) *Reconstructing Individualism: Autonomy, Individuality, and the Self in Western Thought* (Stanford, CA: Stanford University Press), pp. 222–236.

Hall, S. (1996) 'Who needs identity?' in S. Hall and P. du Gay (eds.) *Questions of Cultural Identity* (London: Sage), pp. 1–17.

Hall, S. (ed.) (1997) *Representation* (Milton Keynes: Open University Press).

Hall, S. and P. du Gay (eds.) (1996) *Questions of Cultural Identity* (Milton Keynes: Open University Press).

Hancock, A.M. (2007) 'When multiplication doesn't equal quick addition: examining intersectionality as a research paradigm', *Perspectives on Politics* 5, 63–79.

Hanifan, L.J. (1916) 'The rural school community center', *Annals of the American Academy of Political and Social Science* 67, 130–138. Also L.J. Hanifan (1920) *The Community Center* (Boston: Silver Burdett).

Harman, V. (2010) 'Social work practice and lone white mothers of mixed-parentage children', *British Journal of Social Work* 40(2), 391–406.

Harris, D. and J. Sim (2002) 'Who is multiracial? Assessing the complexity of lived race', *American Sociological Review* 67, 614–627.

Harris, R. and B. Rampton (2009) 'Ethnicities without guarantees: an empirical approach', in M. Wetherell (ed.) *Identity in the 21st Century: New Trends in Changing Times* (Basingstoke: Palgrave Macmillan).

Hartigan, J. (2008) 'Is race still socially constructed? The recent controversy over race and medical genetics', *Science and Culture* 17(2), 163–193.

Heaton, T. and C. Jacobson (2000) 'Intergroup marriage: an examination of opportunity structures', *Sociological Inquiry* 70(1), 30–41.

Heath, A., C. Rothon, and A. Sundas (2010) 'Identity and public opinion', in A. Bloch & J. Solomos (eds.) *Race and Ethnicity in the 21st Century* (London: Palgrave Macmillan), pp. 186–208.

Hein, J. (1993) 'International migrants or welfare clients: the selection of a master status for Indochinese refugees by American voluntary agencies', *Journal of Sociology and Social Welfare* 20(1), 115.

Herman, M. (2004) 'Forced to choose: some determinants of racial identification in multiracial adolescents', *Child Development* 75(3), 730–748.

Herman, M. (2006) 'Racial Categorization, Ancestry, and Context: Implications of Race and Racial Context for Depressive Symptoms and Self-Esteem Among Multiracial Adolescents'. Paper Presented at the Annual Meeting of the American Sociological Association, Montreal, Quebec, Canada, 11 August 2006.

Herman, Melissa R. (2010) 'Do you see what I am? How observers' backgrounds affect their perceptions of multiracial faces', *Social Psychology Quarterly* 73(1), 58–78.

Herring, C., V. Keith, and H. Horton (eds.) (2004) *Skin/Deep: How Race and Complexion Matter in the 'Color Blind' Era* (Urbana: University of Illinois Press).

Herrnstein, R. and C. Murray (1994) *The Bell Curve* (New York: Free Press).

Hewitt, R. (1986) *White Talk, Black Talk* (Cambridge: Cambridge University Press).

Hickman, M. (1998) 'Reconstructing deconstructing "race": British discourses about the Irish in Britain', *Ethnic and Racial Studies* 21(2), 288–307.

Hiller, D.V. (1982) 'Overweight as master status: a replication', *Journal Psychology* 110, 107–113.

Hollinger, D. (1998) 'National culture and communities of descent', *Reviews in American History* 26(1), 312–328.

Holloway, S., R. Wright, and M. Ellis (2012) 'Constructing multiraciality in U.S. families and neighborhoods', in Edwards et al. (eds.) *International Perspectives on Racial and Ethnic Mixedness and Mixing* (London: Routledge).

Home Office (2001) 'People, families, and communities survey' (renamed Citizenship Survey). Dataset SN4754, accessed via the ESDS.

Hughes, E.C. (1945) 'Dilemmas and contradictions of status', *American Journal of Sociology* 50, 353–359.

Humes, K.R., N.A. Jones, and R.R. Ramirez (2011) *2010 Census Briefs: Overview of Race and Hispanic Origin: 2010* (Washington, DC: US Census Bureau).

Hunter, M. (2007) 'The persistent problem of colorism', *Sociology Compass* 1(1), 237–254.

Hylton, K., A. Pilkington, P. Warmington, and S. Housee (eds.) (2011) *Atlantic Crossings: International Dialogues on Critical Race Theory* (Birmingham: CSAP and University of Birmingham).

Ifekwunigwe, J. (1997) 'Diaspora's daughters, Africa's orphans? On lineage, authenticity, and mixed race identity', in H.S. Mizra (ed.) *Black British Feminism: A Reader* (London: Routledge), pp. 127–152.

Ifekwungwe, J. (1999) *Scattered Belongings* (London: Routledge).

Ifekwunigwe, J. (2002) 'An(other) English city: multiethnicities, (post)modern moments and strategic identifications', *Ethnicities* 2(3), 321–348.

Jacobson, J. (1997) 'Religion and ethnicity: dual and alternative sources of identity among young British Pakistanis', *Ethnic and Racial Studies* 20(2), 238–256.

Jackson, K.F., H.C. Yoo, R. Guevarra and B.A. Harrington (2012) 'Role of identity integration on the relationship between perceived racial discrimination and psychological adjustment of multiracial people', *Journal of Counseling Psychology* 59(2), 240–250.

Jenkins, R. (1996) *Social Identity* (London & New York: Routledge).

Jenkins, R. (1997) *Rethinking Ethnicity* (London: Sage).

Jones, J. (2006) *Somewhere to Go? Something to Do? London Borough of Newham Young People's Survey* (Northampton, UK: Mattersoffact).

Jones, S. (1994) *The Language of Genes* (New York: Doubleday).

Joyner, K. and G. Kao (2005) 'Interracial relationships and the transition to adulthood', *American Sociological Review* 70(4), 563–581.

Katz, I. (1996) *The Construction of Racial Identity in Children of Mixed Parentage* (London: Jessica Kingsley Publishers).

Katz, I. and A. Treacher (2005) 'The social and psychological development of mixed parentage children', in T. Okitikpi (ed.) *Working with Children of Mixed Parentage* (Lyme Regis: Russell House Publishing).

Khanna, N. (2004) 'The role of reflected appraisals in racial identity', *Social Psychological Quarterly* 67(2), 115–131.

Khanna, N. (2010) ' "If You're Half Black, You're Just Black": reflected appraisals and the persistence of the one-drop rule', *Sociological Quarterly* 51(1), 96–121.

Khanna, N. (2011) 'Ethnicity and race as "symbolic": the use of ethnic and racial symbols in asserting a biracial identity', *Ethnic and Racial Studies* 34(6), 1049–1067.

Kich, G. (1992) 'The developmental process of asserting a biracial, bicultural identity', in M. Root (ed.) *Racially Mixed People in America* (Newbury Park: Sage).

Kim, C.J. (1999) 'The racial triangulation of Asian Americans', *Politics and Society* 27(1), 105–138.

King, R. and K. DaCosta (1996) 'Changing face, changing race', in M. Root (ed.) *The Multiracial Experience* (Thousand Oaks: Sage), pp. 227–244.

King-O'Riain, R. et al. (eds.) (2013) *Global Mixed Race* (New York: New York University Press).

Kohn, M. (1995) *The Race Gallery: The Return of Racial Science* (London: Jonathan Cape).

Krysan, M. (2000) 'Prejudice, politics and public opinion: understanding the sources of racial policy attitudes', *Annual Review of Sociology* 26, 135–168.

Kuo, W. (1995) 'Coping with racial discrimination: the case of Asian Americans', *Ethnic and Racial Studies* 18(1), 109–127.

Kymlicka, W. (1995) (ed.) *The Rights of Minority Cultures* (Oxford: Oxford University Press).

LaGory, M., K. Fitzpatrick, and F. Ritchey (2005) 'Life chances and choices: assessing quality of life among the homeless', *Sociological Quarterly* 42(4), 633–651.

Lamont, M. (ed.) (1999) 'Above "People Above"? Status and worth among White and Black workers', in *The Cultural Territories of Race* (Chicago: University of Chicago Press).

Lee, J. and F. Bean (2004) 'America's changing color lines', *Annual Review of Sociology* 30, 221–242.

Lewis, G. (2009) 'Birthing racial difference: conversations with my mother', *Studies in the Maternal* 1(1). Available at: www.mamsie.bbok.ac.uk.

Lincoln, B. (2008) *Mix-d uk: A Look at Mixed-race Identities* (Manchester: Multiple Heritage Project and Ahmed Iqbal Ullah Education Trust).

Lopez, A. (2003) 'Collecting and tabulating race/ethnicity data with diverse and mixed heritage populations,' *Ethnic and Racial Studies*, 26(5), 931–961.

Luke, C. and A. Luke (1998) 'Interracial families: difference within difference', *Ethnic and Racial Studies* 21(4), 728–754.

Mahtani, M. (2002) 'What's in a name? Exploring the employment of "mixed race" as an identification', *Ethnicities* 2(4), 469–490.

Mahtani, M. and A. Moreno (2001) 'Same difference: towards a more unified discourse in "mixed race" theory,' in D. Parker & M. Song (eds.) *Rethinking 'Mixed Race'* (London: Pluto), pp. 65–75.

Mengel, L. (2001) 'Triples: the social evolution of a multiracial panethnicity', in D. Parker & M. Song (eds.) *Rethinking 'Mixed Race'* (London: Pluto Press).

Merton, R. (1941) 'Intermarriage and the social structure: fact and theory', *Psychiatry* 4(4), 361–374.

Miethe, T.D. and R.C. McCorkle (1997) 'Gang membership and criminal processing: a test of the "master status" concept', *Justice Quarterly* 14(3), 407–427.

Miles, R. (1984) *Racism* (London: Routledge).

Modood, T. (1994) 'Political blackness and British Asians', *Sociology* 28(4), 859–876.

Modood, T. (1996) 'The changing context of "race" in Britain', *Patterns of Prejudice* 30(1), 3–13.

Modood, T., R. Berthoud, J. Lakey, J. Nazroo, P. Smith, S. Virdee, and S. Beishon (1997) *Ethnic Minorities in Britain: Diversity & Disadvantage* (London: Policy Studies Institute).

Morning, A. (2000) 'Who is multiracial? Definitions and decisions', *Sociological Imagination* 37(4), 209–229.

Morning, A. (2008) 'Ethnic classification in global perspective: a cross-national survey of the 2000 census round', *Population Research and Policy Review* 27, 239–272.

Morris, N. (2012) ' "Absurd adoption barriers" to be broken down', *The Independent*, March 10.

Muttarak, R. and A. Heath (2010) 'Who intermarries in Britain: explaining ethnic diversity in intermarriage pattern', *British Journal of Sociology* 61, 275–305.

Nagel, J. (1994) 'Constructing ethnicity', *Social Problems* 41(1), 152–176.

Nandi, A. and L. Platt (2012) 'How diverse is the UK', in S. McFall (ed.) *Understanding Society: Findings 2012* (Colchester: Institute for Social and Economic Research, University of Essex).

NatCen (2012) *British Social Attitudes 29th Report* (London: Natcen) Available at: http://www.bsa-29.natcen.ac.uk/read-the-report/immigration/views-of-immigration.aspx, 29 September 2012.

Nayak, A. (2003) *Race, Place and Globalization* (Oxford: Berg).

Nobles, M. (2000) *Shades of Citizenship* (Stanford: Stanford University Press).

Office of Management and Budget (1997) *Federal Register*, 7 September 1997, Part II, pp. 36873–36946.

Office for National Statistics (2003) *Ethnic Group Statistics: A guide for the Collection and Classification of Ethnicity Data* (London: ONS).

Office for National Statistics (2005) *Focus on Ethnicity & Identity: Inter-ethnic Marriage* (London: Office for National Statistics). Available at: http://www.ons.gov.uk/ons/rel/ethnicity/focus-on-ethnicity-and-identity/focus-on-ethnicity-and-identity-summary-report/index.html (accessed 11 June 2010).

Office for National Statistics (2008) *Information Paper. Recommended Questions for the 2009 Census Rehearsal and 2011 Census* (London: ONS).

Office for National Statistics (2011) 'Proportion who consider their identity to be British, English, Scottish or Welsh: by ethnic group, 2004, GB', available at: www.statistics.gov.uk

Okitikpi, T. (ed.) (2005) *Working with Children of Mixed Parentage* (Lyme Regis: Russell House Publishing).

Okitikpi, T.T. (2005) 'Identity and identification: how mixed parentage children adapt to a binary world', in T. Okitikpi (ed.) *Working with Children of Mixed Parentage* (Lyme Regis: Russell House), pp. 76–92.

Olumide, J. (2002) *Raiding the Gene Pool* (London: Pluto Press).

Omi, M. and H. Winant (1994) *Racial Formation in the United States* (New York: Routledge).

Oudhoff, K. (2007) *Ethnic Minorities, Discrimination and Well-being in the EES* (Voorburg: Statistics Netherlands). Available at: http://epp.eurostat.ec.europa.eu/portal/page/portal/conferences/documents/33rd_ceies_seminar_documents/3.2%20OUDHOF%20EN.PDF

Owen, C. (2007) 'Statistics: the mixed category in census 2001', in J. Sims (ed.) *Mixed Heritage: Identity, Policy, Practice* (London: Runnymede Trust), pp. 1–5.

Owen, C. and J. Statham (2009) *Disproportionality in Child Welfare – Prevalence of Black and Ethnic Minority Children Within 'Looked After' and 'Children in Need' Populations and on Child Protection Registers in England (No. DCSF-RR-124)* (London: Department for Children, Schools, and Families).

Panico, L. and J.Y. Nazroo (2011) 'The social and economic circumstances of mixed ethnicity children in the UK: findings from the millennium cohort study', *Ethnic and Racial Studies* 34(9), 1421–1444.

Parker, D. and M. Song (2001) *Rethinking 'Mixed Race'* (London: Pluto).

Parker, J.D. et al. (2004) 'Bridging between two standards for collecting information on race and ethnicity: an application to Census 2000 and vital rates', *Public Health Reports* 119(2), 192–205.

Perlmann, J. and M. Waters (eds.) (2002) *The New Race Question: How the Census Counts Multiracial Individuals* (New York: Russell Sage).

Phillips T. (2005) 'After 7/7: sleepwalking to segregation', Speech to the Manchester Council for Community Relations, 22 September. Available at: http://www.humanities.manchester.ac.uk/socialchange/research/social-change/summer-workshops/documents/sleepwalking.pdf

Phinney, J.S., B. Lochner, and R. Murphy (1990) 'Ethnic identity development and psychological adjustment in adolescence', in A. Stiffman & L. Davis (eds.) *Ethnic Issues in Adolescent Mental Health* (Newbury Park, CA: Sage), pp. 53–72.

Phoenix, A. and C. Owen (1996) 'From miscegenation to hybridity: mixed relationships and mixed parentage in profile', in B. Bernstein & J. Brennen (eds.) *Children, Research and Policy* (London: Taylor & Francis), pp. 111–135.

Pilkington, A. (2003) *Racial Disadvantage and Ethnic Diversity in Britain* (Basingstoke: Palgrave Macmillan).

Platt, L. (2009) *Ethnicity and Family: Relationships Within and Between Ethnic Groups: An Analysis Using the Labour Force Survey* (Colchester: ISER, University of Essex).

Platt, L., L. Simpson, and B. Akinwale (2005) 'Stability and change in ethnic group in England and Wales', *Population Trends* 121, 35–46.

Portes, A. and D. Macleod (1996) 'What shall I call myself? Hispanic identity formation in the second generation', *Ethnic and Racial Studies* 19(3), 523–547.

Prevatt-Goldstein, B. (1999) 'Black, with a white parent, a positive and achievable identity', *British Journal of Social Work* 29, 285–301.

Prewitt, K. (2005) 'Racial classification in America: where do we go from here?' *Daedalus* 134, 5–17.

Qian, Z. (2004) 'Options: racial/ethnic identification of children of intermarried couples', *Social Science Quarterly* 85(3), 746–766.

Rattansi, A. (2007) *Racism: A Very Short Introduction* (Oxford: Oxford University Press).

Raz, J. (1986) *The Morality of Freedom* (Oxford: Oxford University Press).

Rees, P. (2008) 'What happens when international migrants settle? Projections of ethnic groups in United Kingdom regions', in J. Raymer & F. Willekens (eds.) *International Migration in Europe: Data, Models and Estimates* (London: John Wiley), pp. 330–358.

Renn, K.A. (2000) 'Patterns of situational identity among biracial and multiracial college students', *The Review of Higher Education* 23(4), 399–420.

Roberts, S. and P. Baker (2010) 'Asked to Declare His Race, Obama Checks "Black"', *The New York Times*, 2nd April.

Rockquemore, K. and P. Arend (2002) 'Opting for white: choice, fluidity, and racial identity construction in post civil-rights America', *Race and Society* 5, 49–64.

Rockquemore, K. and D. Brunsma (2002) *Beyond Black: Biracial Identity in America* (Thousand Oaks: Sage).

Rockquemore, K. and T. Laszloffy (2005) *Raising Biracial Children* (Lanham: Rowman).

Rondilla, J. and P. Spickard (2007) *Is Lighter Better?* (Lanham: Rowman & Little Publishing).

Root, M. (ed.) (1996) *The Multiracial Experience* (Thousand Oaks: Sage).

Root, M. (ed.) (1992) *Racially Mixed People in America* (Thousand Oaks: Sage).

Roth, W. (2005) 'The end of the one-drop rule? Labelling of multiracial children in Black intermarriages', *Sociological Forum* 20(1), 35–67.

Roth, W. (2010) 'Racial mismatch: the divergence between form and function in data for monitoring racial discrimination in Hispanics', *Social Science Quarterly* 91(5), 1288–1311.

Runnymede Trust (2007) 'Mixednness and mixing'. Available at: http://www.runnymedetrust.org/projects/mixed-heritage/mixedness-conference-lsbu.html

Russell, K., M. Wilson, and R. Hall (1992) *The Color Complex* (New York: Anchor Books).

Saenz, R., S. Hwang, B. Aguirre, and R. Anderson (1995) 'Persistence and change in Asian identity among children of intermarried couples', *Sociological Perspectives* 38(2), 175–194.

Sanchez, D., J. Good, and G. Chavez (2011) 'Blood quantum and perceptions of Black/White biracial targets', *Personality and Social Psychology Bulletin* 37, 3–14.

Schenker, N. and J.D. Parker (2003) 'From single-race reporting to multiple-race reporting: using imputation methods to bridge the transition', *Statistics in Medicine* 22, 1571–1587.

Schuman, H. et al. (1997) *Racial Attitudes in America* (Cambridge: Harvard University Press).

Scottish Government and General Register Office for Scotland (2008) *Scotland's New Official Ethnicity Classification* (Edinburgh: GRO(S).

Shih, M. and D. Sanchez (2005) 'Perspectives and research on the positive and negative implications of having multiple racial identities', *Psychological Bulletin* 131, 569–591.

Silva, G.M.D. and E.P. Reis (2012) 'The multiple dimensions of racial mixing in Rio de Janeiro, Brazil: from whitening to Brazilian negritude', *Ethnic and Racial Studies* 35(3), 382–399.

Simpson, L. and B. Akinwale (2004) *Quantifying Stability and Change in Ethnic Group* (Manchester: Cathie Marsh Centre for Census and Survey Research).

Simpson, L. and B. Akinwale (2007) 'Quantifying stability and change in ethnic group', *Journal of Official Statistics* 23(2), 185–208.

Skinner, D. (2007) 'Groundhog day? The strange case of sociology, science and race', *Sociology* 41(5), 931–943.

Small, S. (2001) 'Colour, culture and class', in D. Parker & M. Song (eds.) *Rethinking 'Mixed Race'* (London: Pluto Press).

Smith, D., R. Edwards, and C. Caballero (2011) 'The geographies of mixed-ethnicity families', *Environment and Planning* 43, 1455–1476.

Smith, L. (2006) log – 'finding voice', 6 September 2006, Laura Smith. Available at: http://www.guardian.co.uk/news/blog/2006/sep/13/findingvoice1

Smith, S. and J. Jones (2011) 'Intraracial harassment on campus: explaining between- and within-group differences', *Ethnic and Racial Studies* 34(9), 1567–1593.

Smith, S. and M. Moore (2000) 'Intraracial diversity and relations among African-Americans', *American Journal of Sociology* 106(1), 1–39.

Snow, D. and L. Anderson (1993) *Down on Their Luck: A Study of Homeless Street People* (Berkeley: University of California Press).

Solomos, J. (1993) *Race and Racism in Britain* (London: Macmillan).

Solomos, J. and L. Back (1996) *Racism and Society* (London: Macmillan).

Somers, M.R. (1994) 'The narrative constitution of identity: a relational and network approach', *Theory & Society* 23, 605–649.

Song, M. (2001) 'Do Asian Americans have "more" ethnic options than African Americans?' *Ethnicities* 1(1), 57–82.

Song, M. (2003) *Choosing Ethnic Identity* (Cambridge: Polity Press).

Song, M. (2009) 'Is intermarriage a good indicator of integration?' *Journal of Ethnic and Migration Studies* 35(2), 331–348.

Song, M. (2010) 'Does "race" matter? A study of mixed race siblings' identifications', *Sociological Review* 58(2), May 2010.

Song, M. (2012) 'Making sense of "mixure": states and the classification of "mixed" people', *Ethnic and Racial Studies* 35(4), 565–573.

Song, M. and F. Hashem (2010) 'What does "White" mean? Interpreting the choices of "race" by mixed race young people in Britain', *Sociological Perspectives* 53(2), 287–292.

Spencer, J.M. (1997) *The New Colored People* (New York: NYU Press).

Spencer, R. (2006) 'New racial identities, old arguments: continuing biological reification', in D. Brunsma (ed.) *Mixed Messages* (Boulder: Lynne Reinner Publishers).

Spickard, P. (1989) *Mixed Blood* (Madison: University of Wisconsin Press).

Spickard, P. (1992) 'The illogic of racial categories', in M. Root (ed.) *Racially Mixed People in America* (Thousand Oaks: Sage).

Spickard, P. (2001) 'The subject is mixed race: the boom in biracial biography', in D. Parker & M. Song (eds.) *Rethinking 'Mixed Race'* (London: Pluto Press).

Standen, B. (1996) 'Without a template: the biracial Korean/White experiences', in M. Root (ed.) *The Multiracial Experience* (Thousand Oaks: Sage).

Statistics Canada (2003) *Ethnic Diversity Survey: Content Overview* (Ottawa: Statistics Canada).

Stephan, C. (1992) 'Mixed-heritage individuals: ethnic identity and trait characteristics', in M. Root (ed.) *Racially Mixed People in America* (Newbury Park: Sage).

Stonequist, E. (1937) *The Marginal Man* (New York: Russell and Russell).

Sue, C. (2013) 'Negotiating identity narratives among Mexico's cosmic race', in R. King-O'Riain et al. (eds.) *Global Mixed Race* (New York: New York University Press).

Swidler, A. (1986) 'Culture in action: symbols and strategies', *American Sociological Review* 51, 273–286.

Tajfel, H. (1978) 'The achievement of group differentiation', in *Differentiation between Social Groups. Studies in the Social Psychology of Intergroup Relations* (London: Academic Press), pp. 77–98.

Tashiro, C. (2002) 'Considering the significance of ancestry through the prism of mixed-race identity', *Advances in Nursing Science* 25(2), 1–21.

Taylor, C. (1994) 'The politics of recognition', in D. Goldberg (ed.), *Multiculturalism: A Critical Reader* (Cambridge: Blackwell).

Thornton, M. (1992) 'Is Multiracial status unique?' in M. Root (ed.) *Racially Mixed People in America* (Thousand Oaks: Sage).

Thornton MC. (1996) 'Hidden agendas, identity theories, and multiracial people', in M.M.P. Root (ed.) *The Multiracial Experience: Racial Borders As the New Frontier* (Philadelphia: Temple University Press), pp. 101–120.

Tikly, L. et al. (2004) *Understanding the Educational Needs of Mixed Heritage Pupils.* Research Report RR549 (London: Department for Education and Skills).

Tizard, B. and A. Phoenix (1993) *Black, White or Mixed Race?* (London: Routledge).

Troyna, B. and R. Hatcher (1992) *Racism in Children's Lives: A Study of Mainly White Primary Schools* (London: Routledge).

Tuan, M. (1998) *Forever Foreigners or Honorary Whites?* (New Brunswick: Rutgers University Press).

Tucker, C., R. McKay, B. Kojetin, R. Harrison, M. De la Puente, L. Stinson, and E. Robison (1996) *Testing Methods of Collecting Racial and Ethnic Information: Results of the Current Population Survey Supplement on Race and Ethnicity. Statistical Note No. 40.* (Washington, DC: Bureau of Labor Statistics).

Twine, F.W. (2010) *A White Side of Black Britain: Interracial Intimacy and Racial Literacy* (Durham, NC: Duke University Press).

Twine, F.W. and C. Gallagher (2008) 'Introduction. The future of whiteness: a map of the "third wave"', *Ethnic and Racial Studies* 31(1), 4–24.

Ulmer, C., B. McFadden, and D.R. Nerenz (2009) *Race, Ethnicity, and Language Data: Standardization for Health Care Quality Improvement* (Washington, DC: The National Academies Press).

Van den Berghe, P.L. (1978) 'Race and ethnicity: a sociobiological perspective', *Ethnic and Racial Studies* 1(4), 401–411.

Vertovec, S. (2007) 'Super-diversity and its implications', *Ethnic and Racial Studies* 30(6), 1024–1054.

Waters, M. (1990) *Ethnic Options: Choosing identities in America* (Berkeley: University of California Press).

Waters, M. (1999) *Black Identities: West Indian Immigrant Dreams and American Realities* (Cambridge: Harvard University Press).

Wetherell, M. (ed.) (2009) *Identity in the 21st Century* (London: Palgrave Macmillan).

Wilson, A. (1987) *Mixed Race Children* (London: Allen & Unwin).

Woodward, K. (2004) *Questioning Identity* (Milton Keynes: Open University Press).

Xie, Y. and K. Goyette (1997) 'The racial identification of biracial children with one Asian parent: evidence from the 1990 Census', *Social Forces* 76(2), 547–570.

Yancey, G. (2006) 'Racial justice in a black/nonblack society', in David L. Brunsma (ed.) *Mixed Messages: Multiracial Identities in the 'Color-Blind' Era* (Boulder, CO: Lynne Rienner Publishers, Inc), pp. 49–62.

Young, R. (1994) *Colonial Desire* (New York: Routledge).

Younge, G. (2010) *Who Are We?* (London: Penguin).

Zack, N. (1993) *Race and Mixed Race* (Philadelphia: Temple University Press).

Zack, N. (1996) 'On being and not-being Black and Jewish', in M. Root (ed.) *The Multiracial Experience* (Thousand Oaks: Sage).

Index

Note: Page numbers in bold refer to figures and tables

Printed and bound by CPI Group UK Ltd, Croydon, CR0 4YY